Critical Essays on
NATHANAEL WEST

CRITICAL ESSAYS
ON
AMERICAN LITERATURE

James Nagel, General Editor
University of Georgia, Athens

Critical Essays on

NATHANAEL WEST

edited by

BEN SIEGEL

G. K. Hall & Co. / New York
Maxwell Macmillan Canada / Toronto
Maxwell Macmillan International / New York Oxford Singapore Sydney

Copyright © 1994 by Ben Siegel

G. K. Hall & Co.
Macmillan Publishing Company
866 Third Avenue
New York, New York 10022

Maxwell Macmillan Canada, Inc.
1200 Eglinton Avenue East
Suite 200
Don Mills, Ontario M3C 3N1

Library of Congress Cataloging-in-Publication Data

Critical essays on Nathanael West / Ben Siegel.
    p.   cm. — (Critical essays on American literature)
    Includes bibliographical references and index.
    ISBN 0-7838-0027-4
    1. West, Nathanael, 1903–1940—Criticism and interpretation.
I. Siegel, Ben, 1925– . II. Series.
PS3545.E8334Z63   1994
813'.52—dc20   94-14474
                                                                   CIP

The paper used in this publication meets the minimum requirements of
American National Standard for Information Sciences—Permanence of
Paper for Printed Library Materials. ANSI Z3948-1984.∞™

10   9   8   7   6   5   4   3   2   1

Printed in the United States of America

For RUTH—
who took with her the sunshine and the music and the laughter

Contents

◆

ESSAYS

General Editor's Note

◆

This series seeks to anthologize the most important criticsm on a wide variety of topics and writers in American literature. Our readers will find in various volumes not only a generous selection of reprinted articles and reviews but also original essays, bibliographies, manuscript sections, and other materials brought to public attention for the first time. This volume, *Critical Essays on Nathanael West*, is the most comprehensive collection of essays ever published on one of the most important modern writers in the United States. It contains both a sizable gathering of early reviews and a broad selection of more modern scholarship. Among the authors of reprinted articles and reviews are Edmund Wilson, W. H. Auden, Leslie Fiedler, R. W. B. Lewis, John Hawkes, Gloria Young, Jan Gorak, and Beverly Jones. In addition to a substantial introduction by Ben Siegel, there are also two original essays commissioned specifically for publication in this volume, new studies by David Madden on the narrative method of *Miss Lonelyhearts* and Daniel Walden on Nathanael West as a Jewish satirist. We are confident that this book will make a permanent and significant contribution to the study of American literature.

JAMES NAGEL
University of Georgia, Athens

Publisher's Note

♦

Producing a volume that contains both newly commissioned and reprinted material presents the publisher with the challenge of balancing the desire to achieve stylistic consistency with the need to preserve the integrity of works first published elsewhere. In the Critical Essays series, essays commissioned especially for a particular volume are edited to be consistent with G. K. Hall's house style; reprinted essays appear in the style in which they were first published, with only typographical errors corrected. Consequently, shifts in style from one essay to another are the result of our efforts to be faithful to each text as it was originally published.

Prefatory Note

♦

Nathanael West is something of a phenomenon in American literature. Is there another American novelist who has published so little and engendered so much printed discussion? This collection attempts to give the reader some sense of that criticism's volume and tone, range and direction. To that end I have tried to adhere to as chronological an approach as possible. I have also attempted to be as inclusive as possible, both in the introductory survey and in the selections. But the inevitable space limitations have imposed some obvious restrictions. For example, the first rough draft of the Introduction exceeded 200 pages. Reducing it to a manageable 42 pages has been perhaps the most difficult part of this entire venture. In deciding which essays to include and which to eliminate, I wanted to make certain that each of West's four novels received adequate and balanced discussion. But I was forced to drop a number of pieces whose inclusion could easily be defended. In fact, one could gather a second collection from essays that are neither included nor mentioned here.

There are a number individuals to whom I am indebted for their assistance. As has been true repeatedly in my many years of academic endeavor, I owe a first debt to William H. Davenport (Professor Emeritus, Harvey Mudd College), my mentor and collaborator and friend since my graduate school days at the University of Southern California. Now retired from his long and distinguished career as an outstanding teacher and scholar at the University of Southern California and then Harvey Mudd College, Bill Davenport has always been generous with both help and advice. Few are as adept as he at plunging into the library stacks and emerging with items from dusty journals, newspapers, and microfilm files. If it exists, Bill Davenport finds it. He has made my task here immeasurably easier. He merits much of the credit for whatever contribution to Westiana this modest volume may make.

I should also like to thank David Madden and Daniel Walden. Both were kind enough to take time from other writing, teaching, and editing assignments to contribute original articles to this volume. Like almost everyone else in recent years who has worked on Nathanael West, I am indebted to Jay Martin, not only for his fulsome biography of West but also for his personal kindness and assistance in making materials available to me. I owe a special debt, too, to John Sanford, a distinguished novelist and lifelong friend of West, and to Anthony Buttitta, a former editor of *Contempo* and a literary associate of West. These two worthy men of letters sent me items on West for inclusion here that had not appeared in print since their original publication. Finally, I must thank James Nagel, a most patient and understanding series editor.

On a personal level, I am indebted to my son, Kenneth, my daughter, Sharon, and my son-in-law, Brad, all of whom were discomfited on many occasions because Dad was otherwise occupied. But each tried to help in any way possible. Ultimately, I owe an inexpressible debt to my late wife, Ruth Siegel, who saw the beginning of this project but not its completion. She walks with me still and makes all things possible.

Introduction

◆

BEN SIEGEL

I

Nathanael West devoted much of his short life to running away from his identity. In recent years scholars and critics, led by conscientious biographers like James Light and Jay Martin, have uncovered most of the relevant information illuminating both his life and writings. He was born Nathan Wallenstein Weinstein, on 17 October 1903, in New York City. His parents, Max and Anna Weinstein, were Jewish immigrants from the province of Kovno in Russian Lithuania. Nathan had two sisters, Hinda and Lorraine (whom everyone called Laura and with whom he was very close). Father and son also were very close. Max Weinstein is said to have been "slight, kind, and shy."[1]

Very ambitious for their children, the Weinsteins emphasized education as the key to success. Hence, stated Jay Martin, they regularly presented their seemingly "intelligent and imaginative" young son "with sets of the 'standard' authors."[2] Their gifts were not wasted as Nathan then devoted most of his time to reading. His parents thus had every reason to expect that he would fulfill their highest academic expectations for him. But Nathan apparently determined early on to follow his own agenda. His precocious reading habits failed to carry over to his studies, and he proved a surprisingly poor student at Manhattan's P.S. 81 and P.S. 10. To make matters worse, he was thin and awkward—a sad fact that worked to his disadvantage during his summers in the Adirondacks at Camp Paradox. At De Witt Clinton High he gained the unhappy distinction of being one of the weakest students. He fared little better socially, taking no part in extracurricular activity. Not surprisingly, in June 1920 Nathan left high school without graduating. But having determined that his was to be a life of recognized accomplishment, he could not accept this sign of defeat. To accomplish his ends, Nathan was not above cheating. About a year later he applied to Tufts College, on the basis of what appears to have been a forged transcript from De Witt Clinton. Admitted in September

1921, he withdrew from Tufts after two months because of academic problems. Ever resourceful, he "transferred" to Brown University in February 1922, using the transcript of another Nathan Weinstein at Tufts. Now for the first time, he applied himself to his studies, passing all his courses and graduating from Brown in two and one-half years. During those years Nathan Weinstein cast aside the role of brooding loner to cultivate the personality and character traits of the cultural aesthete the world later would know as Nathanael West.[3]

Indulged by his parents, he affected the sartorial style of an elegant Ivy Leaguer. Generally reserved in manner, he could be friendly, gregarious (he was a competent banjo player), and generous with his sizeable allowance. With girls, however, he is said to have been either too shy or brash. He received little if any formal education in Judaism. It is very likely that he was ritually circumcised, but he did not have a Bar Mitzvah ceremony. The Weinsteins refused to speak Yiddish in their home. At Brown he strived mightily to avoid being identified as Jewish, opting instead to socialize with the elitist Gentile fraternities. He was pathetically eager to be pledged. He never was, and he never got over this rejection.

He did fall in with a group of ambitious young would-be writers like I. J. Kapstein, Quentin Reynolds, and S. J. Perelman. What success West achieved on campus has been described as essentially literary and "aesthetic." He was credited with having the largest personal library of any Brown man at that time, and with lending books readily. He took special delight "in stories about strange weapons and exotic methods of torture and could describe both in considerable detail." A friend remembers that West tended to think " 'in violent terms and in terms of violence' " (Martin, *NWE*, 2). His academic behavior continued to be offbeat and unscrupulous. Using at Brown the "other Nathan Weinstein's" credits in science and economics, he limited himself there almost exclusively to courses in literature, history, and philosophy. His extracurricular activity centered on his work as an editor of *Casements*, the campus literary magazine. Apparently he also wrote an early draft of his first novel, *The Dream Life of Balso Snell*, while still at Brown. Upon graduating in 1924, after "conning a teacher who'd given him a failing mark," West convinced his father to send him to Paris, where he later claimed he spent several years, growing a red beard and living a Henry Miller–like existence. That was simply another of his fantasies. Philip French has pinpointed West's inability to tell or even recognize the truth outside his fiction. "From his early youth" West proved "a fantasist," stated French. He was "almost as incapable of telling the truth about his life as he was incapable of telling anything else in his fiction. There's little he didn't lie about, from his hunting exploits to his uneventful three months in 1926 Paris (transformed into a three-year Milleresque extravaganza)."[4] One of his cousins described West even more cogently as "the master of 'the convincing lie,' a compulsive role player" (Martin, *NW*, 32).

Upon his return to New York from Europe, West worked for a time for his father, a successful building contractor. He would seemingly have been content to live off his family while he wrote his "unprofitable books," but the Wall Street crash forced him out into the world. In 1927, West got a job as an assistant or night manager at Kenmore Hall, an East 23rd Street hotel then owned in part by Morris Jarcho, the brother of his aunt's husband. He received $35 a week plus room and board. Working nights, he was able to spend his time there reading and observing the seedier aspects of urban American life. He was also able to provide free rooms to his college friends and even their needy friends. Included in this latter group was Dashiell Hammett, who completed *The Maltese Falcon* at the Kenmore as one of West's bootleg guests. In 1928 he moved on to the Sutton, a more luxurious residential hotel on East 56th Street, again working the night desk and sheltering at reduced rates or at no cost impoverished writers like Erskine Caldwell and James T. Farrell. But the Depression struck even closer to home: his father was among those ruined by the crash.

Already West was exhibiting the deeply complex and conflicting intellectual and emotional tensions to be found in his novels. In 1929, thanks to S. J. Perelman, he was shown a group of letters written to the lovelorn columnist of a Brooklyn newspaper. He saw immediately that the letters were cries for help to dispassionate journalistic scribblers. Deeply moved by the letters, West started transmuting his reactions into fiction. The going was hard, and he worked on this second novel for four years, completing its final draft only in November of 1932. The experience underscored the very strengths and weaknesses that both attracted and repelled those who knew him. "No one could satisfactorily explain the many clashing elements in his nature and interests," Richard Gehman later noted. "He despised military men, yet was an authority on armies and strategies from the time of Caesar on." He viewed "organized religion as a hoax, but was on intimate terms with the structure, organization and financial condition of the Catholic Church." In appearance, Gehman observed, West "was tall, awkward and disarming," but he compensated by dressing "with excessive propriety in Brooks Brothers clothes." There were more contradictions. West possessed "an acute feeling for words," said Gehman, but he was a poor speller. He disliked "business and workaday occupations," but he "was successful as a hotel clerk for several years." Born and raised on New York's Upper West Side, he was an inept athlete, "but when he finally became an outdoor man he was a comic personification of Nimrod."[5]

Even those who knew him never claimed to have solved the enigma that was Nathanael West. "The chief source of his personal complexity," said Jay Martin, "lay in the contrast between his intellectual and emotional life, between his ability passively to understand experience and his initial lack of capacity for deeply active involvement in it." John Raskolnikov Gilson, a character in *Balso Snell*, describes himself as "on the side of the intellect against the emotions, on the side of the brain against the heart."[6] This internal tension marked most of West's early actions and human relationships. Certainly he presented different faces to his intimate friends and to others. To Philip Wylie, for example, whom he met in 1925, he appeared "a divided person—thin, restless, discontented, sardonic, homely, and very warm and affectionate under that." Some acquaintances, however, found him bitingly sardonic and mean-spirited. His "merciless, intellectual humor," observed Martin, struck such individuals as "intellectual brutalism" (Martin, *NWE*, 3). But others, especially his writer friends, knew him as a warmer, more sympathetic human being. Malcolm Cowley found him essentially "soft and vulnerable," his cynical manner "a cover-up for a real desire to make contact." His sister Laura and her husband, S. J. Perelman, always emphasized West's warm and tender qualities. A slightly more objective view was that of Robert M. Coates, who recognized his friend's conflicting internal tensions. For him the central element of West's character was "his immense, sorrowful . . . all-pervasive pessimism. He was about the most thoroughly pessimistic person I have ever known. . . . But though this colored all his thinking both creatively and critically, it had no effect on his personality, for he was one of the best companions I have ever known, cheerful, thoughtful, and very flexible in all his personal attitudes" (Martin, *NWE*, 3–4).

While at the Sutton, West rewrote his earlier drafts of *The Dream Life of Balso Snell*. He told A. J. Liebling that he considered the novel a protest against the writing of books. Jay Martin has viewed West's first novel in more personal terms. Martin has suggested that it was primarily the product of West's "wit, the sardonic side of his personality" and of his readings in continental literature. Like many of his contemporaries, West admired the Modernist period's brief, tightly structured French novellas. He was drawn to European experimental fiction and the preoccupation of artists and writers like Breton, Picasso, Klee, Joyce, and others with man's "dream life," with his "nightlife of the soul." During the 1920s, has stated Martin, the new literature had turned "values inside out" by declaring "the primacy of dreams over acts, of violence over order, of Sade's sexual gospel over that of the churches." Taking these ideas and values to heart, West fashioned the "travel" narrative of a naive hero who confronts the most cherished conventions of the Western tradition. Citing Proust as his source, West uses as epigraph the Anaxagorean dictum that "life is a journey." He then follows the meanderings of "an American Babbitt . . . through the anus of the Trojan Horse, and of his encounters there with various forms of deception, pretense, and illusion." Originally wishing to fashion a "parody" of the story of Troy, West ends up concentrating on "the deceitfulness of dreams, and thus of the life which these dreams symbolize." Here West was already confronting those ideas central to his later fiction. He was trying to determine "how to satirize illusions" at a time when the modern world appeared in dire need of them, and when each illusion seemed to lead only to "the proliferation" of even greater ones (Martin, *NWE*, 4–5).

In later years a number of West's friends would offer their recollections of his character and personality. To their offerings should be added the thinly veiled and surprisingly candid self-portrait he includes in his first novel. In one telling passage West reveals what has motivated his own unrelenting bitterness. "All my acting has but one purpose, the attraction of the female. If it had been possible for me to attract by exhibiting a series of physical charms, my hatred would have been less. But I found it necessary to substitute strange conceits, wise and witty sayings, peculiar conduct, Art, for the muscles, teeth, hair of my rivals." In other words, he added, "All this much-exhibited intelligence is but a development of the instinct to please." Those he most wanted to please were women he could not get. "Because of women like Saniette," he explains several paragraphs later, "I acquired the habit of extravagant thought. I now convert everything into fantastic entertainment and the extraordinary has become an obsession" (*CW*, 26–27).

In 1931 West had 500 copies of *The Dream Life of Balso Snell* privately printed by the avant-garde firm of Contact Editions. The author was listed as "Nathanael West," marking Nathanael Weinstein's official name change. He explained to William Carlos Williams how he arrived at this name. "Horace Greely said, 'Go West, young man.' So I did." This explanation has often been repeated, but as usual the truth was more mundane. He adopted the name "West" from an older cousin, Sam Wallenstein, noted Martin, "who had been using it for some time in Wall Street" (Martin, *NW*, 179). His Jewish self-hatred had by now progressed to the point where he referred to Jewish girls as "bagels." But the world seemed to care little about his name change or his prejudices. His novel received only two reviews. One was assigned by his editor-friends at *Contempo* to V. N. Garofolo, and the other, written at West's request, was by his childhood buddy Julian Shapiro (John Sanford). Even so, Garofolo's review, while essentially favorable, was mixed. "Perhaps it would be rather impertinent to call this facile, buoyant book a novel," he wrote, but it still amounts to "a distinguished performance in sophisticated writing."[7] Shapiro, in a "letter" to the editors of the *New Review* (Paris), was much more positive. Under the heading of "Tired Men and Dung," he quickly dismissed the "hacks" who had misread West's novel, arguing that if more sophisticated readers were aware of its existence, "it would be very much liked." These "hiredmen, or the tiredmen," have misunderstood the novel and failed to realize it is a funny book. For West has "used parts of the book to fling handfuls of dung in their faces."[8]

West was also having personal troubles. He dedicated *Balso Snell* to Alice Shepard, a Roman Catholic girl who had attended Pembroke College with his sister Laura. They were secretly engaged from 1929 to 1932 and then publicly engaged. For several years West even carried around a marriage license, but they never married. Indeed West was notorious among his acquaintances as a sexual loser. Taking a leave of absence from the Sutton in 1931, West and John Sanford, also an aspiring novelist, headed for a shack in the Adirondacks near Warrensburg, New York. At work on *Miss Lonelyhearts*, West would read "each sentence back aloud" and end up with approximately "a hundred words a day" (Hyman, 213). He rewrote the manuscript at least a half-dozen times— there in the mountains, back at the Sutton, then at Warford House, a small hotel in Frenchtown, New Jersey, after quitting the Sutton.

II

West was now fully committed to writing and editing. In 1932 he became an associate editor (with Robert McAlmon) of *Contact*, William Carlos Williams's short-lived little magazine. That year and the following, he published articles and parts of the first draft of *Miss Lonelyhearts* in it and in *Contempo*. West stirred strong emotions in those encountering him for the first time. Josephine Herbst later would recall that "early fall of 1932," when William Carlos Williams urged her to "look up young West." She found him a reflection of his work's "complexities" and "contraries."[9] His second novel was then much on his mind. In a *Contempo* piece he titled simply "Some Notes on Miss L.," West explained that he had been thinking of his narrative in comic strip terms. Indeed, he chose "as subtitle: a novel in the form of a comic strip. The chapters to be squares in which many things happen through one action. The speeches contained in the conventional balloons." He also tried to explain the sources of his hero's tortured religious yearnings. "*Miss Lonelyhearts* became the portrait of a priest of our time who has a religious experience. His case is classical and is built on all the cases in James' *Varieties of Religious Experience* and Starbuck's *Psychology of Religion*. The psychology is theirs, not mine. The imagery is mine."[10] In August 1933 he was appointed associate editor of *Americana*, a savagely satirical magazine edited by Alexander King and George Grosz. West's connection to this magazine was brief but important. "Some of its raucous and Dadaist quality," observed Daniel Aaron, "is caught in his subsequent novels, together with its bitterness and cynicism and rage born of breadlines and national skullduggery."[11] West then wrote some stories for the slick magazines, but he was unable to sell any. He also applied for a Guggenheim fellowship, but even with F. Scott Fitzgerald as one of his sponsors, he was unsuccessful.

So far 1933 had hardly proved a happy year. In addition to his other disappointments, West saw his new novel, *Miss Lonelyhearts*, caught up in a squabble between publisher and printer. His publisher, Horace Liveright, had gone bankrupt, and the printer, a Liveright creditor, refused to deliver copies of the book to the bookstores. So despite a smattering of generally favorable reviews, *Miss Lonelyhearts* garnered few readers and was quickly remaindered. Also, the inevitable critical dissenters, like T. S. Matthews in the *New Republic*, made themselves heard. Matthews dismissed *Miss Lonelyhearts* in a single brief paragraph that concluded with the observation that West's novel was "a centrifugal extravaganza, patched together by lovelorn letters quite horrible enough to be actual facsimiles."[12] The first truly thoughtful appraisal of the novel was by T. C. Wilson, in the *Saturday Review of Literature*. Wilson also observed that younger writers like Erskine Caldwell and Nathanael West were "attempting to restore the comic view of life to its legitimate place in art." As for West's new novel, it was "a solid work as well as a brilliant one."[13]

In a sense, the critical tide had turned in West's favor, although reviewers still expressed misgivings about his style and tone. William Troy, in a relatively brief assessment in the *Nation*, was somewhat typical. Finding the novel's events to be "all very sad, bitter and hopeless," he was most put off by the style. Were it not for West's "prose, which leans too much to the baroque and for a certain ambiguity of genre ('the actual and the fanciful' are here too often confounded)," Troy complained, *Miss Lonelyhearts* would have proved "a better book." Yet despite this shortcoming, he conceded that the novel was "one of the season's most readable and . . . exceptional books."[14] For Robert Cantwell, himself a novelist, West's "thin little book" seemed "a kind of modernized, faithless, 'Pilgrim's Progress'" that exuded "a sour, hangover humor" suggestive of James Thurber's *New Yorker* cartoons.[15] In a "Symposium" in *Contempo*, Angel Flores, Josephine Herbst, and William Carlos Williams voiced their opinions of the new book. "Nathanael West's most remarkable performance," said Flores, "has been to bring . . . [Dostoyevsky's] dark angels into the Haunted Castle." West did not resort "to the drab realism" that bears responsibility "for the stagnation in the works of the younger American writers." Instead, West has provided his readers with "anguish and terror and fantasy."[16]

For Josephine Herbst, West's novel resembled "a detective story" exhibiting a realism concerned not "with actuality but with the comprehension of a reality beyond reality." Capturing the "entire jumble of modern society," West here depicts that social confusion "like a life-sized engraving narrowed down to the head of a pin."[17] More combative was William Carlos Williams, who rejected the charge that West's novel was "sordid." The truly "sordid piece of business," he flared, was the newspaper advice column itself. West's novel "isn't a perfect book," Williams conceded. "But it is excellently conceived and written and it cannot be thrust aside in such slipshod fashion."[18]

West spent a few months in Hollywood in 1933, working as a junior writer at Columbia Pictures. Not only did he sell the movie rights to *Miss Lonelyhearts* to Twentieth Century–Fox, but he also was given a studio writing contract there at 350 dollars a week. Fortunately for him, he did not work on the script for the film version of his novel. Its title was changed to "Advice to the Lovelorn" and its story turned into a murder thriller for actor Lee Tracy. But West was given a few writing assignments. About this time he conceived the idea of writing a novel about the dream capital's "subterranean life" (Martin, *NWE*, 7). He also put himself on record politically by publishing a Marxist poem in *Contempo*. He returned to New York that July bitter and disenchanted with Hollywood. S. J. Perelman caught some of his brother-in-law's inner turmoil in a satiric portrait in which he claimed there were two Nathanael Wests. One is "a ruddy-cheeked, stocky sort of chap, dressed in loose tweeds . . . six feet in height, a dead shot, a past master of the foils," wrote Perelman. "The other is only 18 inches high. He is very sensitive and somewhat savage."[19]

West likely experienced a slight boost in confidence when two established literary contemporaries, Scott Fitzgerald and Malcolm Cowley, singled him out for praise. In his introduction to a new Modern Library edition of *The Great Gatsby*, Fitzgerald complained of "the growing cowardice of the reviewers" and declared "it's . . . saddening . . . to see young talents in fiction expire from sheer lack of a stage to act on: West, McHugh and many others."[20] Cowley struck the same note in *Exile's Return*. Devoting several pages to West, he referred to *Miss Lonelyhearts* as "a tender and recklessly imaginative novel that had few readers." To cash in on such favorable reactions to his second novel, West quickly wrote *A Cool Million*. A savage attack on the Horatio Alger, rags-to-riches myth of capitalist America's rugged individualism, this work was rejected by his previous publisher, Harcourt, Brace. Its editors considered it a disappointing fall from the level of *Miss Lonelyhearts*. Published instead by Covici-Friede in 1934, *A Cool Million* was savaged by most of the reviewers and almost immediately remaindered. For example, George Stevens, in a brief *Saturday Review* notice, found the opening chapter "mildly amusing" but the rest to be "superfluous." He could see "only a straining for effect and an impenetrable tedium."[22]

West's friends and a few reviewers rallied to its defense. Novelist Jack Conroy purchased several dozen copies of *A Cool Million* and gave them to acquaintances, with the proviso they pass their copies along to others. Another friend, John Chamberlain, used his *New York Times* review to defend the novel (a "wry, piercing, painful" satire) against Lewis Gannett's negative critique in the *New York Herald Tribune*.[23] Another charitable reaction, surprisingly enough, was that of T. S. Matthews, who had disdained *Miss Lonelyhearts*. Perhaps he was compensating for what he now deemed an earlier error in judgment. In any event, Matthews informed his *New Republic* readers that he found West's latest effort to be "a native American work, a crayon cartoon of the Voltairean school."[24] Another affirmative vote was cast by the unidentified reviewer in the *Review of Reviews and World's Work*. He considered *A Cool Million* "a delightful parody, with satire which hits uncomfortably near the truth. It is not a profound book, but it is a funny one."[25] Equally positive was the anonymous reviewer in the *Nation*. "Mr. West is heavy-handed, he conceded, "but his book is stimulating and at times bitterly hilarious."[26]

By 1935 West was more politically active. In effect, a fellow traveler of the Communist party, he went with James T. Farrell, Edward Newhouse, and Leane Zugsmith to join a group of Communist sympathizers in picketing Orbach's department store in Los Angeles and was jailed for a few hours "for obstructing traffic." Luckily for him, Hyman observed, West was "unable to get his political orientation explicitly into his fiction" (Hyman, 215). He now found himself without viable options for making a living. (His first three novels had earned him only $780.) So despite his distaste for Hollywood, he returned there to be a script writer at Republic Studios. Hollywood was now his real home, whether or not he wished to recognize it as such. But whereas novelists like Fitzgerald, Faulkner, and Huxley were at studios such as MGM and Twentieth Century–Fox, West worked mostly at "Poverty Row" film factories like Republic. Only near the end of his life did he make it even to RKO and Universal. By then West had finally found his niche. In the end he derived more from his *shlock* Hollywood experiences than did those writers who were better situated. After all, he was researching and writing *The Day of the Locust* on a daily basis. So he was quite content and amused to grind "out the rather stupefying plots" his Republic, Universal, and RKO bosses demanded. No other American writer, stated Tom Dardis, derived as much from Hollywood as did Nathanael West.[27]

To observe the movie community's seamier elements, West chose to live near Hollywood Boulevard. Continuing his involvement with radical politics in California, he responded to the call of the American Writers Congress, joined the Screen Writers Guild (acting as one of its union organizers), and worked hard for Loyalist Spain and other leftist causes. West also became a regular at the Stanley Rose Book Store, recalled Budd Schulberg. On weekends Rose and West prowled Hollywood's back streets and late-night joints. In addition to "the night-crawling, the cockfights, prizefights, and Gower Gulch nocturnalia that . . . [West] was drawing on for his novel in progress, *The Day of the Locust*," he and Stanley were dedicated hunters who preferred to pursue doves and ducks rather than discuss Proust and Faulkner. What was Nathanael West like in the years 1936–40? In preparing this sketch Schulberg "jotted down a free-association list of adjectives describing Pep: hulking, big, awkward, melancholy, sad, strange, detached, withdrawn, shy, friendly, warm, remote, secretive, shaggy, tweedy, gentle, sardonic, defensive, hurt, bitter, introspective, affectionate, lovable." His was "a bone-deep negativism," stated Schulberg, and a truly "terrible . . . sense of doom."[28]

Yet despite his professed "negativism" and his bitter disappointment over his new novel's poor sales, West continued to work steadily and live comfortably. During the late thirties, alone or in collaboration with Boris Ingster, West turned out screenplays for such low-budget but money-making films as *Five Came Back*, *I Stole a Million*, and *Spirit of Culver*. He was happy with this situation. For "unlike F. Scott Fitzgerald and many other writers," Jay Martin has observed, "he never aspired to make great films. He preferred to work on B- or even C-grade pictures, since these did not touch the sources of the creative energy for his fiction; he regarded movies simply as a source of support" (Martin, *NWE*, 7). For an outspoken Marxist, West was living out his personal interpretation of the American dream. Despite his newfound comforts and pleasures, West continued to proclaim his distaste for Hollywood and the "pants pressers" who ran its studios. He sought to return to the East by working on two plays for Broadway. The first, "Even Stephen" (a collaboration with Perelman) was never produced, and the second, "Good Hunting: A Satire in 3 Acts" (with Joseph Schrank), enjoyed two performances in November 1938. In 1939 West published *The Day of the Locust*, which he had finished between studio assignments, and which he hoped would prove successful enough for him to leave Hollywood. It was not; in fact, it sold only 1480 copies and moved West to complain to F. Scott Fitzgerald: "So far the box score stands: Good reviews—fifteen per cent, bad reviews—twenty-five per cent, brutal personal attacks—sixty per cent."[29] Despite West's self-pitying comments, the reviews were generally positive, even enthusiastic at times. One of the earliest was by his friend, the novelist George Milburn. He found it difficult to understand, said Milburn, why West should have become a "coterie writer." Indeed the "comedy" of his latest work "about forlorn clowns should make it popular, because it has the same ineffable appeal which caused millions to go to see Charlie Chaplin."[30]

Another affirmative vote was cast by the *Nation*'s reviewer, Louis B. Salomon. West does "a great deal more than just pillory the foibles and flimflammery of the movie industry," said Salomon. Indeed, West surrounds young studio painter Tod Hackett with "such a galaxy of spongers, misfits, and eccentrics as will give a sensitive reader the crawling horrors."[31] A similar summation was offered by Edmund Wilson. Writing in the *New Republic*, America's most respected man of letters focused on West's bizarre cast of characters. In his new novel Nathanael West has captured "the emptiness of Hollywood," and "he is, as far as I know, the first writer to make this emptiness horrible," said Wilson. He did find that "the book suffers a little from the lack of a center of the community which it describes" and from a lessening of the "concentration" of *Miss Lonelyhearts*. But the important thing is that Nathanael West has "survived to write another remarkable book."[32] Wilson's emphasis on West's "survival" would soon prove tragically ironic. In fact, even in the short time left to him West was not to enjoy an unqualified literary success. For a few critics were far less complimentary than those cited. *Time*'s anonymous reviewer, for example, did concede that "Author West starts off well," but the trouble is that "well before the last scene . . . his intended tragedy turns into screwball grotesque, and groggy Author West can barely distinguish fantastic shadows from fantastic substance."[33]

The decade of the thirties had not proved especially kind to West, despite his having published four novels that established his literary reputation. The 1940s seemed to hold promise of both greater personal happiness and literary success. For in 1939 he had met and fallen in love with a young widow with a sunny disposition and a son from her previous marriage. She was Eileen McKenney, the heroine of Ruth McKenney's *My Sister Eileen*, widely popular as a book and a movie. They married in April 1940, and West adopted her son. The newlyweds spent three happy months in Oregon hunting and fishing. There West supposedly worked out the rough plot for a fifth novel, which he planned to start when they got home. On their return, West received a higher paying job at Columbia, and shortly thereafter that studio bought the screen rights to *A Cool Million* and its screen treatment, which West had cowritten. But this blissful period was to be short-lived. On December 22, he and his wife were returning from a hunting trip in Mexico, when West, a notoriously poor driver, ran a stop sign near El Centro, California, and crashed their station wagon into another automobile. Eileen died on the spot, and West an hour later on the way to the hospital. He was 37. His body was shipped to New York and buried, ironically enough, in a Jewish cemetery.

In a memorial essay written six years later, John Sanford would recall that tragic day to wish "earnestly to God" his old friend "hadn't been such a damn poor driver." Yet he realized "that Pep's poor driving was Pep," that his friend was awkward and uncoordinated in "everything but writing."[34] Very likely West would find dark humor in his posthumous fame. The year before his death he had summed up his perceptions of his literary career in a letter to George Milburn. There he declared that

all my books always fall between the different schools of writing. The radical press, although I consider myself on their side, doesn't like my particular kind of joking, and think it even Fascist sometimes, and the literature boys, whom I detest, detest me in turn. The highbrow press finds that I avoid the big, significant things and the lending library touts in the daily press think me shocking and what, in the novels of Michael Arlen, is called 'bad hat.' The proof of all this is that I've never had the same publisher twice—once bitten, etc.— because there is nothing to root for in my work and what is even worse, no rooters. (Gehman, *IDL*, xxii–xxiii)

West was right in that, during his lifetime, his publishing record resembled one of his own black comedies. But his reputation has continued to grow, as have the sales of his novels. Scholarly books and essays, not to mention doctoral dissertations, appear in ever-increasing numbers. An unsuccessful playwright, West would find it ironic that *Miss Lonelyhearts* was made into a play and an opera, and a second, more serious film. Translated into French by Marcelle Siobon, as *Mademoiselle Coeur-Brise* (1946), with an introduction by Philippe Soupault, the novel has been credited with exerting a discernible influence on French postwar fiction. In England West's books soon found similar success. As early as 1950, Richard Gehman could claim that "Today West is at last getting just recognition for his special, remarkable talent; more and more rooters, ten years after his death, are helping his reputation to come into its own. Ten years after his death: that is the final ironic, tragic, Westian joke" (*IDL*, xxiii). But perhaps the biggest boost to his literary reputation occurred in America in 1957, when all four novels were reissued in a single volume. Singing his praises, reviewers then proclaimed him one of this country's most significant writers of the 1930s.

III

Yet the Nathanael West critical industry started slowly. A few months after West's death, Edmund Wilson commented on the loss. In a "Postscript" to his *The Boys in the Back Room*, he offered brief estimates of West and of his own good friend, F. Scott Fitzgerald, who had died on 21 December, the day preceding West's demise. After a few brief comments on West's first three novels, followed by his 1939 review of *The Day of the Locust*, Wilson moved on to Fitzgerald. He concluded his piece with a familiar accusation. "Both West and Fitzgerald were writers of a conscience and with natural gifts rare enough in America or anywhere," he declared, "and their failure to get the best out of their best years may certainly be laid partly to Hollywood, with its already appalling record of talent depraved and wasted."[35] More than a decade later, David D. Galloway would repeat and extend this Fitzgerald/ West comparison. "Both men had an agonized sense of the ironies of life," he wrote, "and their heroes all embarked on the fatal race for a green light or a silver screen image that continuously receded before them."[36] In repeating this cherished canard of East Coast writers concerning Hollywood's pernicious effect on novelists, Wilson fails to mention that despite their "natural gifts," both West and Fitzgerald needed Hollywood much more than Hollywood needed them. Wells Root, himself a screenwriter, offered a more realistic appraisal of the effects of screenwriting on his friend West. "Whatever happened to him in pictures, good or bad, up to the time of his death," Root observed, "had affected in no way his real work, which was writing novels" (Gehman, *IDL*, xix).

West's death was not big news in literary circles, neither in Hollywood nor elsewhere. The *1940–41 International Motion Picture Almanac*, for example, listed eight movies on which he had worked, together with the dates and studios. The next year's issue mentioned him under "Deaths of the Year."[37] The 1940 edition of *Current Biography* treated him little better, devoting most of the eight-line entry to his and Eileen's fatal accident.[38] America was now at war, and seemingly little critical attention could be spared for a recently dead writer of bitter novellas and scripts for second-rate films. But by 1946 the war was over, returning veterans were jamming college campuses, and the publishing industry was expanding. The nation's intellectual mood was now expansive enough to accept West's dark comedy. Among the first to note this cultural shift was an old West admirer and friend, Robert M. Coates. Introducing the 1946 New Directions edition of *Miss Lonelyhearts*, Coates characterized West as "fundamentally, a pessimist"—a quality characteristic of his "between-wars" generation. Coates discerned "something a little unhealthy" in West's "insistence on the unpleasantness of all primary human relations." Yet Coates also felt it was "the savagery that gives bite to his work and the unhealthiness that gives it color."[39]

Not until the next year, however, did academe—in the person of Daniel Aaron—discover Nathanael West. Writing in *Partisan Review* rather than in an academic journal, Aaron turned out one of the first critical essays on West that was not meant as a review or an introduction to a new volume. He was prompted by English critic Cyril Connolly's description of *Miss Lonelyhearts* as a neglected but "defiant masterpiece of futility" suffering the fate of many other worthy novels "little known or underrated." Aaron fully agreed, and declared that Edmund Wilson alone had adequately treated West's "strange and remarkable talent." Yet Aaron wished *The Dream Life of Balso Snell* had not been published, since it lacks most of the merits of West's other novels. Still it does illustrate "West's predilection for the perverse and the grotesque." In *Miss Lonelyhearts* West is "less fantastic," Aaron continued, but the world he depicts remains "intensely personal" and resembles "a wasteland" lacking any "signs of spring." West makes this wasteland even more evident in his third novel, *A Cool Million: or The Dismantling of Lemuel Pitkin*. But this "unpleasantly genial parody," Aaron declared, proves a mere "weak tour de force which is hardly saved by its serious undertones and occasional insights." With *The Day of the Locust*, however, West returns "to a more significant level of writing." This final novel may lack "the concentration and focus of *Miss Lonelyhearts*, "said Aaron, but it still reveals "a detachment, a curious and penetrating discernment." Aaron admired West's novels, but, ever the cautious academic, he was careful not to overrate them. West's works cannot match, for instance, "the colorful and violent documentations of Dos Passos or the grim tracts of Farrell" (*TTM*, 99–106).

Despite the interest displayed by critics like Edmund Wilson and Daniel Aaron in West's work, most American literary histories and reference books either ignored or dismissed him in a sentence or two. Across the Atlantic, however, the English began to pay attention. Alan Ross was first, with a piece in *Horizon*. West's underlying rationale derives from a "disgust" near to "hysteria," stated Ross, and in *The Dream Life of Balso Snell* this disgust is coupled with a complete disregard for any audience. Still West could swing from this unimpressive exercise in "intellectual gauchery," Ross added, to a work with "the direct and economic intensity of *Miss Lonelyhearts*." But then he could follow up immediately with *A Cool Million*, at best "a hurried, exaggerated allegory without a phrase of distinction." Then again, only a few years later, with *The Day of the Locust* West could suggest he was "merging his bitterness and savagery into a wider, more organic pattern without losing his edge."[40]

Nathanael West had been dead for nine years when the first English edition of *Miss Lonelyhearts* appeared (with the Ross article as introduction) in

1949, 16 years after the novel's initial publication. Michael Swan, reviewing it in the *New Statesman and Nation*, was properly respectful: he found the novel to be "as shapely as a sonnet, as concentrated as an epigram." It is a kind of "Christian parable, the product of that interesting type of mind which seems controlled by a Christian background and yet is repelled by it."[41] But for West devotees, a new era began in 1950, with several tangible signs of his growing critical and public acceptance. In his *A Literary History of Southern California*, Franklin Walker noted the "serious intent" reprsented by "the works of two promising writers who died young—*The Day of the Locust*, by Nathaniel (*sic*) West, and *The Last Tycoon* (by) F. Scott Fitzgerald." Walker then offered up a familiar lament: "Although they vary in degree of satire, humor, and shock, the novels about Hollywood nearly all agree that life in the movie colony is artificial, the art meretricious, and the industry the graveyard of talent."[42]

More substantial was Richard Gehman's Introduction to the New Directions edition of *The Day of the Locust*. Gehman adroitly summed up some significant differences between the "philosophy . . . climate and character" of West's novels and those of his literary contemporaries. Like them, West also "deplored the emptiness" of American life in the 1930s. Yet he focused on "characters who were, in the blindness of their lives, so tragic as to be true comic figures." Echoing Alan Ross, Gehman reasoned that his characters' unrelenting intensity may have been one of the reasons for West's never winning a wide audience in his lifetime (Gehman, *IDL*, ix–xi, xix). An unidentified reviewer in *Newsweek* took exception to Gehman's comments. "In his otherwise interesting introduction," the writer stated, "Richard Gehman tries to make West a typical example of the neglected genius, but the characterization never quite fits." Still the reviewer found West's work to be "distinctive and original," especially *The Day of the Locust*.[43] Much more certain and specific was the tough-minded Isaac Rosenfeld. In *Partisan Review* he lamented the inability of American intellectuals to write effectively on the nation's popular culture. Only one man, Nathanael West, truly "knew what he was doing" and made this evident by the validity of his theme: "the secret inner life of the masses." The aesthetic result is work of "independent status, the nearest thing to a new art form ever to be derived from the materials of a mass culture."[44]

The next year a half-dozen pieces on West appeared, but several were slight notices or merely revisions or expansions of earlier efforts. In his *American Literature in the Twentieth Century*, Swiss literary historian Heinrich Straumann devoted a single paragraph to West, focusing primarily on *Miss Lonelyhearts*.[45] In *The Modern Novel in America*, American scholar Frederick J. Hoffman included only two quick references to *The Day of the Locust*. One was a footnote, but in the other he stated that "Though Nathanael West's *Day of the Locust* (1939) has its own reasons for failure, it is much more successful in isolated scenes and in sharpness of focus than Fitzgerald's fictional view of Hollywood."[46] In his revised edition of *Exile's Return*, which he now subtitled *A*

Literary Odyssey of the 1920's, Malcolm Cowley updated his 1934 comments to declare *The Day of the Locust* "still the best of the Hollywood novels" and *Miss Lonelyhearts* "a tender and recklessly imaginative novel that had few readers" (*ER*, 237–40). Some fresh biographical details did appear in Erskine Caldwell's *Call It Experience: The Years of Learning How to Write*. Caldwell briefly recalled his three-week stay at the Sutton in 1931 and his friendship with West.[47]

The most substantial 1951 offering was a *Hudson Review* evaluation of *The Day of the Locust* by Daniel Aaron. Trying again for a balanced appraisal, Aaron repeated much of his earlier essay and reached the same conclusions. West is "a comic writer who can be droll if never unabashedly joyous, and he is as much impressed by the ludicrousness of life as he is by its horror." Aaron did not find this final effort "really a satisfactory novel." West never fuses "his image of the 'dream dump' with the more revealing symbol of the cockfight."[48] Richard McLaughlin was also interested in West's view of Hollywood. In his rather florid "West of Hollywood," McLaughlin claimed that West's deep natural pessimism had been compounded by his exposure to the Surrealists in Paris. Their "derisive, destructive nay-saying" had inspired his "strikingly vivid, perversely original" fantasy *The Dream Life of Balso Snell*. Later, needing "a theme worthy of his fury to bring out the acid in his pen," West rediscovered one in *The Day of the Locust*, "the most biting, disturbing book to come out of Hollywood."[49]

In 1955, Cyril M. Schneider, making adroit use of earlier criticism, published a survey of West's life and work in the *Western Review*. While he did mention some critics and reviewers by name, Schneider included no footnotes or bibliography and was later accused of plagiarism.[50] Attempting to pinpoint the qualities that set West apart from his contemporaries, Schneider stated that everywhere he looked West saw "evil and stupidity" triumph over good, to such an extent that he found "no hope of redemption or escape."[51] James Light, who would later publish the first book-length study of West, shifted critical attention back to West's obsessive use of violence. In his "*Miss Lonelyhearts*: The Imagery of Nightmare," Light reasoned that this novel's postwar popularity "is understandable" in a "world increasingly dominated by violence." Relying on "a succinct, imagistic style," West portrays a suffering hero spiritually adrift in a "decayed world" whose "basic reality is violence." He becomes a man "split between the spirit and the flesh, between the devil and the saint."[52] Arthur Cohen, writing in the Catholic magazine *Commonweal*, was less interested in West's debt to surrealistic imagery than to Dostoyevsky and the figure of the "holy fool." Calling his piece "The Possibilities of Belief: Nathanael West's Holy Fool," Cohen declared that the Russian "provides the paradigm of West's creative activity." The Dostoyevskian hero is a pilgrim of the dialectical "opposition of the perfect sinner and the perfect saint." A similar "hero of the dialectic, albeit the modern dialectic," is at the center of West's novels.[53] The next year W. H. Auden, in his "Interlude: West's Disease," offered his special perspective on West and his work. Declaring that "Nathanael West is not, strictly speaking a novelist," Auden explained that West "does not attempt an accurate description either of the social scene or of the subjective life of the mind." West is for Auden a "specialist who knows everything about one disease and nothing about any other." In short, his major characters all "suffer from the same spiritual disease." This malady, or "West's Disease," is one "of consciousness." It not only renders its victim "incapable of converting wishes into desires," but also every wish has "the same and unvarying meaning: 'I refuse to be what I am.'"[54]

IV

Critical interest in West and his work continued to rise. The 1957 one-volume edition of *The Complete Works of Nathanael West*—with Alan Ross's *Criterion* piece as introduction—brought a new wave of reviews and essays.[55] "Is a Nathanael West Revival under way?" asked the "News and Ideas" section of *College English*.[56] The answer was a resounding "Yes." In his *New Yorker* review, Norman Podhoretz flatly declared that this volume of "only four hundred and twenty-one pages . . . contains some of the best writing . . . by an American in this century." Yet many readers fail to grasp that "West was first and last a writer of comedy." For West's " 'particular kind of joking,' " noted Podhoretz, proves primarily to be his means "of saying that the universe is always rigged against us and that our efforts to contend with it invariably lead to absurdity."[57]

Podhoretz wished to explain West's comedy. Edward Greenfield Schwartz focused on why contemporary critics attacked West personally and also misread his novels. Shortly before his death, West had "complained to F. Scott Fitzgerald that most of the reviews of *The Day of the Locust* were 'brutal personal attacks.' " But, as Schwartz rightly pointed out, West had little cause for surprise. He had aligned himself with those venomous "laughing morticians" of the satiric monthly *Americana*, who had determined that all of modern civilization exuded "a miasmic stench." Hence his novels lacked "dogma, hope, and idealism and seemed anachronistic in a decade dominated by proletarian fiction." Critics may also have been "embarrassed by his self-abasement, which seems at times to border on an almost virulent anti-Semitism."[58] These factors may help explain why critics and readers took so long to recognize West's importance. "Work as original and remarkable as West's," claimed William Bittner in the *Nation*, "almost always fails to strike an audience when it first appears. But if the artist's insight is sound . . . and . . . if his technique is valid . . . the audience will grow into appreciation of it." West delves deeper than does Melville, said Bittner, "into the ingrained confidence game of American civilization" to reveal the ever-growing "split between aspiration and actuality."[59] An indication of the validity of West's satire, added Roger H. Smith in the *Saturday Review*, is that his works seem increasingly relevant. West's "saving grace" as man and writer, declared Smith, was his "detached" treatment of "the dreams by which man attempts to live and of the violence which perverts these dreams."[60]

In a piece in the *Reporter* titled "He Might Have Been A Major Novelist," Ralph Russell lamented the loss of West's potential. His fictional method is the more effective, said Russell, "precisely because it is a caricature." His thought and action were seemingly "derived from the picaresque novel," and they suggest "that everything is empty and dreadful" and essentially "a fraud." Yet for all his cynicism, West's portrait of suffering people in New York and Hollywood is "deeply, heartbreakingly sympathetic and . . . in places magnificently comic."[61] Also emphasizing West's bitter anger was *Time* magazine's anonymous reviewer. Under the heading of "The Great Despiser," the writer pointed out that amid "the whimpers" of the Depression "West raised a man's voice in savage rage against the general condition of man." In America's bland literary climate of the 1950s, "the chilling ferocity of West's satirical attack . . . involves not only a total rejection of common American ideals, but a Swiftian loathing for the texture of life itself." The *Time* staffer did not find this anger excessive. "A hard man is good to find," the reviewer concluded, "and such a one was West."[62] William Peden essentially agreed. Writing in the *Virginia Quarterly Review*, he stated that despite the varied techniques and subject matter of West's novels, they are all "savage indictments of . . . the 'horrible emptiness of mass lives.' "[63]

The single volume of West's collected novels was published not only in America but also in England, where the critics found the same strengths and weaknesses in his work as did their American colleagues. Simon Raven, in a brief note in the *Spectator*, observed that West centers on "the power of a hostile universe to reduce mankind to mere waste-bags of lechery and absurdity."[64] In the *New Statesman* V. S. Pritchett offered a longer and more thoughtful appraisal. He declared West to have been "preoccupied with hysteria as the price paid for accepting the sentimentalities of the national dream." West drew his material from dreams and their "terrible deceits." Pritchett also credited West with being "a delicate student of the American bitch," as well as with exhibiting "comic powers," a flair for "inventing extraordinary scenes," and, interestingly enough, a "sadistic streak." What he lacked was "the breadth for full-length works."[65]

In a lengthy but essentially revisionist overview, the unidentified reviewer in the *Times Literary Supplement* argued that West's posthumous reputation was unmerited. He may have been "underestimated" while alive, said the *TLS* reviewer, but West has been "grossly over-praised in recent years." Essentially a "sad moralist," he is frequently too "facetious, . . . careful and even finicky to develop "a personal style." In fact, his fiction, "beneath the chromium brightness of its surface," offers little but "a self-corrosive despair."[66] A much briefer and even harsher reaction was that of Graham Hough. Informing his *Encounter* readers that he regarded the West "omnibus" as essentially "a period piece," he conceded that *Miss Lonelyhearts* has enjoyed "a justified minor celebrity." But he dismissed as "surely absurd" any ranking of West among this century's greatest Ameican writers.[67] But back in New York, playwright Howard Teichmann offered West devotees his stage version of *Miss Lonelyhearts* at the Music Box theatre. The critics were scathing. "As a dramatic transcript of West's book," declared Henry Popkin, in the *New Republic*, Teichmann's play "is consistently inaccurate . . . in transmitting the spirit, although the letter sometimes survives."[68] In the *Commonweal*, Richard Hayes was more penetrating and charitable than Popkin, but ultimately he was disappointed for the same reasons. Howard Teichmann's adaptation, Hays lamented, while "gallant and honorable and committed," lacked West's "authenticity of first-hand experience."[69]

Of course, America's literary critics continued to voice their opinions, in ever-increasing numbers. Looking for fresh insights, some now felt pressed to discern and elaborate on West's literary sources, beyond the Surrealists. Dostoyevsky quickly proved a clear favorite. For example, James F. Light published a second article on West's dependence on violence and dreams, adding a section on his indebtedness to Dostoyevsky. In an essay for *College English* titled "Violence, Dreams, and Dostoyevsky: The Art of Nathanael West," Light observed that at his universe's "dark center" West places the conjunction of "violence and dreams." In the background hovers "the shadow of Fyodor Dostoyevsky," whose Grand Inquisitor charges that God has given man not happiness but freedom." This very freedom causes West's people to seek something in which to believe. Failing that, they are "doomed to total misery."[70]

The same year, in his much-heralded essay "The Breakthrough," Leslie Fiedler traced the emergence of the Jewish novelist in America. Placing West within a Jewish literary context, in sharp contrast to Malcolm Cowley, Fiedler related him to the literary violence of the 1930s. For Fiedler the essential truth was that Nathanael West, "despite his own disclaimers, [remains] in a real sense, a Jew." No other writer reveals "so absolute a sense of the misery of being human."[71] However, Malcolm Cowley, in his Introduction to the Avon paperback edition (1959) of *Miss Lonelyhearts*, linked Pep West, whom he knew personally, not to his Jewish background but to the literary spirit of the decade preceding the Depression. For Cowley, West's novels reveal "the spirit of the 1920's, with all their reckless experimentation, their effort to be outrageous, their interest in wildly personal dreams, their sympathy for the individual oppressed not by social forces but by the laws of life itself."[72]

V

By the 1960s so much had been written on West that whether knowingly or not, critics were recycling earlier insights. They also resorted to enlarging—

often exaggerating—West's historical importance and his specific indebtedness to earlier poems and stories or novels. These elements are to be seen in one of the decade's earliest pieces, Marc L. Ratner's " 'Anywhere Out of This World': Baudelaire and Nathanael West." The "European tone" of West's fiction, said Ratner, "that is, his rejection of reform and his belief in the absurdity of existence, has its source in the French Symbolists and particularly Baudelaire." More specifically, Ratner claimed that the "pivotal" discussion of the "alternatives of escape" in chapter 7 of *Miss Lonelyhearts* derives from Baudelaire. Indeed, he claimed that a comparison of Baudelaire's prose poem "Anywhere Out of This World" and West's *Miss Lonelyhearts* would shed light on the latter's "theme and format," as well as on its hero's "absurd, ironic death."[73]

Death as a theme was also very much on Leslie Fiedler's mind. Fiedler helped launch the new literary decade with his memorable survey *Love and Death in the American Novel*. Recasting and dividing his earlier views on West, Fiedler found in the early fiction "traces of queasiness before woman's surrender of her traditional role, her usurpation of male privileges which so disturbed Faulkner." This gender shift proves indicative of things to come. West's later "fiction contains a series of . . . travesties of the teasers and betrayers and lady rapists who assault and torment his male protagonists." Fay Greener, for example, "is the blond bitch in all her archetypal purity." Not surprisingly, Fiedler again linked West with a Jewish literary tradition. Despite his strenuous efforts at denial, West remained, claimed Fiedler, "enough the child of a long [Jewish] tradition of nonviolence to be racked by guilt in the face of violence." Yet despite his gifts, West did not strike Fiedler as a truly "achieved writer."[74] Ihab Hassan sounded a somewhat similar note. For Hassan, the attitudes West and other American novelists express toward love and sexuality are senseless and pathetic. In his "Love in the American Novel," Hassan observed that James T. Farrell, John O'Hara, John Dos Passos, and Nathanael West use "sexual activity, brutalized and random," to suggest the pathetic failure of modern human relations.[75] For Edmond L. Volpe the most interesting element in *Miss Lonelyhearts* was not the lack of satisfying love or sex but its echoes of T. S. Eliot. Volpe did not know whether West intended "a reply" to Eliot's *The Waste Land*, but the "similarities in theme and imagery seem too obvious to be accidental." Volpe did discern one important difference. In Eliot's poem "regeneration is possible," whereas in West's fiction "there is no hope of salvation."[76]

V. L. Lokke found West's lack of hope even more pronounced in *The Day of the Locust*. In "A Side Glance at Medusa" (one of the more pessimistic readings of this novel), Lokke agreed with Edmund Wilson that West was not only the first novelist to catch Hollywood's "emptiness" but also the first to make "this emptiness horrible." Lokke declared that West's analysis rests in part on his view of "Hollywood as a symbol rather than as a peculiar institution, industry, or city." There the restive hordes of the marginal and disenfranchised embody "the anarchic energy which can destroy our society."[77] Lokke's article appeared early in 1961. That year was marked by the first book-length study of West: James F. Light's groundbreaking *Nathanael West: An Interpretative Study*. His was not an attempt at "a comprehensive biography," explained Light, but at an analysis of the "interrelationship between West's life and . . . art." He wished to illuminate "the work, basically, and the life, subordinately." In doing so, he found "biographically relevant . . . the theme of the Quest," a theme that "runs through each analysis of the novels."[78] Like Leslie Fiedler and many critics to follow, Light emphasized West's Jewishness. He attributed West's lifelong rejection of his ethnic heritage to his having been denied fraternity membership at Brown because he was a Jew. Later biographers and critics have amplified and even corrected Light's study, but all are indebted to him for having provided the initial road map through West's life and work.

The Autumn 1961 issue of *Kenyon Review* contained a lengthy verbal portrait by Josephine Herbst of the young West, whom she had met in 1932. She also compared his ideas with those of the Surrealists and Dostoyevsky, and analyzed *Miss Lonelyhearts* and *The Day of the Locust*. West's novels are "dark parables" devoid of heroes, big shots, tycoons, or even rich people. His lack of public acceptance, Herbst believed, can be attributed to the savagery of his criticism and lack of a counterbalancing hope.[79] In 1962, Stanley Edgar Hyman published a 40-page monograph, *Nathanael West*, that is noteworthy primarily for its succinct summaries of West's life and four novels and a Freudian reading of his fiction. Relying for biographical information primarily on Light and acquaintances of West, such as Richard B. Gehman, A. J. Liebling, Ruth McKenney, and John Sanford, Hyman nevertheless failed to challenge West's personal fabrications, that later biographers would correct. Hyman considered *Miss Lonelyhearts*, along with *The Great Gatsby* and *The Sun Also Rises*, as among this century's "three finest American novels." He found both Oedipal and latent homosexual tendencies in West's hero and concluded that West's basic strength derives from "his vulgarity and bad taste, his pessimism, his nastiness."[80]

In a symposium paper on experimental novelists, published in the *Massachusetts Review*, John Hawkes also focused on these dark aspects of West's fiction. Comparing West with Djuna Barnes and Flannery O'Connor, Hawkes declared these three very different American writers to be unique "in their uses of wit, their comic treatments of violence and their extreme detachment."[81] Continuing his comparison of West and O'Connor in an essay for the *Sewanee Review* titled "Flannery O'Connor's Devil," Hawkes saw West as the novelist "who, along with Flannery O'Connor, deserves singular attention as a rare American satirist." These two comic writers may differ in their visions, but they alone share an "inverted attraction for the reality of our absurd condition."[82] Focusing on *The Day of the Locust*, David D. Galloway also probed West's dark vision, at much greater length. In his "Nathanael West's Dream Dump,"

Galloway argued that West nurtures the "theme of man's self-delusionment in a world of frustrating and finally destructive dreams." Indeed the dreams West chronicles "inevitably metamorphosed into nightmare." In place of ideology, West offers a warning "that life is a hoax, an April-fool purse embroidered with dreams."[83]

R. W. B. Lewis was also not much concerned with West's ideology, dealing instead with his use of the clown or Fool. In "Hart Crane and the Clown Tradition," Lewis observed that in his poem "Chaplinesque," Crane introduced his generation to the figure "of the clown, of the poet as clown, or of the poet, perhaps of Everyman, as Fool." Transformed into "the artist as comedian" by Wallace Stevens and E. E. Cummings, and later by Henry Miller and Nathanael West (in *Miss Lonelyhearts*), "the figure of the poet, and of the human being, as clown has seemed singularly appropriate in a world where . . . the human being [is turned] into a grotesque."[84] For Alvin Kernan, West was essentially a satirist who melds fantasy and nightmare. In "The Mob Tendency in Satire: *The Day of the Locust*," Kernan explained that West is a very different type of "moralist" than, say, an Alexander Pope. As a novelist West develops his effects "in blocks of semi-realistic description of scenes, characters and actions." Yet the final effect in both satirists is "to show folly's disorganization of all that is fundamental to life."[85] In 1964, David D. Galloway followed up his article of the previous year with "A Picaresque Apprenticeship: Nathanael West's *The Dream Life of Balso Snell* and *A Cool Million*." Wishing to rescue West's lesser two novels from their "critical limbo," Galloway insisted that despite their "lack of restraint [and] contrived picaresque structures," these novels reveal, even "in raw form," West's basic "themes, techniques, and influences." West was "a great despiser" who satirized what he despised. His targets were less the men themselves than the masks they wore.[86]

In his *Nathanael West: The Ironic Prophet* (1964), Victor Comerchero explained that his is "a critical discussion" and "lengthy introduction" rather than "a thorough study of West." Sounding much like Stanley Edgar Hyman, whose West monograph he praised, Comerchero also provided a Freudian reading of West and attempted to trace the influence of French surrealists and symbolists, of Jessie L. Weston's *From Ritual to Romance*, and of T. S. Eliot's *The Waste Land* on his work. Commerchero cited a basic flaw in West. Although he displays "much ingenuity," West shows "little variety" or "range" and repeatedly strikes a single "note"; it amounts to a "a half-warning, half-despairing cry" for the "victim" of our modern age whom Comerchero dubbed "Westian Man."[87] By 1965 Westian Man appeared to many readers as the prime symbol of modern man *in extremis*. But the West critical boom was causing some critics to scramble to find new significance in West's much-disparaged first novel. In his essentially negative "Nathanael West's *The Dream Life of Balso Snell*," A. M. Tibbetts, like Galloway, claimed that in this "long short story" all West's "themes and techniques" are present "in embryonic form." Tibbetts concluded that, like Jonathan Swift, West allowed his hatred for man to "overrule his sense of artistic form and propriety," and express his hatred "by a fascination for man's lowest functions." For these and other reasons, West was for Tibbetts "a writer who has lost artistic control of his work."[88]

At this point, Daniel Aaron, one of West's earliest academic critics, updated his initial impressions in "Late Thoughts on Nathanael West." He was not claiming that West was "misunderstood and neglected," he stated. West belonged to a select group of socially committed novelists and poets like Edward Dahlberg, Kenneth Fearing, and S. J. Perelman. West supported the Left's objectives but retained "the verbal exuberance, the unplayful irony, the nocturnal surrealist fancies associated with a certain school of expatriate writing in the 'twenties." Aaron then discussed the influence of William James, Tolstoy, and John Bunyan on West. Yet no matter how closely he followed his literary masters, West failed to impress his fellow radicals. For them the real problem with *A Cool Million*, as with his other novels, Aaron concluded, was that "the real culprit is not capitalism but humanity."[89] Then, in a particularly telling piece, Douglas H. Shepard made clear that West's reliance on his sources could amount at times to word-for-word borrowing. Those early reviewers who had recognized the derivation of *A Cool Million* from Horatio Alger's formula fiction, Shepard claimed in "Nathanael West Rewrites Horatio Alger, Jr.," were "more correct than they realized." But what they and even later critics had failed to notice is that West's novel depends not merely "on a parody of Alger's prose style" but also on passages lifted directly from Alger's novels "without . . . acknowledgment." Refraining from the charge of plagiarism, Shepard argued that it must have cost West "as much effort, if not more, to adapt and tinker with the original . . . than to invent out of whole cloth."[90] R. W. B. Lewis, who earlier had been concerned with West's use of the clown as Everyman, was now interested in his use of Satan. In his "Days of Wrath and Laughter," Lewis stated that "the Satanic character" in *The Day of the Locust*, "the harnesser of all that hatred, goes in fact unnamed." Yet readers are made aware that he will prove to "be an even greater scoundrel . . . serving the bitter frustrations of the aging California citizenry." This "California super-promiser" will prove "a successor as well to West's earlier Antichrists, the editor Shrike in *Miss Lonelyhearts* (1933) and Shagpoke Whipple in *A Cool Million* (1934)."[91]

In Fall 1966, Thomas M. Lorch published the first of three essays drawn from his Yale dissertation on West. In "The Inverted Structure of *Balso Snell*," he refocused attention on West's first novel, to join those critics taking a fresh view of West's "least understood and least appreciated book." Disagreeing with those who "find it significant . . . only insofar as it anticipates West's later works," Lorch declared *Balso Snell* to be "a worthwhile short fiction" whose faults are of "execution" rather than "fundamental conception." This novel represents not "a dismissal of literature," Lorch insisted, "but rather a scathing critique of its misuses, abuses, and perversions."[92] In his next essay,

"West's *Miss Lonelyhearts*: Skepticism Mitigated?," Lorch considered the influence of Edwin Diller Starbuck's *Psychology of Religion* and especially William
James's *The Varieties of Religious Experience* on West's second novel. For here,
Lorch stated, West has "followed James . . . in denying the existence of
supernatural reality." Still, neither James nor West totally rejects religion. The
religious development of West's hero adheres not only to the pattern delineated
by William James, argued Lorch, but also exhibits "basic characteristics"
advocated by such Christian mystics as the medieval St. John of the Cross and
the modern theologian Jacques Maritain. The very intensity of West's own
religious needs cause him to suggest through his hero "that religion may be
a positive source of insight and creativity as well as a destructive illusion."[93]
A very different view of the religious elements in *Miss Lonelyhearts* was offered
by Robert J. Andreach, in his "Nathanael West's *Miss Lonelyhearts*: Between
the Dead Pan and the Unborn Christ." Relating West's novel to the "Pan-
Christ antagonism," he saw the story's "unifying principle" as that struggle
which pits "the virile, sexual, natural paganism against the effeminate, ascetic,
materialistic Christianity." In *Miss Lonelyhearts*, the cynical editor Shrike is
identified as "the dead Pan" and is suggestively satanic in his behavior. In
fact, said Andreach, that all of the novel's other characters, except Betty, prove
"inhibited worshipers" unable to "reconcile their Pan instincts" with their
awareness of the sinfulness of these instincts.[94]

   In a *Massachusetts Review* interview in Summer 1966, John Hawkes turned
again to Nathanael West to clarify the nature of his own comedy. Hawkes
recognized a special bond with West. He explained that "comedy works in
two ways." In his own work and in that of West, Flannery O'Connor, and
Joseph Heller comedy appears "a self-inflicting affair." Yet comedy also can
suggest "a saving attitude," as in Bernard Malamud. Any act that seems
"pathetically humorous or grotesquely humorous" draws the reader "back into
the realm . . . of . . . the one or two really deep permanent human values."
Every "writer of worth," Hawkes insisted, "is concerned with these things."[95]
It was not West's comedy, but rather his reliance upon psychology that
intrigued Roger D. Abrahams. In "Androgynes Bound: Nathanael West's
Miss Lonelyhearts," Abrahams labeled that novel "one of the most demanding
and perplexing reading experiences of American letters." In it West unfolds
a deeply "real moral dilemma in psychologically realistic terms," as he moves
his reader to sympathize with and laugh at the pathetic hero. The protagonist
recognizes that his "utter despair" or "malaise" derives from a failure to
"harmonize the dictates of head . . . [and] heart." He lacks a course of action
to "synthesize" these inner needs. His "sado-masochistic pattern," Abrahams
claimed, contributes to "an important inner rhythm" in the novel's structure.[96]

   Book-length studies of West were appearing in a steady trickle. In *The
Fiction of Nathanael West: No Redeemer, No Promised Land*, Randall Reid lucidly
traced West's literary and cultural sources. West was for him a curiously
paradoxical writer. He "repudiated social realism but focused on sociological

themes, dismissed psychological novels but was an acute literary psychologist, laughed at art but was a conscious and dedicated artist. He was a dandy with proletarian sympathies, a comic writer who specialized in unfunny jokes."[97] Following up the insights of earlier critics, Reid probed West's indebtedness to William James, Dostoyevsky, Aldous Huxley, James Branch Cabell, Sherwood Anderson, the French symbolist poets (especially Baudelaire and Rimbaud), Joris-Karl Huysmans, the Ritual Theater, the Comic-Strip Novel, and the Waste Land myth. While not the most original West scholar, Reid provided the most detailed and precise account of West's sources.

Freudian psychology, as well as Kafka, was the focal point of Leslie Fiedler's "Master of Dreams." Here Fiedler's basic purpose was to show how Kafka and Freud, "the crippled poet and the triumphant savant," have helped "shape . . . Jewish-American writing in the first half of the twentieth century." Though the critics of the 1930s did not suspect it, West began "the great take-over by Jewish-American writers of the American imagination." These writers were undertaking to dream "aloud the dreams of the whole American people." Hence *The Dream of Balso Snell* proves "a fractured and dissolving parable of the very process by which the emancipated Jew enters into the world of Western culture." It is also West's "last . . . explicit declaration of Jewishness."[98] In sharp contrast to Fiedler's view of West as a "Jewish" writer was Thomas Lorch's perception of him as a "Judeo-Christian" one. In his "Religion and Art in *Miss Lonelyhearts*," Lorch disagreed with those who find a rejection of "Christian belief and action" in the novel. These readers give inadequate weight either to the protagonist's "Christian development and improvement," said Lorch, or to "the inseparability of his positive growth" from those "equally real negative forces" (irony and skepticism) which challenge that growth.[99]

Concentrating on West's "violent pessimism," Kingsley Widmer offered a much darker reading. In "The Sweet Savage Prophecies of Nathanael West," Widmer saw West's "apocalyptic comedies" as "precursors of the despairing laughter" later to be "called 'black humor' and of several of the post-30s modes of poetic-naturalism." Still West's melancholy losers lack substance, reflecting their society's lack of both "human depth . . . [and] communal values."[100] Satiric devices rather than sex, religion, or violence were the central interest of James W. Nichols in his "Nathanael West, Sinclair Lewis, Alexander Pope and Satiric Contrasts." A familiar organizing "device" used in such satiric works as *A Cool Million, Babbitt,* and *The Rape of the Lock*, Nichols argued, is one "of playing one set of ideas or values against another." West draws upon the Horatio Alger novels to contrast their "ethos with the one embodied in *A Cool Million*." He provides "simultaneously a commentary upon the [earlier] kind of American optimism typified by Alger and a commentary upon the world of the 1930's."[101]

In 1968, the reprinting in England of the 1957 British edition of West's *Complete Works* (as well as the appearance there of Randall Reid's *The Fiction of Nathanael West*) resulted in a number of belated reviews. Two merit attention here. In his *Spectator* piece, "Prophet of Black Humour," Martin Seymour-Smith wrote as if he were unaware of West scholarship on the same topic. Certainly he did not acknowledge his own obvious debt to Leslie Fiedler. A stylistic and conceptual innovator, West was "the original black comedian," said Seymour-Smith, as well as "the prophet of the Jewish American novel of the 'fifties and 'sixties." In spite of his also being the inventor of "sick" humour, and "a prophet of doom," West inevitably "displays a poet's awareness" of his hapless characters' "truly human standards and sadly celebrates their innate vitality."[102] If Stanley Reynolds agreed that West was a true "master of black humour," in his review of the *Collected Works* in the *New Statesman*, he was moved to add that West has "no ear for real speech," while his fantasy and major characters "are all borrowed." A prime example is "Homer in *The Day of the Locust,* who is a straight steal from *Hands* in Sherwood Anderson's *Winesburg Ohio.*" West's psychology is equally unoriginal, insisted Reynolds, coming "literally word for word from William James's . . . *Varieties of Religious Experience.*" Even West admitted that he cut with " 'a pair of shears' " the "structure and characters" of *Miss Lonelyhearts* from *Crime and Punishment*, with entire "paragraphs of speech and emotions" derived in the same manner "from Huysmans, Aldous Huxley and others." But the prime problem is with the collective message of West's novels, Reynolds concluded: it is "life sans everything."[103]

As the 1960s wound to a close, West was garnering so much critical attention that even his two "neglected" novels were no longer neglected. Not surprisingly, critics by then often simply expanded on earlier observations and comparisons. In his "A Surfeit of Shoddy: Nathanael West's *A Cool Million*," for example, Robert I. Edenbaum, like so many critics before him, declared *A Cool Million* to be "a latter-day *Candide*," with Lemuel Pitkin taking the place of "Voltaire's innocent." Still *A Cool Million* does project the perspective of the American "lower-middle class" as then embodied in the schizophrenic "yellow journalism" of the Hearst press. To this end, West intends this novel to be "not an image of a world at all," claimed Edenbaum, "but an image of an image—a portrait of William Randolph Hearst's 'own self-portrait' of the lower-middle class."[104] One of the stronger critiques of those years was that of Max Schulz. In his *Radical Sophistication: Studies in Contemporary Jewish-American Novelists*, Schulz devoted a chapter to West. Calling his essay "Nathanael West's 'Desperate Detachment,'" Schulz argued that unlike most later Jewish-American writers West could not "rest content in the human suspension between heavenly aspirations and earthly limitations, belief and skepticism, order and disorder." Hence his novels, despite their basic satire, are weakened by West's "search for absolutes" and his inability "to control his own sense of outrage and despair."[105]

This decade of West criticism was rounded off by a 28-page monograph in the Seabury Press "Religious Dimensions in Literature" series. In his *Nathanael*

West's Miss Lonelyhearts: An Introduction and Commentary, Robert M. Perry offered four possible interpretations of *Miss Lonelyhearts*. Perry first advanced a secular summary of an "alienated" and "neurotic" young journalist experiencing "an identity crisis." The second interpretation described the religious quest of a young man who wishes to be "like Christ," but who exhibits "an unconscionable amount of violence." The third possible interpretation was even "more discouraging" than the previous two, said Perry. Viewing "our world as already in a post-Christian phase of history," West suggests Christ's suffering no longer has meaning for our culture, with Christ and Christianity now mere "decoration." Finally, Perry offered what he terms "the post-anti Christian interpretation" as closest to his own view. Whereas the modern novelist-critic may ask "what kind of God would tolerate the [human] condition," the needy human being insists that a higher "Something" must exist. Hence *Miss Lonelyhearts* can be read as a "trustworthy pointer toward a new emphasis in religion."[106]

VI

The new decade saw no decline in West criticism. Indeed, several banner years in both scholarship and criticism followed. In 1970, for example, Jay Martin published his *Nathanael West: The Art of His Life*, which was quickly recognized as the benchmark "life" of the novelist. Martin had been given access to West's papers by the novelist's sister Laura and her husband, S. J. Perelman. The approximately 700 items he examined included letters, notebooks and scrapbooks, unpublished plays and short stories, poems, film scenarios, and plans for novels. Martin also interviewed or corresponded with several hundred individuals who had known West. Martin's book not only gave new impetus to West criticism but also has served other critics as a prime source of information on the various ways West incorporated his dreams and experiences into his fiction. Also in 1970 Harold P. Simonson published a slender volume he called *The Closed Frontier: Studies in American Literary Tragedy*. In his concluding essay, "California, Nathanael West, and the Journey's End," Simonson related West's work to the California or "frontier" version of the American Dream. West's fiction, he stated, should "be read as a profound interpretation of how the great myth of the West comes to an end." Indeed, no angrier American novel than *The Day of the Locust* "has been written since *The Confidence Man* and *The Mysterious Stranger*."[107] Taking an even darker view of West's persistent negativism was Bruce Olsen. In "Nathanael West: The Use of Cynicism," Olsen complained that West assaults, like "a soured infant, not only Horatio Alger but also grassroots democracy, Christian compassion, and Hollywood's dream of America." He offers neither hope nor "positive feeling."[108]

If 1970 had proved an important year in West scholarship, so did 1971. In addition to a cluster of articles, two monographs and two collections of articles appeared. The most significant contribution was the revised edition of James F. Light's pioneer monograph, *Nathanael West: An Interpretative Study*, which had originally been published in 1961. Light now decided that there was "no easy answer" to explain the continuing growth of the Westian cult. West's vision may be "limited," Light noted, but it remains a vision whose "despair cries out from the heart" with enough honesty, seriousness, and power to render it memorable.[109] The other monograph was by Nathan A. Scott, Jr., and ostensibly offered another religious analysis of West and his work, comparable to the efforts of Perry and other critics. But in a 43-page pamphlet, *Nathanael West: A Critical Essay*, written for the Eerdmans "Contemporary Writers in Christian Perspective" series, Scott instead presented a succinct secular reading of West, based primarily on the work of Light and Martin.[110]

Jay Martin followed up his biography of the preceding year with *Nathanael West: A Collection of Critical Essays*, which brought together 19 previously published essays by various critics and four pieces by West himself. Martin set the tone for his essentially biographical introduction by observing that the novelist's "description of the hero of *The Day of the Locust* as 'really a very complicated young man with a whole set of personalities, one inside the other like a nest of Chinese boxes,' aptly characterizes West himself."[111] Actually, Martin's volume was one of two devoted to West and published in 1971 by Prentice-Hall. The other, *Twentieth Century Interpretations of Miss Lonelyhearts: A Collection of Critical Essays*, was edited by Thomas H. Jackson. As its title suggests, it is more narrowly focused than the Martin collection. Its 11 essays all deal with West's second novel. In his introduction Jackson summarized each of the essays.[112] Five appeared in the Martin collection and most have been discussed here.

A more regional approach to West is that taken by Lawrence Clark Powell in his "Nathanael West: The Day of the Locust." Using Jay Martin's biography of West as his guide, Powell, longtime director of the UCLA university library, placed that book within the context of the "Hollywood novel." Powell found *The Day of the Locust* to be "like a series of paintings by Hieronymous Bosch, etched in brilliant detail, terrible and compassionate, and rising to the apocalyptic denouement of an orgiastic movie premiere." Still the "pornographic novelists," he added, could learn much from West. His themes may be "sex and violence, alienation and disillusionment," but West handles them "fastidiously, surgically," with a total absence of "four-letter words."[113] The next year Irving Malin opened his monograph, *Nathanael West's Novels*, by declaring his departure from West's earlier critics. Those critics have not "read the novels in a chronological way, from the opening chapter to the end." Malin thus found "dangerous" their assumption "that the text is not the last word." Some critics have also misread West's ambivalence as resulting "from his sexual tensions" rather than from his Jewishness. Malin conceded only that

"West is as ambivalent toward Freud as he is toward the Jew." His novels may be "written with great authority," but they prove essentially "childish." His heroes find themselves in a "closed dreamworld" where they end in "nightmarish failure." Nathanael West is then "the spiritual father (or brother) . . . [and] inspirational guide" of the more recent American Gothic writer.[114]

Budd Schulberg continued in the same vein. Near the end of his biographical sketch, "Pep West: Prince Myshkin in a Brooks Brothers Suit" (discussed above), Schulberg compared West with S. J. Perelman and some of the writers Malin mentions. "It may be no accident that Pep and his brother-in-law, Sid Perelman, were such intimate friends," Schulberg observed. "[F]or artistically there is a definite connection between them," as "a savage rejection of human foibles" flows also through Perelman's humor. In addition to his "true gallows humor," West "anticipated the style of Becket and Ionesco." He was "an innovator" as well as "a perfectionist," with the "ingenious ability to combine pratfall comedy with impacted realism" (Schulberg, 164–67).

Early in 1973 Mike Frank, in his "The Passion of Miss Lonelyhearts According to Nathanael West," insisted that *Miss Lonelyhearts* was a "profoundly anti-Christian novel." In it the world proved "a perennial wasteland . . . [with] heroism . . . meaningless and martyrdom futile. . . . [F]leeing the corrupt city to seek redemption in nature," Miss Lonelyhearts and Betty discover the "pastoral myth" to be "just that, a myth." In West's universe then "the only reasonable alternative to the protagonist's furious despair is cynicism," Frank stated, so that Shrike's repulsive responses "at least have the virtue of making sense." With no true Christ in which to believe, Miss Lonelyhearts is driven to assume the savior's role himself.[115]

The most comprehensive work published on West in 1973 was a critical collection edited by David Madden and titled *Nathanael West: The Cheaters and the Cheated*. Several years earlier these 14 essays had been entries in a competition for the best essay on West, sponsored by Everett / Edwards publishers and the *Southern Review*. The winning essay had appeared in the *Southern Review*; the rest were making their first appearance in print. Instead of a conventional introduction, editor Madden opted for "A Confluence of Voices"—that is, for a carefully selected and imaginatively melded series of quotations from West's fiction, letters, friends, and critics (including the volume's own contributors' essays), as well as from a wide variety of writers. The tightly screened essays and creative introduction make this volume the strongest collection of West criticism to date.[116]

At the same time, Walter Wells focused on *The Day of the Locust* as not only the quintessential Hollywood novel, but also one wrested from the nature of a place. In "Shriek of the Locusts," a chapter in *Tycoons and Locusts*, his study of 1930s Hollywood fiction, Wells emphasized the close relationship between West's narrative and its "Hollywood-Southland" setting. Here is where the corruption of the American Dream proves contagious enough to pervert traditional forms of religion, love, or sexuality. Hence *The Day of the Locust* is "a novel which does not measure good against bad, or bad against worse," stated Wells. Rather, it's a novel "where all is nightmare."[117] For Daniel R. Brown, however, Hollywood's influence seemed less important than the influence of naturalism and existentialism. In "The War Within Nathanael West: Naturalism and Existentialism," Brown insisted that both movements left strong imprints on West's work. But instead of "exist[ing] separately or in pure, unadulterated form," they "combine, usually in confused and even contradictory ways." Thus West can be at times "as darkly pessimistic as the most pessimistic existentialists," but on other occasions he may be truly "hopeful." Differing from Jean Paul Sartre, however, West sees little freedom in his characters' choices. His response "to the metaphysical shriek . . . is neither suicide nor acceptance. It is thin, ironic laughter."[118]

A tangible example of West's suspension between hope and disillusion is his use of the *Anima Christi* prayer in *Miss Lonelyhearts*. In an extended note in *The Explicator*, David R. Mayer pointed out that in *The Dream Life of Balso Snell* West satirically incorporates three Latin verses from the *Anima Christi* into his tale of St. Puce, the "flea who lives in the armpit of Christ." This brief citation becomes a parody of the full text in *Miss Lonelyhearts* through the character of the cynical editor Shrike, whose ongoing "parody represents in miniature Miss Lonelyhearts' fumbled search."[119] In another *Explicator* note, Herb Russell added to our understanding of West's use of characters' names. In *The Day of the Locust*, Russell stated, West used the maiden name of Emily Dickinson's discoverer, Mabel Loomis, for his "Maybelle Loomis," whose spoiled child starts the novel's riot. West also uses Mabel Loomis's married name, Todd, in naming his central character "Tod." In dragging her child "from casting office to casting office," Maybelle Loomis is guilty of the same kind of selfish advancement that Mabel (Loomis) Todd may have been."[120]

Rounding off 1975 was the indefatigable William White with his *Nathanael West: A Comprehensive Bibliography*. Building on his own earlier bibliographies and checklists, White provided an invaluable research tool for all students of Nathanael West. Listing West's writings chronologically and critical material about him alphabetically, White filled 181 pages with information on West's plays and movies, his unpublished stories and miscellaneous writings, theses and dissertations devoted to him, title pages from West's novels, and an appendix of uncollected writings. In a work of this scope, errors of omission and commission are inevitable, but all subsequent critics, reviewers, editors, and bibliographers of West are indebted to White for his pioneering efforts.[121] The following year, Dennis P. Vannatta readily acknowledged his indebtedness to White. In his *Nathanael West: An Annotated Bibliography of the Scholarship and Works*, Vanatta listed and often annotated "over 500 books, articles in periodicals, reviews, theses, and dissertations which concerned West in one degree or another." The student of West had to be struck, Vanatta stated, "as much by the repetition of West scholarship as by its variety."[122]

Jay Martin then added an unexpected coda to his comprehensive biography by tracing the influence of the burlesque stage on West. In "Nathanael West's Burlesque Comedy," Martin argued that West's work is best seen in the light of his familiarity with standard burlesque stage routines. West loved the form and in *The Dream Life of Balso Snell* tried "to suffuse fiction with burlesque episodes and burlesque style." Burlesque illustrated that on stage as in life "improvisation is the rule since experience is only provisional."[123] J. A. Ward was concerned with S. J. Perelman's influence on West. In "The Hollywood Metaphor: The Marx Brothers, S. J. Perelman, and Nathanael West," Ward contended that West's critics and biographers had ignored definite parallels in the fiction of the two friends. Both offer "naive and passive" narrators who "are either writers or painters, reduced to hack work." Both see in show business a true "metaphor for American culture" and "a set of rhetorical and structural techniques" for their own fiction. It is significant, for example, that "the funniest and fiercest of the comedians, Shrike, is Nathanael West's incorporation of Groucho Marx into the real world."[124]

Whatever his opinion of Hollywood, West enjoyed a comfortable living writing for the movies. His plays, however, had proved commercial failures. He would have been surprised then to find a 1977 adaption of *A Cool Million* meeting with some success on the London stage. In a magazine review of current productions, Geoff Brown noted that as a novelist West had "abandoned himself too much to vicious parody, to unrelenting mocking laughter." Hence his book "is an unrewarding read." Yet without West's "deliberately plodding narration," the book takes to the stage brilliantly.[125] West would likely have been pleased by such a favorable, if mixed, response to a stage presentation of his first novel. He would have had less cause to be satisfied with Hollywood's posthumous treatment of his work, especially *Miss Lonelyhearts*. This novel merited an effective movie treatment, suggested Michael Klein, as it was written in a "fast-paced . . . B-film style." In his "Miss L. Gets Married," Klein reasoned that despite West's political leanings, his fiction is devoid of "political or ideological solutions" to the societal issues it raises. So was the 1933 film version of *Miss Lonelyhearts* (entitled *Advice to the Lovelorn*). But in 1958 Dore Schary made a more serious version titled simply *Lonelyhearts*. Montgomery Clift as Miss Lonelyhearts and Robert Ryan as Shrike acquitted themselves well, said Klein. But the book's concerns were internalized, softened, and sentimentalized, and the familiar West "contradictions" were muted.[126]

Schary's distortion of his novel would have angered West, but he would likely have been amused by the thread of hope Martin Tropp found in his novels. In his "Nathanael West and the Persistence of Hope," Tropp declared that West's losers discern "half-hidden indications of . . . a way out of their nightmare labyrinth." Emphasizing this point in *A Cool Million*, West points up "the absurdity of optimism in the face of physical suffering" by having Lemuel Pitkin retain "his boyish pluck and cheery good nature" while being "systematically dismantled by a heartless society." Finally, in *The Day of the*

Locust, Tropp claimed, West comes closest to defining man's inner "music" by extending it to the lyric song of birds, despite the fact that his main characters "are corrupted, and the 'dance of life' is parodied in a brutal cockfight."[127] Martin Tropp may have been intrigued by possible glimmers of "belief and love" in West's fiction, but Deborah Wyrick was more taken with the Dadaist influence on his narrative structure. In her "Dadaist Collage Structure and Nathanael West's *Dream Life of Balso Snell*," she argued that critics have ignored the novel's structure. Yet the fact that the visual arts provided West with the "architectural principles" of his other novels suggests "a similar structural matrix for *Balso Snell*." In this first work "West translates visual collage into literary collage" by "filch[ing] freely" a variety of "snippets" from "a plethora of other authors." But then his "aesthetic sensibilities transform [his] ugly material into a beautiful "Dadaist collage that, by its very artistry, celebrates that which it wishes to destroy."[128]

VII

In recent years West's critics have strived mightily not to repeat what had already been said. They have proved tireless and undaunted in their efforts to sustain his relevance for contemporary readers. In "American Dreams and American Cities in Three Post–World War I Novels," Sidney H. Bremer placed West among those American novelists who, in the three decades following World War I, saw Western civilization as breaking up and their own country as cut off from its shaping "myths of communalism, pastoralism, and individualism." Edith Wharton, F. Scott Fitzgerald, and Nathanael West, who set some of their novels in New York, considered that city's "old dreams" to be "bankrupt and lost."[129] In an essay dealing primarily with the significance of Harry Crews and Erskine Caldwell as Southern novelists, John Seeley also pointed to Nathanael West's influence on writers in the South. Seeley saw the South and California as having long been intimately connected "as literary regions." The "Hollywoodization of Southern writing" was graphically depicted for Seelye in the novels of Harry Crews, "a Georgia boy with impeccable credentials." In his third novel, *This Thing Don't Lead to Heaven*, Crews reveals his unacknowledged "debt to the California tradition . . . of Nathanael West and Evelyn Waugh's *The Loved One*."[130]

The year 1982 brought another book-length study, albeit a slender one, Kingsley Widmer's *Nathanael West* in the Twayne's United States Authors Series. Adhering to the Twayne format of combining biography and criticism, Widmer offered a Freudian interpretation of West's rejection of his Jewishness. A self-proclaimed "contentious" critic, Widmer was much given to deprecating the efforts of other critics in his notes. But students of West should find Widmer's "Notes and References" and "Selected Bibliography" useful.[131] Gordon Bordewyk also emphasized West's Jewishness. Picking up where Leslie Fiedler left off, he argued for West's influence upon so prominent a Jewish writer as Saul Bellow. In his "Nathanael West and *Seize the Day*," Bordewyk insisted that not only are the Westian "verbal echoes" in *Seize the Day* "too significant to be ignored," but that they also add "another perspective and . . . layer" to Bellow's "remarkable novel." Bordewyk thought it possible, therefore, "that Bellow was working directly from the text of *Miss Lonelyhearts*."[132]

Bordewyk was correct in suggesting that West criticism in recent years has focused increasingly on *The Day of the Locust*. For instance, three contributors to the 1984 volume entitled *Los Angeles in Fiction* dealt primarily with that novel. In his Introduction, editor David Fine placed it within its cultural and literary context, as had Walter Wells. The "first significant generation of Los Angeles writers," stated Fine, published novels in which they "established a way of reading the Southern California landscape." He referred to James M. Cain, Horace McCoy, Aldous Huxley, and Christopher Isherwood, as well as "earlier settlers" like Raymond Chandler and Budd Schulberg. The contrast between the place these people left behind and the place they discovered plays a strong role in their fiction. Certainly *The Day of the Locust* "makes the interaction quite explicit."[133] In the same volume Richard Lehan, in his "The Los Angeles Novel and the Idea of the West," stated that West differs from Scott Fitzgerald in believing that beneath Hollywood's "false glamor . . . is a brutal violence just waiting to erupt." Not surprisingly, therefore, no other "Los Angeles novel ends on a more violent note than *The Day of the Locust*."[134] Gerald Locklin, the volume's final contributor to deal with West, was more interested in the structure of West's fiction that in its regional setting or religiosity, or its concern with happiness, dreams, or death. In "The Day of the Painter; the Death of the Cock: Nathanael West's Hollywood Novel," Locklin did battle with critics like Stanley Edgar Hyman and A. M. Tibbetts who had lamented the "lack of focus" in *The Day of the Locust*. Locklin argued that the novel's "major structural principle" is the unfolding of events through "'the painter's eye,' the eye of Tod Hackett's imagination."[135]

In the 1984 volume of the *Dictionary of Literary Biography*, Daniel Walden—like Leslie Fiedler and Victor Comerchero, Max Schulz and Kingsley Widmer, among others—focused on West's problems with his Jewishness. While West did not draw characters and plots "from the essence of the Jewish experience," Walden conceded, he could not "have written as he did had he not been Jewish, hated being Jewish, and suffered from the fact that he could not escape being Jewish."[136] Robert Emmet Long then joined Gerald Locklin and those other critics wishing to keep West's reputation in the "first rank" of American writers. Long concluded his slender 1985 monograph, *Nathanael West*, by citing West's effect upon a dozen contemporary writers, and his "anticipation . . . [of and] actual influence upon, the Theater of the Absurd." He helped provide "a context for the grotesque conceptions of Carson McCullers" and proved a direct influence upon the early Flannery O'Connor and John Hawkes and Edward Lewis Wallant. More significantly, West was an obvious progenitor of the black humorists of the 1960s and film comics like Lenny Bruce and Woody Allen. In addition, West had "a seminal role in the development of American Jewish fiction after World War II."[137] West's influence upon others was of less interest to Patricia Mesch than his emphasis on man's need to confront reality's harsh truths. His novels may be "uncomfortable to read," she stated in "Recommended: Nathanael West," but in them West did force his readers "to confront actuality," assuring them that only in the loss of innocence lay "choices . . . and . . . hope."[138]

Finding more despair than hope in West was Helge Normann Nilsen, of Norway's University of Trondeim. She began her "A Novel of Despair: A Note on Nathanael West's *Miss Lonelyhearts*" with the quixotic declaration that "Of all Jewish-American novels, *Miss Lonelyhearts* . . . is perhaps the darkest and most despairing." For in it West has produced "an appalling vision" that mixes "religious intensity" and the "hopelessness of belief."[139] Also emphasizing West's bleak outlook was Gloria Young. In "*The Day of the Locust*: An Apocalyptic Vision," she credited West with creating in his final novel "an apocalyptic vision of impending twentieth-century Holocaust." He alludes repeatedly to Christian and Jewish apocalyptic works, and uses Tod Hackett's canvas, "The Burning of Los Angeles," to refer to "painters of madness, decay, and apocalypse" like Goya, Rosa, Desiderio, Guardi, El Greco, and Durer. West establishes "a background reminiscent of Sodom, Babylon, and Hell" for a vision "too black for satire, too bleak for hope."[140] Another attempt to turn West into a "Jewish writer," albeit a reluctant one, was by the ubiquitous Harold Bloom. In his offbeat introduction to a slender nine-essay collection devoted to *Miss Lonelyhearts*, editor Bloom declared it to be "a melancholy paradigm that West, who did not wish to be Jewish in any way at all, remains the most indisputably Jewish writer yet to appear in America." Bloom also agreed with Stanley Edgar Hyman's view "that the book's psychosexuality is marked by a repressed homosexual relation[ship] between Shrike and Miss Lonelyhearts."[141]

Thomas Strychacz concerned himself not with West's bleak vision or rejected Jewishness but with the subtle craftsmanship underlying the apparent structural confusion in West's final novel. In "Making Sense of Hollywood: Mass Discourses and the Literary Order in Nathanael West's *The Day of the Locust*," Strychacz argued that the novel's "cinematic narrative fragments" are not "slipshod artistry" but "deliberate and finely crafted narrative strategies." West demonstrates the "ability of the literary text to confront and 'rewrite' the botched 'texts' of Hollywood." So if *The Day of the Locust* proves "no supreme fiction in which . . . [an] artistic harmony balances the disintegration of mass culture," it still embodies West's ability to transform "fragmentation itself into narrative strategy."[142] Showing little interest in West's melding of narrative fragments, Jan Gorak focused instead on his knack for confusing his critics. Devoting two chapters to West in his *God the Artist: American Novelists in a Post-Realist Age*, Gorak stated that West feared his fiction "had been at best only half successful . . . [and] unclassifiable." He proved rather prescient, Gorak lamented, for since his death West's fiction has been "dismantled and reconstituted" to fit the "ideological persuasions" of his commentators. By bending West to his own interpretation, each critic has contributed to the "grossly distorted" apprehension of him as an artist of "disorder."[143]

West's use of illusion or dream attracted Robert Wexelblatt, who discussed the influence of Paul Valery upon the novelist's conception of illusion. In his "Nathanael West, Paul Valery, and the Detonated Society," Wexelblatt noted that West's four novels are epitomized by the "three elements of cultural disintegration, violence, and suicide." But Paul Valery should be recalled when one judges West's effort "to depict cultural disintegration in an orderly fashion." For Valery's ideas help explain "the tremendous artistic improvement" of *Miss Lonelyhearts* "over the sophomoric *Balso Snell*." Wexelblatt claimed that from Spengler and Valery West learned how to portray "a culture which is fallen and in which falseness, like a cancer, penetrates everything."[144]

The year 1989 marked the fiftieth anniversary of "two slim novels," noted David M. Fine, "that put Los Angeles on the national literary map." In his "Lotus Land or Locust Land?," Fine redefined the Westian view of the American dream-turned-nightmare. West's *The Day of the Locust* and Raymond Chandler's first hard-boiled L. A. detective story, *The Big Sleep*, both appeared in 1939. Chandler adapted the crime novel to the movie city's "peculiar geographic and psychic terrain." But West, in his final work, fashioned the "severest literary indictment" in American fiction "of the Hollywood dream." Later novelists writing about Los Angeles have started from West's "sense of the dream gone haywire" and his realization that one can lose as well as find oneself "in the fluidity of Southern California."[145]

VIII

Scholars and critics in the 1990s are still intrigued by West's sparse fiction and short, troubled life. For instance, West's life was again an object lesson in Gerald Howard's "Let This Be a Lesson to You: The Snakebit Life of Nathanael West." The novelist's literary career, noted Howard, an editor, was one "so ill starred, so beset by bad timing, botched calculations, dark ironies, dashed hopes and all-around rotten luck . . . that it is worthy of a novel by . . . Nathanael West." Yet West bore some responsibility for his bad luck and poor book sales. A comparison of *The Day of the Locust* and *The Grapes of Wrath*, the major American literary success of 1939, reveals why the former sold so poorly on publication. Steinbeck, despite his bleak material, viewed " 'the people' as America's salvation." West saw his countrymen as "material for a social apocalypse." Still if West's personal story ends in disaster, his professional one ends in triumph. His novels since his death have not only sold "in the hundreds of thousands," but they also have found their place in the American literary pantheon.[146]

David Fine returned to the theme of West's use of the California landscape in "Nathanael West, Raymond Chandler, and the Los Angeles Novel." Southern California fiction truly began in the 1930s, Fine explained, when the studios began scouring America and England for writers to create dialogue for sound movies. Viewing themselves as "outsiders" and temporary residents, these new screenwriters quickly created the Los Angeles novel. Southern California attracted not only invalids and the elderly, but also "the healers, spiritualists, quacks . . . and cults." In *The Day of the Locust*, Tod Hackett measures his Hollywood experiences "against his New England past and training" and decides the entire town strongly resembles "a vast movie lot." Together Raymond Chandler and West revealed "a dark, shadow side to the American Dream and to the intensified, California version of it." Each told us "we can escape the past and reinvent our lives."[147] Beverly Jones shifted the focus back to West's earlier work. In "Shrike as the Modernist Anti-Hero in Nathanael West's *Miss Lonelyhearts*," she sided with revisionist critics who view the novel's hero not as a Christ figure but as a "restless Satan." Shrike is for her the more likely Christ figure, as he exposes Lonelyhearts' religious "hypocrisy and irrationality." Shrike's "glib rhetoric," or "insipid tripe," Jones wrote, "becomes the Logos . . . [and] the modernist Word."[148]

The first "West" book published in this decade was a slender monograph by Alistair Wisker. Relying heavily on Jay Martin, James Light, Victor Comerchero, Randall Reid, and Leslie Fiedler, Wisker placed West within the familiar crucible of American-Jewish writing. He also related him to postmodernist criticism and insisted on his relevance for later social satirists. He then compared West with contemporaries like Scott Fitzgerald and William Carlos Williams and explored his influence on later "poets of perversity" such as Carson McCullers, Joseph Heller, John Barth, John Hawkes, and Thomas Pynchon. This slender volume's strongest selling point is an appendix of 14 pieces by West which were either previously unpublished in their entirety or simply uncollected.[149]

Judging by the two essays written for this volume, this decade's critics will be striving to put earlier critical readings of West's novels into fresh perspective. For example, in "The Shrike Voice Dominates *Miss Lonelyhearts*," novelist David Madden, the editor of another collection of essays on West, found "discordant" the "cynical tough-guy voice" of that novel's narrator. "Miss Lonelyheart's own actions, thoughts, and dialogue," he explained, "are incongruent with the style in which West as narrator describes them." Filtering his entire narrative through his protagonist's perceptions, West should offer a style reflecting his character's personality. Instead, he offers a "hard-boiled style" more appropriate for Shrike than Miss Lonelyheart. This incongruity renders West's novel "aesthetically flawed." The Shrike voice dominates not only *Miss Lonelyhearts*, Madden concluded, but also West's general prose style.

In his "Nathanael West: A Jewish Satirist in Spite of Himself," Daniel Walden returned to the one subject that would most likely have made West squirm: his Jewishness. He may have lacked a "meaningful Jewish heritage," Walden stated, but his society still treated West "as a Jew and an outsider." Nathan Weinstein grew into "an angry young man because of the cruel trick fate and his family had played on him," Walden added. "Yet he could not have written as he did had he not been Jewish." West tried hard "to laugh through his tears at his 'misfortune,' but his outrage and despair overwhelmed his laughter." He remained on the most basic level "an outsider." Ironically, "as a Jew who did not want to be a Jew, he became, almost instinctively, a moral teacher, that most Jewish of vocations." In effect, "this Jew who did not want to be a Jew became one in spite of himself."

West also has become a greater literary success than he could possibly have imagined. Critical essays and occasional books devoted to him and his four short novels continue to appear. Most represent attempts to "rescue" a literary reputation that for many years now has had no need of rescue. This salient fact likely would have made even that dour black humorist laugh out loud. Indeed, in the cosmic drama governing his special world, Nathanael West appears to be having the last laugh.

Notes

1. Stanley Edgar Hyman, "Nathanael West," in *Seven Modern American Novelists*, ed. William Van O'Connor (New York: The New American Library, 1964), 211. This essay was originally published in the series of University of Minnesota Pamphlets on American Writers.

2. Jay Martin, introduction to *Nathanael West: A Collection of Critical Essays*, ed. Jay Martin (Englewood Cliffs, N.J.: Pentice-Hall, 1971), 1–2. Subsequent references are abbreviated in the text as *NWE*.

3. Jay Martin, *Nathanael West: The Art of His Life* (New York: Farrar, Straus and Giroux, 1970), 53. Subsequent references are abbreviated in the text as *NW*.

4. Philip French, "Locust Years," *New Statesman*, 14 May 1971, 674.

5. Richard Gehman, "Introduction," *The Day of the Locust* (New York: New Directions, 1950), xii–xiii. Subsequent references are abbreviated *IDL* in the text.

6. *The Complete Works of Nathanael West* (New York: Farrar, Straus and Cudahy, 1957), 24. All subsequent references are abbreviated in the text as *CW*.

7. V. N. G[arofolo], review of *The Dream Life of Balso Snell*, *Contempo* 21 August 1931, 3.

8. Julian L. Shapiro, "Tired Men and Dung," *New Review* (Paris) 1 (Winter 1931–32): 395–97.

9. Josephine Herbst, "Nathanael West," *Kenyon Review* 23 (Autumn 1961): 621.

10. Nathanael West, "Some Notes on Miss L.," *Contempo* 15 May 1933, 1–2.

11. Daniel Aaron, "'The Truly Monstrous': A Note on Nathanael West," *Partisan Review* January–February 1947, 99.

12. T. S. Matthews, "A Fortnight's Grist," *New Republic*, 26 April 1933, 314.

13. T. C. Wilson, "American Humor," *Saturday Review of Literature*, 13 May 1933, 589.

14. William Troy, "Four Fewer Novelists," *Nation*, 14 June 1933, 673.

15. Robert Cantwell, "Outlook Book Choice of the Month," *New Outlook*, July 1933, 58.

16. Angel Flores, "Miss Lonelyhearts in the Haunted Castle," *Contempo* 25 July 1933, 1.

17. Josephine Herbst, "Miss Lonelyhearts: An Allegory," *Contempo* 25 July 1933, 4.

18. William Carlos Williams, "Sordid? Good God!" *Contempo* 25 July 1933, 5, 8.

19. S. J. Perelman, "Nathanael West: A Portrait," *Contempo* 25 July 1933, 1, 4.

20. For West's letter of appreciation to Scott Fitzgerald for the latter's kind words, see William Goldhurst, *F. Scott Fitzgerald and His Contemporaries* (Cleveland: World Publishing, 1963), 236.

21. Malcolm Cowley, *Exile's Return: A Literary Odyssey of the 1920's* (New York: Viking Press, 1951; rpt. New York: Compass Books, 1959), 237.

22. George Stevens, "The New Books," *Saturday Review of Literature*, 30 June 1934, 784.

23. John Chamberlin, "Books of the Times," *New York Times*, 19 June 1934, 17. See also Lewis Gannett, review of *A Cool Million*, *New York Herald Tribune*, 21 June 1934, 19.

24. T. S. Matthews, "A Gallery of Fools," *New Republic*, 18 July 1934, 271–72.

25. *Review of Reviews and Word's Work*, August 1934, 6–7.

26. "Shorter Notices," *Nation*, 25 July 1934, 112.

27. Tom Dardis, "The Scavenger of the Back Lots," *Some Time in the Sun* (New York: Scribner's, 1976), 154, 181.

28. Budd Schulberg, "Pep West: Prince Myshkin in a Brooks Brothers Suit," *The Four Seasons of Success* (Garden City: Doubleday, 1972), 147–53.

29. William White, *Nathanael West: A Comprehensive Bibliography* (Kent OH.: Kent State University Press, 1975), vii.

30. George Milburn, "The Hollywood Nobody Knows," *Saturday Review of Literature*, 20 May 1939, 14–15.

31. Louis B. Salomon, "California Grotesque," *Nation*, 15 July 1939, 78–79.

32. Edmund Wilson, "Hollywood Dance of Death," *New Republic*, 26 July 1939, 339–40.

33. "Truly Monstrous," *Time*, 19 June 1939, 84.

34. John Sanford, "Nathanael West," *Screen Writer*, December 1946, 10–13.

35. Edmund Wilson, "Postscript," *The Boys in the Back Room* (San Francisco: The Colt Press, 1941), 67, 72.

36. David D. Galloway, "Nathanael West's Dream Dump," *Critique: Studies in Modern Fiction* 6 (Winter 1963): 60, 62.

37. Terry Ramsey, ed., "West, Nathaniel [sic]," *1940–41 International Motion Picture Almanac* (New York: Quigley Publishing Company, 1940), 635. See also the 1941–42 issue, 1098.

38. Maxine Block, ed., "West, Nathanael," *Current Biography: Who's News and Why, 1941* (New York: H. W. Wilson Company, 1941), 912.

39. Robert M. Coates, "Introduction," *Miss Lonelyhearts* (New York: New Directions, 1946), xi–xii.

40. Alan Ross, "The Dead Centre: An Introduction to Nathanael West," *Horizon*, October 1948, 289.

41. Michael Swan, "New Novels," *The New Statesman and Nation*, 6 August 1949, 153.

42. Franklin Walker, *A Literary History of Southern California* (Berkeley: University of California Press, 1950), 259.

43. "Neglected Novelist," *Newsweek*, 4 September 1950, 77–78.

44. Isaac Rosenfeld, "Faulkner and Contemporaries," *Partisan Review*, January–February 1951, 109–10.

45. Heinrich Straumann, *American Literature in the Twentieth Century* (London: Hutchinson's University Library, 1951), 80, 87.

46. Frederick J. Hoffmann, *The Modern Novel in America: 1900–1950* (Chicago: Henry Regnery Company, 1951), 140. See also p. 125n.

47. Erskine Caldwell, *Call It Experience: The Years of Learning How to Write* (New York: Duell, Sloan and Pearce, 1951), 110–12.

48. Daniel Aaron, "Waiting for the Apocalypse," *Hudson Review* 3 (Winter 1951): 634–36.

49. Richard McLaughlin, "West of Hollywood," *Theatre Arts*, August 1951, 46–47, 93.

50. See Edward Greenfield Schwartz, "*The Novels of Nathanael West*," Accent 17 (Autumn 1957): 251.

51. Cyril M. Schneider, "The Individuality of Nathanael West," *Western Review*, 20 (Autumn 1955): 7.

52. James Light, "Miss Lonelyhearts: The Imagery of Nightmare," *American Quarterly*, 8 (Winter 1956): 317–18, 323–24.

53. Arthur Cohen, "The Possibilities of Belief: Nathanael West's Holy Fool," *Commonweal*, 15 June 1956, 276.

54. W. H. Auden, "Interlude: West's Disease," *The Dyer's Hand & Other Essays* (New York: Random House, 1962), 238–43. This essay was published originally in *Griffin*, May 1957, 4–11.

55. *The Complete Works of Nathanael West*. Introduction by Alan Ross (New York: Farrar, Straus and Cudahy, 1957), vii–xxii.

56. "News and Ideas," *College English*, May 1957, 430.

57. Norman Podhoretz, "Nathanael West: 'A Particular Kind of Joking,' " *Doings and Undoings: The Fifties and After in American Writing* (New York: Noonday Press, 1964), 66–67. This essay was originally published in slightly different form in *New Yorker*, 18 May 1957, 144–53. It appears also in Jay Martin, ed. *Nathanael West: A Collection of Critical Essays* (Englewood Cliffs, N. J.: Prentice-Hall, 1971), 154–60.

58. Edward Greenfield Schwartz, "The Novels of Nathanael West," *Accent* 17 (Autumn 1957): 251, 259, 262.

59. William Bittner, "Catching Up with Nathanael West," *Nation*, 4 May 1957, 394.

60. Roger H. Smith, "Complete Works of Nathanael West," *Saturday Review*, 11 May 1957, 13–14.

61. Ralph Russell, "He Might Have Been A Major Novelist," *Reporter*, 30 May 1957, 45–46.

62. "The Great Despiser," *Time*, 17 June 1957, 102, 104, 106.

63. William Peden, "Nathanael West," *Virginia Quarterly Review* 33 (Summer 1957): 468–72.

64. Simon Raven, "Sub-Men and Super Women," *Spectator*, 6 December 1957, 810.

65. V. S. Pritchett, "Miss Lonelyhearts," *New Statesman*, 7 December 1957, 791–92.

66. "Nathanael West," *Times Literary Supplement*, 24 January 1958, 44.

67. Graham Hough, "New Novels," *Encounter*, February 1958, 86.

68. Henry Popkin. "The Taming of Nathanael West," *New Republic*, 21 October 1957, 19.

69. Richard Hayes, "Dear Miss Lonelyhearts," *Commonweal*, 25 October 1957, 98.

70. James F. Light, "Violence, Dreams, and Dostoevsky: The Art of Nathanael West," *College English*, February 1958, 208–13.

71. Leslie A. Fiedler, "The Breakthrough: The American Jewish Novelist and the Fictional Image of the Jew," *Midstream* 4 (Winter 1958): 20–23.

72. Malcolm Cowley, Introduction, *Miss Lonelyhearts* (New York: Avon Books, 1959), iii, 96.

73. Marc L. Ratner, " 'Anywhere Out of This World': Baudelaire and Nathanael West," *American Literature* (January 1960): 456–63.

74. Leslie A. Fiedler, *Love and Death in the American Novel* (New York: Criterion Books, 1960), 316–17, 461–65.

75. Ihab Hassan, "Love in the American Novel: Expense of Spirit and Waste of Shame," *Western Humanities Review* 14 (Spring 1960): 156.

76. Edmond L. Volpe, "The Waste Land of Nathanael West," *Renascence* 13 (Autumn 1960): 69–70, 112.

77. V. L. Lokke, "A Side Glance at Medusa: Hollywood, the Literature Boys, and Nathanael West," *Southwest Review* 77 (Winter 1961): 35–36, 42–45.

78. James F. Light, *Nathanael West: An Interpretive Study* (Evanston: Northwestern University Press, 1961), vii–viii.

79. Josephine Herbst, "Nathanael West," *Kenyon Review* 23 (Autumn 1961): 611–14.

80. Stanley Edgar Hyman, *Nathanael West* (Minneapolis: University of Minnesota Press, 1962), 45–46, 27.

81. John Hawkes, "Notes on the Wild Goose Chase," *Massachusetts Review* 3 (Summer 1962): 787.

82. John Hawkes, "Flannery O'Connor's Devil," *Sewanee Review* 70 (Summer 1962): 396.

83. David D. Galloway, "Nathanael West's Dream Dump," *Critique* 6 (Winter 1963): 46–47, 52–53, 63.

84. R. W. B. Lewis, "Hart Crane and the Clown Tradition," *Massachusetts Review* 4 (Summer 1963): 745, 764.

85. Alvin Kernan, "The Mob Tendency in Satire: *The Day of the Locust*," *Satire News Letter* 1 (Fall 1963): 11–13, 15–16.

86. David D. Galloway, "A Picaresque Apprenticeship: Nathanael West's *The Dream Life of Balso Snell* and *A Cool Million*," *Wisconsin Studies in Contemporary Literature* 5 (Summer 1964): 110–22, 125–26.

87. Victor Comerchero, *Nathanael West: The Ironic Prophet* (Syacuse: Syracuse University Press, 1964), xi–xii, 167–71.

88. A. M. Tibbetts, "Nathanael West's *The Dream Life of Balso Snell*," *Studies in Short Fiction*, 2 (Winter 1965): 105–08, 110–12.

89. Daniel Aaron, "Late Thoughts on Nathanael West," *Massachusetts Review* 6 (Winter-Spring, 1965): 307–10, 312, 316.

90. Douglas H. Shepard, "Nathanael West Rewrites Horatio Alger, Jr.," *Satire News Letter*, 3 (Fall 1965): 13–14, 17, 27–28.

91. R. W. B. Lewis, "Days of Wrath and Laughter," *Trials of the Word: Essays in American Literature and the Humanistic Tradition* (New Haven: Yale University Press, 1965), 213, 215–16.

92. Thomas M. Lorch, "The Inverted Structure of Balso Snell," *Studies in Short Fiction*, 4 (Fall 1966): 33–41.

93. Thomas M. Lorch, "West's *Miss Lonelyhearts*: Skepticism Mitigated?" *Renascence* 18 (Winter 1966): 99–101, 103, 105–06, 108–09.

94. Robert J. Andreach, "Nathanael West's Miss Lonelyhearts: Between the Dead Pan and the Unborn Christ," *Modern Fiction Studies* 12 (Summer 1966): 251–56, 258–59.

95. John Hawkes, "On His Novels," *Massachusetts Review* 7 (Summer 1966): 461.

96. Roger D. Abrahams, "Androgynes Bound: Nathanael West's *Miss Lonelyhearts*," *Seven Contemporary Authors*, ed. Thomas Whitbread (Austin: University of Texas Press, 1966), 51–58, 66–67.

97. Randall Reid, *The Fiction of Nathanael West: No Redeemer, No Promised Land* (Chicago: University of Chicago Press, 1967), 10, 12.

98. Leslie A. Fiedler, "Master of Dreams," *Partisan Review* 34 (Summer 1967): 346–48.

99. Thomas M. Lorch, "Religion and Art in *Miss Lonelyhearts*," *Renascence* 20 (Autumn 1967): 11.

100. Kingsley Widmer, "The Sweet Savage Prophecies of Nathanael West," *The Thirties: Fiction, Poetry, Drama*, ed. Warren French (Deland, Florida: Everett-Edwards, 1967), 97–106.

101. James W. Nichols, "Nathanael West, Sinclair Lewis, Alexander Pope and Satiric Contrasts," *Satire Newsletter* 5 (Spring 1968): 119, 121.

102. Martin Seymour-Smith, "Prophet of Black Humour," *Spectator*, 19 July 1968, 94–95.

103. Stanley Reynolds, "Life sans Everything," *New Statesman*, 11 October 1968, 469.

104. Robert I. Edenbaum, "A Surfeit of Shoddy: Nathanael West's *A Cool Million*," *Southern Humanities Review*, 2 (Fall 1968): 427–38.

105. Max F. Schulz, "Nathanael West's 'Desperate Detachment,' " *Radical Sophistication: Studies in Contemporary Jewish-American Novelists* (Athens: Ohio University Press, 1969), 36–37, 40–48, 52–54.

106. Robert M. Perry, *Nathanael West's Miss Lonelyhearts* (New York: Seabury Press, 1969), 12–15, 20–21, 24–32.

107. Harold P. Simonson, "California, Nathanael West, and the Journey's End," in *The Closed Frontier: Studies in American Literary Tragedy* (New York: Holt, Rinehart and Winston, 1970), 100–7; 118–20.

108. Bruce Olsen, "Nathanael West: The Use of Cynicism," *Minor American Novelists*, ed. Charles A. Hoyt (Carbondale: Southern Illinois University Press, 1970), 81–82.

109. James F. Light, *Nathanael West: An Interpretative Study* (Evanston: Northwestern University Press, 1971), 206–13.

110. Nathan A. Scott, Jr., *Nathanael West: A Critical Essay* (Grand Rapids: William B. Eerdmans, 1971).

111. Jay Martin, "Introduction," *Nathanael West: A Collection of Critical Essays* (Englewood Cliffs, N. J.: Prentice-Hall, 1971), 1. The critical essays contained in this volume are: S. J. Perelman, "Nathanael West: A Portrait"; Josephine Herbst, "Nathanael West"; David D. Galloway, "A Picaresque Apprenticeship: Nathanael West's *The Dream Life of Balso Snell* and *A Cool Million*"; William Carlos Williams, "A New Writer"; Carter A. Daniel, "West's Revisions of *Miss Lonelyhearts*"; Angel Flores, "Miss Lonelyhearts in the Haunted Castle"; Josephine Herbst: "*Miss Lonelyhearts*: An Allegory"; William Carlos Williams, "Sordid? Good God!"; Marcus Smith, "Religious Experience in *Miss Lonelyhearts*"; Edmond L. Volpe, "The Wasteland of Nathanael West"; Marc L. Ratner, " 'Anywhere Out of This World': Baudelaire and Nathanael West"; Phillipe Soupault, "Introduction to *Mademoiselle Coeur-Brise (Miss Lonelyhearts)*"; Jay Martin, "The Black Hole of Calcoolidge"; William Carlos Williams, "*The Day of the Locust*"; Edmund Wilson, "The Boys in the Back Room"; Carvel Collins, "Nathanael West's *The Day of the Locust* and *Sanctuary*"; W. H. Auden, "West's Disease"; Norman Podheretz, "Nathanael West: 'A Particular Kind of Joking' "; Daniel Aaron, "Late Thoughts on Nathanael West." The pieces by West are "Through the Hole in the Mundane Millstone," "Some Notes on Violence," "Some Notes on Miss L," and "Bird and Bottle."

112. Thomas H. Jackson, "Introduction," *Twentieth Century Interpretations of Miss Lonelyhearts: A Collection of Critical Essays* (Englewood Cliffs, N. J.: Prentice-Hall, 1971), 1, 11. The essays here are: James F. Light, "The Christ Dream"; Josephine Herbst, "Nathanael West"; Arthur Cohen, "The Possibility of Belief: Nathanael West's Holy Fool"; Robert Andreach, "Nathanael West's *Miss Lonelyhearts*: Between the Dead Pan and the Unborn Christ"; Robert I. Edenbaum, "To Kill God and Build a Church: Nathanael West's *Miss Lonelyhearts*"; Stanley Edgar Hyman, "Nathanael West"; Edmond L. Volpe, "The Wasteland of Nathanael West"; Randall Reid, "No Redeemer, No Promised Land"; Josephine Herbst, "Miss Lonelyhearts: An Allegory"; Angel Flores, "Miss Lonelyhearts in the Haunted Castle"; William Carlos Williams, "Sordid? Good God!"

113. Lawrence Clark Powell, "Nathanael West: *The Day of the Locust*," *California Classics:*

The Creative Literature of the Golden State (Los Angeles: The Ward Ritchie Press, 1971), 345, 355–56.

114. Irving Malin, "Approaches to the Novel," in *Nathanael West's Novels* (Carbondale: Southern Illinois University Press, 1972), 1–7, 9–10.

115. Mike Frank, "The Passion of Miss Lonelyhearts According to Nathanael West," *Studies in Short Fiction* 10 (Winter 1973): 67–73.

116. David Madden, ed., *Nathanael West: The Cheaters and the Cheated* (Deland, Florida: Everett / Edwards, 1973). The essays included here are: Gerald Locklin, "The Man Behind the Novels"; John M. Brand, "A Word Is a Word Is a Word"; Lawrence W. DiStasi, "Nowhere to Throw the Stone"; Marcus Smith, "The Crucial Departure: Irony and Point of View"; James W. Hickey, "Freudian Criticism"; T. R. Steiner, "West's Lemuel and the American Dream" (winner of the competition); Kingsley Widmer, "The Last Masquerade"; Robert I. Edenbaum, "Pavlovian Nightmare"; Lavonne Mueller, "The Dream Dump"; Max Apple, "History and Case History in Babel's *Red Cavalry* and West's *Day of the Locust*"; Donald T. Torchiano, "The Painter's Eye"; James H. Bowden, "No Redactor, No Reward"; Warwick Wadlington, "Nathanael West and the Confidence Game"; and, as a bonus, Helen Tayor, "An Annotated Bibliography."

117. Walter Wells, "Shriek of the Locusts," *Tycoons and Locusts: A Regional Look at Hollywood Fiction of the 1930s* (Carbondale: Southern Illinois University Press, 1973), 49–70.

118. Daniel R. Brown, "The War Within Nathanael West: Naturalism and Existentialism," *Modern Fiction Studies* 20 (Summer 1974): 181–88, 193–202.

119. David R. Mayer, "West's *Miss Lonelyhearts*," *Explicator* 34 (October 1975): item 11.

120. Herb Russell, "West's *The Day of the Locust*," *Explicator* 33 (January 1975): item 36.

121. William White, *Nathanael West: A Comprehensive Bibliography* (Kent, OH.: Kent State University Press, 1975).

122. Dennis P. Vannatta, *Nathanael West: An Annotated Bibliography of the Scholarship and Works* (New York: Garland Publishing, 1976), xiii.

123. Jay Martin, "Nathanael West's Burlesque Comedy," *Studies in American Jewish Literature* 2 (Spring 1976): 6–7, 9.

124. J. A. Ward, "The Hollywood Metaphor: The Marx Brothers, S. J. Perelman, and Nathanael West," *Southern Review* 12 (July 1976): 659–60, 666, 672.

125. Geoff Brown, "American Images," *Plays and Players* 25 (October 1977): 32.

126. Michael Klein, "Miss L. Gets Married," *The Modern American Novel and the Movies*, ed. Gerald Peary and Roger Schatzkin (New York: Frederick Ungar, 1978), 19–22, 24, 26, 28.

127. Martin Tropp, "Nathanael West and the Persistence of Hope," *Renascence* 31 (Summer 1979): 205–6, 210–13.

128. Deborah Wyrick, "Dadaist Collage Structure and Nathanael West's *Dream Life of Balso Snell*," *Studies in the Novel* 11 (Fall 1979): 349–56.

129. Sidney H. Bremer, "American Dreams and American Cities in Three Post–World War I Novels," *South Atlantic Quarterly* 79 (Summer 1980): 275.

130. John Seelye, "Georgia Boys: The Redclay Satyrs of Erskine Caldwell and Harry Crews," *Virginia Quarterly Review* 4 (Autumn 1980): 613, 617–26.

131. Kingsley Widmer, *Nathanael West* (Boston: Twayne Publishers, 1982).

132. Gordon Bordewyk, "Nathanael West and *Seize the Day*," *English Studies*, April 1983, 153–59.

133. David Fine, "Introduction," *Los Angeles in Fiction*, ed. David Fine (Albuquerque: University of New Mexico Press, 1984), 2–4.

134. Richard Lehan, "The Los Angeles Novel and the Idea of the West," in Fine, ed., *Los Angeles* 33–34.

135.   Gerald Locklin, "The Day of the Painter; the Death of the Cock: Nathanael West's Hollywood Novel," in Fine, ed., *Los Angeles*, 67–68, 70–73, 79–80.

136.   Daniel Walden, "Nathanael West," *Twentieth-Century American-Jewish Fiction Writers*, ed. Daniel Walden. *DLB* Series 28 (Detroit: Gale Reearch, 1984): 324–29.

137.   Robert Emmet Long, *Nathanel West* (New York: Ungar, 1985), 148–70.

138.   Patricia A. Mesch, "Recommended: Nathanael West," *English Journal* 75 (March 1986): 99–100.

139.   Helge Norman Nilsen, "A Novel of Despair: A Note on Nathanael West's *Miss Lonelyhearts*," *Neophilologus* 70 (July 1986): 475–78.

140.   Gloria Young, "The Day of the Locust: An Apocalyptic Vision," *Studies in American Jewish Literature* 5 (1986): 103–06, 108, 110.

141.   Harold Bloom, "Introduction," *Modern Critical Interpretations: Nathanael West's Miss Lonelyhearts*, ed. Harold Bloom (New York: Chelsea House publishers, 1987), vii, 1–2. The essays included in the volume are: Stanley Edgar Hyman, *Miss Lonelyhearts*; Roger D. Abrahams, "Androgynes Bound: Nathanael West's *Miss Lonelyhearts*"; Marcus Smith, "Religious Experience in *Miss Lonelyhearts*"; John R. May, "Words and Deeds"; James W. Hickey, "Freudian Criticism and *Miss Lonelyhearts*"; Jeffrey L. Duncan, "The Problem of Language in *Miss Lonelyhearts*"; Martin Tropp, "Nathanael West and the Persistence of Hope"; Mark Conroy, "Letters and Spirit in *Miss Lonelyhearts*"; and Douglas Robinson "The Ritual Icon."

142.   Thomas Strychacz, "Making Sense of Hollywood: Mass Discourses and the Literary Order in Nathanael West's *The Day of the Locust*," *Western American Literature* 22 (1987): 149–52, 155–60.

143.   Jan Gorak, "The Art of Significant Disorder: The Fiction of Nathanael West," and "Nathanael West: Godly Maker in a Commercial World," *God the Artist: American Novelists in a Post-Realist Age* (Urbana: University of Illinois Press, 1987), 37–38, 40–45, 78–79.

144.   Robert Wexelblatt, "Nathanael West, Paul Valery, and the Detonated Society," *English Language Notes* 25 (March 1988): 66–69, 71–73.

145.   David M. Fine, "Lotus Land or Locust Land?" *Los Angeles Times Book Review*, 31 December 1989, 4.

146.   Gerald Howard, "Let This Be a Lesson to You: The Snakebit Life of Nathanael West," *New York Times Book Review*, 23 December 1990, 3, 17.

147.   David Fine, "Nathanael West, Raymond Chandler, and the Los Angeles Novel," *California History* 68 (Winter 1989–90): 196–201.

148.   Beverly Jones, "Shrike As the Modernist Anti-Hero in Nathanael West's *Miss Lonelyhearts*," *Modern Fiction Studies* 36 (Summer 1990): 218–23.

149.   Alistair Wisker, *The Writing of Nathanael West* (New York: St. Martin's Press, 1990).

REVIEWS AND BRIEF NOTES

◆

The Dream Life of Balso Snell

◆

A Distinguished Performance

V. N. G[AROFOLO]*

This is a first novel. And, considering the usual unevenness of first novels, Mr. West has effected a splendid and craftsmanlike book. Perhaps it would be rather impertinent to call this facile, buoyant book a novel, but whatever the author ordains to baptize his work it is, not too superlatively, a distinguished performance in sophisticated writing. True, there is nothing tremendously significant in it either of style or technique. Yet there is a suavity of phrase and execution in *The Dream Life of Balso Snell* that makes for excellent reading. It is with enthusiasm that we look for Mr. West's next work.

*Reprinted from *Contempo*, 21 August 1931, 3. Permission granted by Anthony Buttitta.

Tired Men and Dung

Julian L. Shapiro*

A few months ago, Contact Editions published *The Dream Life of Balso Snell*, a first novel by Nathanael West. Since its appearance, I've read several notices and reviews of it in the New-York press; the hacks have generally misunderstood it, or made statements about it that usually swamp a book out of circulation. If it came to the attention of those who know more about a book than its price, I think it would be very much liked. This is the story of the novel:

Balso Snell, *a lyric poet by trade*, while wandering in the tall grass outside the ancient city of Troy, discovers and enters the wooden horse of the Greeks. Inside, he has a series of adventures. His first encounter is with a guide, who tells him a story apotheosizing the dummy who bears letters of recommendation to those he doesn't know, in the hope of getting the keys to the city. The story, *Visitors*, is short enough to be quoted in full. "A traveller, while visiting Tyana, saw a snake enter the lower part of a man's body.

'Pardon me, my good man,' he said, 'but a snake just entered your. . . .'

'Yes,' was the astounding rejoinder, 'he lives there.'

'Ah, then you must be the sage Apollonius of Tyana. Here is a letter of introduction from my brother George. May I see the snake, please. Now your rectum. Perfect!'"

After leaving the guide, he meets a man who is attempting to crucify himself with thumbtacks. This man is Maloney the Areopagite, biographer of Saint Puce, a flea that lived in the armpit of our Lord. Maloney tells Balso, in the language of the hagiographers and of Huysmans, of the life and martyrdom of Saint Puce. Balso then continues on his way, but is stopped by JohnRaskolnikov Gilson, who reads him a theme written in public school for a teacher named McGeeny. Gilson explains that the lady had just loved Dostoevsky and that he had wanted to sleep with her despite that. The title of the theme is *Crime Journal*, an example of youthful selftorture. Further up the intestine of the horse, Balso finds the McGeeny gal. She, too, is a writer and forces him to listen to her story of Samuel Perkins, a man who wrote the biography of

*Reprinted, with permission of the author, from *The New Review* (Paris), 1 (Winter 1931–32): 395–97.

the man who wrote the biography of Boswell, each in his turn hoping to go down into posteriority a tin can on the tail of the great doctor. Balso, tired of listening to authors in search of an audience, falls asleep and in his dream reads two letters written to a girl named Janey Davenport by Tiger Darwin, who had seduced her while her folks were visiting in Plainfield, New-Jersey. Balso awakens to find the McGeeny sitting near him. She asks him what he thinks of the letters and tells him they are part of a novel she is writing in the manner of Richardson; she wants to know whether Balso thinks the epistolary style too archaic. When she confesses to having poured gravy on the flowers of her garden in order to attract flies rather than butterflies or bees, Balso recognizes in her an old sweetheart and seduces her to the tune of varied seduction speeches, while the seducee turns the pages for him with all known methods of refusal.

One of the reasons why the hiredmen, or the tiredmen, have failed to understand is because West used parts of the book to fling handfuls of dung in their faces. That may have been an error on West's part, not because the critics didn't deserve it, but because the stuff probably got in their eyes. Mr. Pound recently wrote in one of your issues that Mr. Joyce had complained that no reviewer had ever said he enjoyed *Ulysses*. Well, the same's true here. West's book is at least funny, but no one has written about that. It's a good sort of literary fooling, a nonsense both above and below what the critics sweat for, what to go after with tongues hanging out, *solutions and answers; ah, saviour, you've given me the why of it at last*. This book doesn't try to explain anything; all the way it's fooling and funny, but with plenty under the nonsense to offend those who always have *the high seriousness*. Sometimes the book gets hard and what the critics call *daring*, and whenever that happens they remember the bum novels they've got stuffed away in their trunks, the rejection slips and the earnest advice to try another profession. Then they rear up hollering about *young* and about *the lad will grow up*. They'd say that about satire even if they knew the man who wrote it was a hundred and four. For them, The Dream Life isn't a needle; it's a club. Its funny to hear the hired-tiredmen say *fine talent but perverted*. Let us pray for them in the words of Balso Snell: 'O beer! O Meyerbeer! O Bach! O Offenbach! Stand me now as ever in good stead.'

Cordially yours,
Julian L. SHAPIRO.
Warrensburgh, New-York.
August 9 th, 1931.

Lamb Story

♦

American Periodicals

Hugh S. Davies*

[The stated purpose of *Contact* magazine is] "to cut a trail through the American jungle without the use of a European compass." The use of an American compass has involved most of the contributors in violence, some of them in unnecessary violence. Mr. West's story, for example, of the clumsy sacrificial slaughter of a lamb by drunken students has the typical faults of the latest realistic manner; the thing is incredible, as an event, in spite of its careful detail, simply because such things cannot happen without arousing the strongest emotions in the spectator. Accordingly, only an emotional description of the scene will be credible, and this attitude of impersonal observation, of scientific and photographic reproduction defeats its own object; in extreme cases (like this), [it] robs the account of all realism, and leaves the reader not impressed, but reflective: if it really happened, then it must be regretted that Mr. West feels like that about it; if, on the other hand, it is imaginary, as it seems to be, then it is almost pathological. . . .

*Reprinted from the *Criterion* 11 (July 1932): 772. Copyright © Hugh S. Davies, courtesy of Faber and Faber Ltd.

Miss Lonelyhearts

♦

A New American Writer

WILLIAM CARLOS WILLIAMS*

No. I don't mean *another* American writer, I mean a *new* one: Nathanael West. When another of the little reviews that appeared in the United States during the last quarter of the century died, I thought it was a shame. But now I think differently. Now I understand that all those little reviews ought by necessity to have a short life, the shorter the better. When they live too long they begin to dry up. But they have had at least one excuse for their existence— they have given birth to at least one excellent writer who would not otherwise have had the means to develop. *Contact* has produced N. West. Now it can die.

The special strength of West, apart from his ability to maneuver words, is that he has taken seriously a theme of great importance so trite that all of us thought there would be no life in it: I mean the terrible moral impoverishment of our youth in the cities.

But to do that he has discovered that the way to treat this theme is to use the dialect natural to such a condition. Since the newspapers are the principal corruptors of all that has value in language, it is with the use of this very journalistic "aspect" and everyday speech that language must be regenerated. West has taken as his material the idiom of the reporters, the tough men of the newspapers, and has counterpointed it with the pathetic

*William Carlos Williams: "A New American Writer." Copyright © 1994 by William Eric Williams and Paul H. Williams. Reprinted by permission of New Directions Publishing Corp.

letters and emotions of the poor and ignorant city dwellers who write to the newspapers to obtain counsel for their afflictions and poverty.

After all, what is the urban population made up of? Of seduced and corrupted, nothing more. They have been gathered together so that they may be better exploited, and this is West's material. But no, his "material" is writing itself—he has invented a new manner, he has invented a medium that allows him the full expression of his sentiments in a language which a journalist would recognize. It conveys the real, incredibly dead life of the people and the incredibly dead atmosphere of the book itself and—my God!—we understand what scoundrels we've become in this century. "Don't be deceived" could be West's motto. Don't think yourself literate merely because you write long books and use correct English. Here are the problems, do something with them that will not be a lie. Don't deceive yourself: you don't see because you don't look. These things are there just the same. And if you think you can write poems while you live in a sewer, and at the same time think you're lying in a bed of roses—well, go ahead and be happy!

The cities are rotten and desperate—so is most polite, "literary" literature. So? Nothing much. Only a little review that publishes good material. I don't think that many will find it. It [West's writing] would offend the paying subscribers if it appeared in the large monthly magazines. Which makes one wonder if they will ever let it enter their consciousness.

[Dirt Under the Skin]

T. S. MATTHEWS*

A great many people, in these disgraceful years, are openly cynical about their jobs. Few have a better right than newspapermen. It is hard to see, for instance, how a man whose daily job it is to write a column of advice to the lovelorn can at the same time take this job seriously and do it well (that is, acceptably to his employers). It is a dirty job, in the plainest sense of the words. What happens to such a man when the dirt begins to get under his skin is the subject of *Miss Lonelyhearts*, a centrifugal extravaganza, patched together by lovelorn letters quite horrible enough to be actual facsimiles.

*Reprinted, with permission, from the *New Republic*, 74 (26 April 1933): 314.

American Humor

T. C. Wilson*

American literature of recent years has produced very little vigorous humor. There are indications, however, that certain of the younger writers, notably Erskine Caldwell and Nathanael West, are attempting to restore the comic view of life to its legitimate place in art—Caldwell with his novels "Tobacco Road" and "God's Little Acre," and West with his robust satire, "Miss Lonelyhearts." Their works may ultimately form a contribution to our literature and enrich the tradition of native humor.

"Miss Lonelyhearts" is a comedy with tragic implications. Beneath their surface absurdities the people in this tale are pitifully ineffective and frustrated. The problems and disappointments which they bring to Miss Lonelyhearts, conductor of a New York newspaper column of advice to the distressed, in the belief that he can help them, reveal the futility of their lives. Broken-hearted, Desperate, Disillusioned-with-tubercular husband, and the rest are laughable in their naive letters, but their suffering is depressing. Mr. West presents them with much power. In the character of Miss Lonelyhearts he also exposes the civilization which has produced them. When Miss Lonelyhearts no longer considers his job a joke and circulation stunt, and begins to think of himself as the spiritual adviser to millions of inarticulate sufferers, a kind of modern Christ, he is compelled to search for values to base his philosophy on. He examines various ideals—art, Christ, the soil—but rejects one after another when he finds them all without meaning for him. He is left as helpless and inarticulate as those starved souls he hoped to lead to the light of a new faith.

It is an ironic and bitter humor that arises from such a dilemma—quite unlike the merely amusing type of *New Yorker* fun-poking at superficialities. Mr. West pierces beneath the surfaces of his material. The tragic lives of his characters impress us even more powerfully because they are made to seem stupid and comic. We may laugh with the author at these people, but we recognize the essential seriousness which has given his writing its impetus. "Miss Lonelyhearts" is a solid work as well as a brilliant one. Mr. Dreiser would have made a tragedy out of this material; Mr. West, in making a satiric comedy of it, has perhaps given a more adequate rendering of men whose warped lives do not offer any theme considerable enough for tragedy.

*From the *Saturday Review of Literature* 9 (13 May 1933): 589. Reprinted by permission of General Media, Inc.

Some Notes on Miss L.

NATHANAEL WEST*

I can't do a review of *Miss Lonelyhearts*, but here, at random, are some of the things I thought when writing it:

As subtitle: "A novel in the form of a comic strip." The chapters to be squares in which many things happen through one action. The speeches contained in the conventional balloons. I abandoned this idea, but retained some of the comic strip technique: Each chapter instead of going forward in time, also goes backward, forward, up and down in space like a picture. Violent images are used to illustrate commonplace events. Violent acts are left almost bald.

Lyric novels can be written according to Poe's definition of a lyric poem. The short novel is a distinct form especially fitted for use in this country. France, Spain, Italy have a literature as well as the Scandinavian countries. For a hasty people we are too patient with the Bucks, Dreisers and Lewises. Thank God we are not all Scandinavians.

Forget the epic, the master work. In America fortunes do not accumulate, the soil does not grow, families have no history. Leave slow growth to the book reviewers, you only have time to explode. Remember William Carlos Williams' description of the pioneer women who shot their children against the wilderness like cannonballs. Do the same with your novels.

Psychology has nothing to do with reality nor should it be used as motivation. The novelist is no longer a psychologist. Psychology can become something much more important. The great body of case histories can be used in the way the ancient writers used their myths. Freud is your Bulfinch; you can not learn from him.

With this last idea in mind, Miss Lonelyhearts became the portrait of a priest of our time who has a religious experience. His case is classical and is built on all the cases in James' *Varieties of Religious Experience* and Starbuck's *Psychology of Religion*. The psychology is theirs not mine. The imagery is mine. Chapt. I— maladjustment. Chapt. III—the need for taking symbols literally is described through a dream in which a symbol is actually fleshed. Chapt. IV—deadness and disorder; see Lives of Bunyan and Tolstoy. Chapt. VI—self-torture by conscious sinning: see life of any saint. And so on.

I was serious therefore I could not be obscene.
I was honest therefore I could not be sordid.
A novelist can afford to be everything but dull.

[Mixing Dostoevski and Gin]

WILLIAM TROY*

The hero of *Miss Lonelyhearts* is a young man who earns his living devising replies to "Desperate," "Brokenhearted," "Sick-of-it-all," and others of the lovelorn who write to him for advice. But it must not be gathered that Mr. West's book is the sort of rollicking, whimsical Arabian Nights' Adventure into the modern Bagdad that Christopher Morley, let us say, might write. There is no color in the bazaars of this Bagdad; the creatures who inhabit it have the shaggy contours of a James Thurber drawing. The hero himself suffers from what he calls a "Christ-complex"; he keeps primed for his task on a heavy mixture of Dostoevski and gin. When in a halfhearted gesture of compassion he attempts to help one of the frustrated people who have appealed to him he is rewarded with death. It is all very sad, bitter, and hopeless. If it were not for Mr. West's prose, which leans too much to the baroque, and for a certain ambiguity of genre ("the actual and the fanciful" are here too often confounded), "Miss Lonelyhearts" would be a better book. As it stands, however, it is one of the most readable and one of the most exceptional books of the season. . . .

*William Troy, "Four Fewer Novelists," *The Nation* magazine/The Nation Company, Inc., 14 June 1933.

[Pouring Salt Into Wounds]

ROBERT CANTWELL*

But the really unusual novel of the recent past is a thin little book called *Miss Lonelyhearts*, by Nathanael West (Harcourt), superficially a picture of the psychological torments of a reporter who conducts a column of advice to the distressed, actually a kind of modernized, faithless, "Pilgrim's Progress." It has a sour, hangover humor that suggests James Thurber's drawings in the *New Yorker*, and revolves around Miss Lonelyhearts' attempts to help the people who come to him for guidance, his relationship with Shrike, his editor, who is a master at the art of pouring salt into wounds, and with several women who seem to fade away like the figures in adolescent nightmares. It is a picture of a man suffering the torments of Hell, surrounded by demons he doesn't recognize as demons. A typical review was that by William Troy in *The Nation*, in which Mr. Troy said, in effect, that while *Miss Lonelyhearts* was one of the most original of recent novels, he wasn't very enthusiastic about it. . . .

*Reprinted from *New Outlook* 162 (July 1933): 58.

Miss Lonelyhearts in the Haunted Castle

Angel Flores*

Somebody mentioned Dostoevski and Cocteau as *Miss Lonelyhearts* progenitors. I had never seen such names coupled before. I re-read *Miss Lonelyhearts* and gradually the statement elucidated itself. In *Miss Lonelyhearts* do appear the hairshirts worn by Fyodor's heroes, and the air rings with antiChristian catapults, bloody guffaws and mystical quavers. The author of *Miss Lonelyhearts* has not tried to conceal his admiration for the Russian master. In fact the most exciting section in his earlier work, *The Dream Life of Balso Snell,* was significantly entitled *Journal of John Raskolnikov Gilson.* Dostoevski *is* a concomitant of *Miss Lonelyhearts*—but how about Cocteau? I did not see the point clearly perhaps because Cocteau has so many sides and the side my friend had in mind was not predominantly Cocteauan. What my friend really meant was that peculiar nightmarish quality, that pervasive uncanniness which hovers over the canvasses of Giorgio de Chirico and Salvador Dalí. In literature it existed, coarsely, in the terrorists of the XVIIIth century, in the Walpole-Reeve-Radcliffe trio, and, more particularly, in Lewis' *The Monk.* Later it entered the chapel of the Symbolists via Poe-Coleridge, and now reigns, stylized, in surrealisme. Mystery saturates the finest works of the day. Ribemont-Dessaignes Jouhandeau, René Char, Péret, Desnos, and to a lesser degree, Drieu la Rochelle and Henri Poulaille. And though at some distance from, say, *Confiteor*—one can sense it in such vastly different creations as *Der Steppenwolf* and *Geheimnis eines Menschen* . . .

Nathanael West's most remarkable performance has been to bring Fyodor's dark angels into the Haunted Castle. He did not recur to the drab realism which is so responsible for the stagnation in the works of the younger American writers—a realism which generally produces accurate reporting, easy-to-handle bulletins and timetables, and ALSO bed literature. Mr. West has given us anguish and terror and fantasy (Dostoevski-Ribemont-Dessaignes?) at the very crucial moment when the current vanguard taste insists on directing literature towards the casehistory, gravymashpotato tradition.

---

*Reprinted from *Contempo* 3 (25 July 1933): 3–4. Permission granted by Anthony Buttitta.

Miss Lonelyhearts: An Allegory

JOSEPHINE HERBST*

*M*iss *Lonelyhearts* reads like a detective story. Its realism is not concerned with actuality but with the comprehension of a reality beyond reality. The furniture of the speakeasy, the upside-down quality of New York night and day life provide a background that only a fine movie camera could actually interpret. This crazy pattern fits the nightmare quality of the story of Miss Lonelyhearts, the newspaper columnist, who under a sentimental name acts high priest to the broken hearted whose letters begging advice pour into his sanctum. Actually *Miss Lonelyhearts,* the book, is a sort of allegory.

Miss Lonelyhearts floundering among the problems of humanity, stuck in the Slough of Despond of bankrupt emotionalism to the accompaniment of high powered motors, jazz music, weeping drunks and men out-of-work reflects much more than his own minute destiny. The entire jumble of modern society, bankrupt not only in cash but more tragically in emotion, is depicted here like a life sized engraving narrowed down to the head of a pin. Miss Lonelyhearts, stricken with the suffering of the underdog, seeks an answer. Flagellating himself with suffering, he in turn incurs suffering. His sadism breeds back upon himself and in bewilderment he turns to God, symbol of crucifixion and death. The pathological intensity of this seeking leads him to the desire to embrace humanity and that embrace pitches him to death. The ecstatic moment, realistically furnished, in which this occurs approaches the miracle of the old Mystery Plays.

It is significant that although all the scenes are not night scenes, in retrospect they appear to take place in semi-darkness, in that sort of twilight that occurs in dreams. The characters too are those of the dream, faces out of line, some distortion. Miss Lonelyhearts himself, in his dilemma, seeking a way out, is without distinct features. As he goes down, he seems to be someone wearing the huge nose of a clown who has been tightropewalking and has suddenly been discovered to have broken legs. He falls into the pit and even as he sinks the clown nose tortures us with a desire to laugh, the same kind of laughter that hysterically crops up in a tragic moment. If the characters are not sharpened in an individualistic way it is because they much more nearly serve their purpose in this book as types. They are not Mrs. Jones or Miss

*Reprinted from *Contempo* 3 (25 July 1933): 4–5. Permission granted by Anthony Buttitta.

Smith or Mr. Brown but the Desolates, the Heartaches, the Anxious of the world whose faces mask identical suffering more poignant than any individual difference.

Doomed by the society that roars around them to live ignominiously and alone in rabbit hutches, poking their heads out to wail to their father confessor, who, like them is lost, they are not puppets so much as they are representatives of a great Distress. Let anyone who thinks this implies a grotesqueness out of line with the strictest contemporary reality pick up any newspaper. Terror accompanied by the great wash of indifference is in every line. The Tom Mooneys rot in jail to an indifferent California, the Scottsboro boys wait in a destiny quite outside their comprehension or control. That Miss Lonelyhearts in his great need clutches at nothing better than God is symptomatic also. As he goes down in his bad luck the unsolved problems of Abandoned, Expectant and Despair must await some other deliverance.

Sordid? Good God!

WILLIAM CARLOS WILLIAMS*

It's not only in the news section but among the feature sections also that newspapers show they have been published to conceal the news. West takes for his theme "The Miss Lonelyhearts of The New York *Post-Dispatch* (Are-you-in-trouble? Do-you-need-advice? Write-to-Miss-Lonelyhearts-and-she-will-help-you)." It is of course a man who runs the column.

Now this is a particularly sordid piece of business, this sort of feature, for it must be obvious that no serious advice can be given to despairing people who would patronize and even rely on such a newspaper office. The fact is that the newspaper by this means capitalizes misfortune to make sales, offering a pitiful moment's interest to the casual reader while it can do nothing but laugh at those who give it their trust.

Imagine a sensitive man running such a column, a man of imagination who realizes what he is doing and the plot is wound up. What cure? Why the only cure, so far as Nathanael West is concerned, the only truth possible is "the truth"—along with the effects of the evil upon his protagonist. A particularly interesting short novel.

And for this, because the subject matter is sometimes rather stiff, a critic (after all, one must call them something) writing in one of our daily papers has branded the book itself as "sordid." Good God.

How much longer will it take, I wonder, for America to build up a cultural ice of sufficient thickness to bear a really first rate native author? It will happen sooner or later, it must, for we already have a few excellent craftsmen. But—to paraphrase the late Bert Williams—when? Apparently we still make the old and puerile error of finding a work, because its subject matter is unsmiling, serious or if the matter smiles then naturally the book must be light. And so, taking a sordid truth of city making and carrying the facts of the case through to an engrossing climax in brilliant fashion, the book cannot be anything else but sordid also!

If this is so, why then so is *Macbeth* sordid, so *Crime and Punishment,* so nearly the whole of Greek tragedy. And so's your old man. Blah. And that's what our standard American criticism amounts to: Roxy and the statues. Thin ice. We fall through it into mud up to our knees. And there is scarcely a place we can turn to for relief.

This isn't a perfect book, few first books are. But it is excellently conceived and written and it cannot be thrust aside in such slipshod fashion. There are many reasons why nearly everyone who would pick it up would enjoy it.

One thing which has perhaps aided in a careless dismissal of the book is West's insistence on extreme types in his narrative—really the people that newspapers do get letters from: the girl without a nose, the simpleminded child who was raped on the roof of a tenement, "Sick-of-it-all," "Broken-hearted," "Desperate," "Disillusioned-with-tubercular-husband." But after all the use of such extreme types is preeminently the business of literature or we should never have had either Romeo and Juliet, Klytemnestra or Lazarus, whose function it has been to reveal and emphasize a point under observation from a logical intelligence of the facts. Even Betty the innocent if battered girl of the story must be carried down by this dreadful logic also. The fact that she does not become hard-boiled to the end being in itself an interesting sidelight on West's objective.

The letters-to-the-papers which West uses freely and at length must be authentic. I can't believe anything else. The unsuspected world they reveal is beyond ordinary thought. They are a terrific commentary on our daily lack of depth in thought of others. Should such lives as these letters reveal never have been brought to light? Should such people, like the worst of our war wounded, best be kept in hiding?

The characters in West's book, these people whom the newspapers make a business of deceiving, are the direct incentive to his story, the seriously injured of our civic life—although the cases occur everywhere, even worse, perhaps, in the rural districts. The unbearable letters are cited and then the moral bludgeoning which they entail is rapidly sketched out before our eyes. Nothing more clearly upon the track of classical precedent.

If our thought would evade such matters West doesn't. But it is done with skill and virtuosity. It can skate. What is the figure that Dante uses in the Inferno? It is Virgil. It is poetry (that is, good writing) which permits a man, but no ordinary man, to descend to those regions for a purpose. It is the art of writing, in other words, which permits the downward motion since when writing is well made it enlivens and elevates the whole reader—without sweetening or benumbing the sense—while he plunges toward catastrophe.

I'm not dragging in Dante to say West writes poetic prose. He doesn't. But I am saying the book is writtten with skill, we are not wiped around by sloppy narrative. The story, dreadful as it is, is presented tolerably to us, do what we may about the things presented. It's no treatise, no cold dissection. It is the intelligence feelingly going beside us to make it possible for us at the very least to look and to understand.

Although Mary always grunted and upset her eyes, she would not associate what she felt with the sexual act. When he forced this association, she became very angry. He had been convinced that her grunts were genuine by the change that took place in her when he kissed her heavily. Then her body gave off an odor that enriched the synthetic flower scent she used behind her ears and in the hollows of her neck. . . .

He found himself in the window of a pawnshop full of fur coats, diamond rings, watches, shotguns, fishing tackle, mandolins. All these things were the paraphernalia of suffering. . . .

Perhaps I can make you understand. Let's start from the beginning. A man is hired to give advice to the readers of a newspaper. The job is a circulation stunt and the whole staff considers it a joke. He welcomes the job, for it might lead to a gossip column, and anyway he's tired of being a leg man. He too considers the job a joke, but after several months of it, the joke begins to escape him. He sees the majority of the letters are profoundly humble pleas for moral and spiritual advice, that they are inarticulate expressions of genuine suffering. He also discovers that the correspondents take him seriously. For the first time in his life, he is forced to examine the values by which he lives. This examination shows him that he is the victim of the joke and not its perpetrator.

Then someone started a train of stories by suggesting that what they all needed was a good rape.
"I knew a gal who was regular until she fell in with a group and went literary. She began writing for the little magazines about how much Beauty hurt her and dished the boy friend who set up pins in a bowling alley. The guys on the block got sore and took her into the lots one night. About eight of them. They ganged her proper."

Take it or leave it. It's impossible to quote effectively for anything but a minor purpose but that's approximately what the prose is like. It's plain American. What I should like to show is that West has a fine feeling for language. And this is the point I shall stop on. Anyone using American must have taste in order to be able to select from among the teeming vulgarisms of our speech the personal and telling vocabulary which he needs to put over his effects. West possesses this taste.

A Cool Million: or the Dismantling of Lemuel Pitkin
[An Impenetrable Tedium]

G[EORGE] S[TEVENS]*

The opening chapter of this novel is mildly amusing; the rest seems superfluous. It is difficult to be very uproarious in a burlesque of something which nobody takes seriously anyhow, and the idea of putting Horatio Alger in reverse is not exactly fraught with subtlety. Mr. West proceeds from extravagance to extravagance, with a touch that grows heavier as the events proceed. This author's previous novel, *Miss Lonelyhearts*, was much admired, and a fraction of the admiration was deserved. Those who overpraised *Miss Lonelyhearts* may well find *A Cool Million* full of mad humor and esoteric significance. The present reviewer finds only a straining for effect and an impenetrable tedium.

*From the *Saturday Review of Literature,* 10 (30 June 1934): 784. Reprinted by permission of General Media, Inc.

[An Idealistic Simpleton]

T. S. MATTHEWS*

Now let me call your attention to a native American work, a crayon cartoon of the Voltairean school. It is true that *Candide* is an etching whose lines are both more subtle and more biting than the broad strokes of *A Cool Million*, but Mr. Nathanael West has the heart of the matter in him. Though his satire is laid on with a thicker-than-Gallic pencil, and the drawing is more violent than firm, though his manner is more mock-Alger than Voltairean, his picture as a whole makes the same kind of impression. As in *Candide*, his hero is an idealistic simpleton whose head is swimming with the copy-book patter of his day. Lemuel Pitkin continues to believe in rugged individualism, homespun American virtues and home-made American fortunes in spite of a succession of misadventures that twice land him in jail, lose him his teeth, an eye, a leg, his scalp and finally his life. Mr. West pokes a good deal of unkindly fun along the way at intellectuals, social workers, bankers, politicians, and fascists, some of whom he drags into his foreground by the hair of their heads. *A Cool Million* is not so successful a caricature as his earlier *Miss Lonelyhearts*, and it can be taken in at a glance, but the glance is worth it.

*Reprinted, with permission, from the *New Republic* 79 (18 July 1934): 271–72.

[A Rustic Candide]

Horatio Alger is not dead. Americans reared on the trials and tribulations of such heroes as Paul the Peddler and Phil the Fiddler have long missed such familiar characters as the hero's mother, the shabbily dressed stranger, the lad with frank and open countenance, or the honest village banker. But these legendary folk live again in Nathanael West's new satire, *A Cool Million or the Dismantling of Lemuel Pitkin*. Today, however, the hero is constantly in hot water. The old success story formula doesn't work. He saves the squire's daughter from the attention of a bully and loses an eye for his trouble. Sobriety, frugality, and industry help him not. He loses his teeth, his scalp, and is finally shot by an agent of the Third International while making a speech for the new political order of Leather Shirts. The Leather Shirts aimed to restore the truly American virtues extolled by Horatio Alger, Dr. Frank Crane and others. Only posthumously, in the manner of Horst Wessel, does Lemuel Pitkin become a national hero, with all the trappings. *A Cool Million* is a delightful parody, with satire which hits uncomfortably near the truth. It is not a profound book, but it is a funny one.

*Reprinted from *Review of Reviews and World's Work,* 90 (August 1934): 6–7.

[Horatio Alger Revisited]

Anonymous*

There is a story that a Communist, walking in Central Park early one morning last winter, met a young man who had spent the rainy night sleeping on one of the rocks there. When asked what he thought of having to sleep out all night, while so many apartments within view on Fifth Avenue were empty, the vagrant answered: "I guess the landlords are having a hard time too." Lemuel Pitkin, hero of the present satire, is in a way such a man: content to follow the dictates of his heart and of outworn shibboleths rather than of reason. Lem (a rustic Candide) left Vermont to seek his fortune after he had been assured by "Shagpoke" Whipple, shyster banker in the town where he lived and ex-President of the United States, that America was the land of opportunity and that industry and fair play would be justly rewarded. His trials, such as twice being railroaded into jail, imprisoned in a brothel, persecuted, and exploited, were excessive; his rewards consisted in losing first his teeth, then an eye, afterwards, a leg, a thumb, his scalp, and finally his life when he was killed by an agent of the Third International. Nevertheless, he became the martyr-hero of Shagpoke's Fascist party, the Leather Shirts of America, and like the less naive Horst Wessel, his name came to be sung throughout a nation, his birthday being celebrated by battalions of young men marching up Fifth Avenue in coonskin hats, leather shirts, and with squirrel guns in their hands, singing the Lemuel Pitkin song. Probably, since we have no Voltaire and would be unlikely to appreciate one, present day satire can only be written in a wisecracking style. Mr. West is heavy-handed but his book is stimulating and at times bitterly hilarious.

*Anonymous, ["Horatio Alger Revisited"] *The Nation* magazine/The Nation Co., Inc., 139 (25 July 1934): 112.

The Day of the Locust

◆

The Hollywood Nobody Knows

GEORGE MILBURN*

It is hard to understand why Nathanael West should ever have become (borrowing that dark term Bernard DeVoto once used on me) a "coterie writer." The comedy of his novel about forlorn clowns should make it popular, because it has the same ineffable appeal which caused millions to go to see Charlie Chaplin. But the chances are that comparatively few readers will greet this novel by the author of "Miss Lonelyhearts" with the enthusiasm it deserves.

This is too bad. Mr. West's latest book is about the Hollywood nobody knows, except for an occasional resolute explorer who has straggled back from there. It has very little to tell about the motion picture industry as such, although one of the main characters is a studio employee, and there is one memorable chapter about his getting lost in the maze of a movie lot—the only passage in fiction I know of like it is Stephen Dedalus's vision of hell.

It is, for the most part, the story of a lost bookkeeper from Iowa and his curious misadventures among the ordinary followers of an extraordinary industry: a cocksure dwarf, a purple cowboy, a dying vaudeville comedian, a luscious little extra, Mme. Jenning and her cote of dry-cleaned doves, a Hollywood landlady whose hobby is funerals, a repulsive child actor and his even more monstrous mother—all against a Hogarthian background of food faddists, aged perverts and religious fanatics.

*From the *Saturday Review of Literature* 20 (20 May 1939): 14–15. Reprinted by permission of General Media, Inc.

The worst fault of the book is that it follows the choppy, episodical technique of a movie scenario. It has that peculiar disorganization that most movies have. Maybe this was deliberate on the part of the author; if so, I think it was ill-advised. The story, for example, is not long enough to carry the shifting back and forth from the lives of Tod Hackett, the studio designer, to Homer Simpson, the Iowa bookkeeper, without losing force. And the reader is likely to wonder why so much space was given to an irrelevent visit to a brothel, interesting though it is, if Tod Hackett's excursions among brain-breathers and other odd cults are to be passed by with only the briefest mention. This gives "The Day of the Locust" an effect of hasty, disjointed writing that may disappoint some people.

But when Mr. West really gives a scene all he's got, it is something that will stick in your memory for a while. His description of the cockfight, or of the old clown's funeral, or of Hackett's finding the dwarf—such chapters are miniature masterpieces.

And the book ends on a crescendo, narrating what happens in a mob gathered for a Hollywood premiere, a picture of an American Walpurgis Eve that must make anyone who reads it feel that he was there, too, and remember it as vividly.

Truly Monstrous

ANONYMOUS*

In the 25 years Hollywood has been waiting, no novelist has yet written a good book about it. Few serious novelists have even tried. A harder try than most is *The Day of the Locust,* by a 35-year-old Manhattan-born novelist who became a screen writer three years ago, after writing a talented satire called *Miss Lonelyhearts.*

A tale of Hollywood's lunatic fringe, *The Day of the Locust* regards its characters as the human equivalent of Hollywood's architecture: "It is hard to laugh at the need for beauty and romance, no matter how tasteless, even horrible, the results of that need are. But it is easy to sigh. Few things are sadder than the truly monstrous."

Author West starts off well, with wit, a nimble imagination, shrewd slants on the social roots of Hollywood's crackpottery. But well before the last scene—a world première which turns into a savage riot—his intended tragedy turns into screwball grotesque, and groggy Author West can barely distinguish fantastic shadows from fantastic substance. At a similar stage of trying to get Hollywood on paper, William Saroyan before him merely folded his arms, admitted with rare humility that Hollywood had given him "the smiling heart of an idiot and the good nature of a high-class phony."

*Reprinted from *Time* 33 (19 June 1939): 84.

California Grotesque

Louis B. Salomon*

Hollywood baiting is a branch of literature that began brilliantly with "Once in A Lifetime" and is still drawing noteworthy contributions, some good-humored and some bitter. But here is a book that attempts to do a great deal more than just pillory the foibles and flimflammery of the movie industry. While its setting is Hollywood and the miasma of the studio naturally permeates the lives of all the people concerned, Mr. West has sketched an acidulous melange of Southern California grotesques, including not only the usual figures of the disillusioned artist and the self-centered ham actress and the mother of the would-be child star, but some samples of the folk you don't read so much about: the Middle Westerners who have saved up a few thousand dollars and moved to California to end their days basking in its vaunted sun. These people, mostly middle-aged, often semi-invalid, invariably bored with their self-chosen life of idleness, inhabit an appalling spiritual wasteland in which the only plants that take firm root are the "crank" cults you will find advertised flamboyantly in cheap psychology magazines under names like "The Search for Truth," "The Quest for Life," "Power Through Mental Force," and, on a slightly different plane, the "Ham and Eggs" Utopias.

Around the central character of Tod Hackett, a young painter attached to one of the big studios, Mr. West has grouped such a galaxy of spongers, misfits, and eccentrics as will give a sensitive reader the crawling horrors. Even Tod himself, while generous and likable, suffers from lack of willpower; though he recognizes the cheapness and artificiality of blond Faye Greener, he has not the strength either to put her out of his mind or to demand from her the favors she withholds only from those who are considerate of her. The story ends on a particularly nighmarish note, when Tod, trying to help a poor lumbering dolt who has also been blighted by Faye's fascination, is injured by the star-worshipping, irresponsible mob outside a world premiere.

There is abundant material here for scathing satire or careful social study, and the principal objection to *The Day of the Locust* is apt to be that it merely scratches the surface. To make the picture less sketchy, less like the strongly highlighted scenes of a bad dream, it needs more thorough characterization,

*Louis B. Salomon, "California Grotesque," *The Nation* magazine/The Nation Co., Inc., 149 (15 July 1939): 78–79.

more documentation—most of all, perhaps, a few ordinary, everyday people (of whom there must be a few even in Hollywood), to lend perspective. Perhaps this very sketchiness was part of the author's plan, but by presenting only a two-dimensional picture it detracts from the impressiveness of what could well be a very striking arraignment of America's most unbelievable menagerie.

Hollywood Dance of Death

EDMUND WILSON*

Almost nothing that is any good gets written about the life of Hollywood. The authors who keep away don't know it. The authors who work there accept it; the authors who have succeeded in escaping don't want to put themselves on record for fear they may want to go back. Anita Loos never published in book form the eviscerating Hollywood satire called "The Better Things of Life," which came out in *The Cosmopolitan* and soon after she went back to the better things. Even people who live in Southern California and who have little or no stake in the movies find it difficult to put that world on paper. It turns out that, as they travel West, a transformation, imperceptible but basic, like the change from Eastern to Western time, has taken place in their point of view. They come to themselves every now and then, aware that sensational things are going on all about them; but they no longer have the standards to judge them, the convictions which spur one to judge. Is it the changeless and insipid sun?—the organized and disciplined stupidity?—the flimsiness of the buildings and people? Certainly a number of factors have combined to produce a state of mind in which it is difficult for the writer not only to register his reactions but even to have reactions at all. It takes only a few years of Hollywood to render him incapable of anything but turning up at the League of American Writers and delivering bosom-beating speeches, reminiscent of the Moscow trials, in which he repudiates the frivolity of his past career and excoriates the Fascists in Spain, without ever, however, doing anything to expose that other campaign against art, education and social justice, which is being successfully carried on by his employers no further away than Hollywood.

Nathanael West, the brilliant author of *Miss Lonelyhearts,* went to Hollywood some years ago, and his silence had been causing his readers alarm lest he, too, might have faded out. But Mr. West, as this new book happily proves, is still alive out there beyond the mountains, and can still tell what he feels and sees—has still, in his heart, remained an artist. His new novel, *The Day of the Locust,* deals with the nondescript characters on the fringe of the Hollywood studios: an old comic who sells shoe polish and his film-struck daughter; a quarrelsome dwarf; a cock-fighting Mexican; a Hollywood cowboy and a Hollywood Indian; and an undeveloped hotel clerk from Iowa, who has come

*Reprinted from the *New Republic* 99 (26 July 1939): 338–39.

to the Coast to enjoy his savings—together with a sophisticated screen-writer, who lives in a big house that is "an exact reproduction of the old Dupuy mansion near Biloxi, Mississippi." And these people have been painted as precisely and polished up as brightly as the figures in Persian miniatures. Their speech has been distilled with a sense of the flavorsome and the characteristic which makes John O'Hara seem pedestrian. Mr. West has footed a precarious way and has not slipped at any point into relying on the Hollywood values in describing the Hollywood people. The landscapes, the architecture and the interior decoration of Beverly Hills and vicinity have been handled with equal distinction. Everyone who has ever been in Los Angeles knows how the mere aspect of things is likely to paralyze the esthetic faculty in providing it with no *point d'appui* from which to exercise its discrimination, if not actually to stun the sensory apparatus itself, so that accurate reporting become impossible. But Mr. West has stalked and caught some fine specimens of these cross-eyed-making Hollywood lepidoptera and impaled them on fastidious pins. Here are Hollywood restaurants, apartment houses, funeral churches, brothels, evangelical temples and studios—in this latter connection, an extremely amusing episode of a man getting nightmarishly lost in the Battle of Waterloo. Mr. West's surrealiste beginnings have stood him in good stead on the Coast.

The doings of these people are bizarre, but they are also sordid and senseless. Mr. West has caught the emptiness of Hollywood; and he is, as far as I know, the first writer to make this emptiness horrible. The most impressive thing in the book is his picture of the people from the Middle West who have passed on from their meager working lives to the sunlit leisure of the Coast, wanting something more than they have had but not knowing what they want, with no capacity for the enjoyment of anything except gaping at movie stars and listening to Aimee McPherson's sermons. In the last episode, a crowd of these people, who have come out to see the celebrities at an opening, is set off by an insane act of violence on the part of the cretinous hotel clerk, and gives way to an outburst of mob mania. The America of the murders and rapes which fill the Los Angeles papers is only the obverse side of the America of the inanities of the movies. Such people—Mr. West seems to say— dissatisfied, yet with no ideas, no objectives and no interest in anything vital, may in the mass be capable of anything. The daydreaming purveyed by Hollywood, the easy romances that always run true to form, only cheat and exacerbate their frustration.

I think that the book itself suffers a little from the lack of a center of the community which it describes. It has less concentration than *Miss Lonelyhearts*. Mr. West has introduced a young Yale man who, as an educated and healthy human being, is supposed to provide a normal point of view from which the deformities of Hollywood may be criticized: but it is precisely one of the points of the story that this young man should find himself swirling around in the same aimless eddies as the others. I am not sure that it is really possible to do anything substantial with Hollywood except by making it, as Dos Passos did in *The Big Money,* a part of a larger picture which has its center in a larger world. But in the meantime Nathanael West has survived to write another remarkable book—in its peculiar combination of amenity of surface and felicity of form and style with ugly subject and somber feeling, quite unlike—as his other books have been—the books of anyone else.

Having given Random House as bookmakers a bad mark on Isherwood's *Goodbye to Berlin,* I must give them a good mark on *The Day of the Locust.* It is attractively proportioned, shows a fine page of type and is handsomely bound in scarlet. I have noted only one misprint—on page 115.

Faulkner and Contemporaries

ISAAC ROSENFELD*

Most of the books and articles that have come out of the intellectuals' recent interest in popular culture have been so bad that one might well think of them as the intellectuals' own form of popular culture. These lubrications have been self-conscious or condescending or inspired by a mawkish concern over the fate of culture. In nearly every case, the writer has been disinclined or unable to participate in the life he was talking about. Hollywood, radio, television, detective stories, the comic strips, etc., are no place for the alienated; you either like this sort of thing or you leave it alone. The only man who, in my opinion, really knew what he was doing was Nathanael West, and this is because of his theme—it runs through both *Miss Lonelyhearts* and *The Day of the Locust,* and it makes him unique among American novelists—the secret inner life of the masses.

West's credentials for writing *The Day of the Locust* were painfully earned. He came to Hollywood to write for the movies, when the three novels he had already published, including *Miss Lonelyhearts,* failed to sell. But there isn't a streak of self-pity in *The Day of the Locust,* though it is derived from an experience of Hollywood that must have been up to his ears. He went beyond the personal irritation; in fact, Hollywood didn't seem to have irritated him at all. There is so much gusto in his satire, so much taste for the very thing he was destroying, that he achieved in this book a kind of serenity, as a man will when his love and his hate work together.

Though West did not want to be considered a surrealist, it is a fairly accurate classification; there is the same compression of meaning in his images, often several layers thick, and the compression achieves for him a similar effect, incandescent and explosive. Now this is by no means an estrangement from the popular, the surrealists themselves having made extensive use of devices from popular culture. In West's use of this imagery he straddles the two worlds of his own sensibility, the poetic and the popular, and the grotesques who fill his work, the dwarf bookie, the girl with a hole in her face instead of a nose ("no boy will take me out . . . although I am a good dancer and have a nice shape and . . . pretty clothes"), the family of performing Eskimos, etc., are derived from this juxtaposition. This not only gave West access to an existence

*Reprinted from *Partisan Review* 18 (January–February, 1951): 109–11.

usually closed to intellectuals; it worked both ways, showing him the limitations of the intellectuals' ordinary position. His conscious characters are by the measure of their own elevation above the mass cut off from the necessary contact with common life. The result is neither an apology for nor a condemnation of the popular. It has independent status, the nearest thing to a new art form ever to be derived from the materials of a mass culture. It is a pity that he had not fully brought it off at the time of his early death, for with West went one of our few real chances to salvage something from commercialization; and we are not likely to have another writer so gifted and so well situated.

But this puts it all too placidly. West's art was closer to nightmare. He saw, as everybody has seen, the starvation latent in the popular media, but he stayed clear of the platitudes and condolences over the death of culture. He showed the death of everything with the walls tumbling down. The starvation is not only for good books and fine music; it is a starvation for all of life, for sexual fulfillment, for decent work, for pleasure and happiness and relief from the desolation that drives people insane. (West had a religious sense of this need, which must have worked in him as it does in the mass, making him peculiarly sensitive to the symbols of holy violence. *The Day of the Locust* is foaming with prophecy.) Out of this starvation swarm the locusts, the mobs gone mad and descending on the cities to revenge themselves on the make-believe of effortless satisfaction that inflamed their hunger. Nathanael West was in touch with the popular culture over its whole range, and he has so far remained the only one who has drawn the whole conclusion.

Waiting for the Apocalypse

DANIEL AARON*

Now that Nathanael West's *Miss Lonelyhearts* has attained the status of a "minor classic," he is not likely to be slighted by the literary historians and critics who until recently have pretty much ignored him. His last novel, however, is less well know. New Directions' reissue of *The Day of the Locust,* first published in 1939, should remove any doubts about West's perverse genius and extend his still limited audience.

Readers familiar with any of West's earlier writing will recognize in this Hollywood-Los Angeles extravaganza the tone and mannerisms which always distinguished his books, bizarre and ferocious, from the more popular "proletarian" novels of the thirties. West apparently admired the left-wing propagandists who solemnly documented the decay of capitalist society, and he sympathised with their aims, too, but he was saved from being naive and doctrinaire by his compulsive irony, by his delight in the incongruous, and perhaps most of all by his profound disgust with life itself. These very qualities separated him from a generation who either preferred the exposures of the radical pamphleteers or the literature of escape. West's books never sold well although he had a small cult of admirers.

Unlike most of his contemporaries, West is not easy to place or to categorize. It is true that his obsession with the grotesque, his studies of people suddenly seized and ridden by private demons, suggest Sherwood Anderson; that the meticulous way in which he delineates the atrocious reminds us of Huysmans; and that there is something akin to a Chagall-like mysticism in his disciplined nightmares. But at the same time his vision of a foul and arid world is intensely personal and quite underivative, for he is a comic writer who can be droll if never unabashedly joyous, and he is as much impressed by the ludicrousness of life as he is by its horror.

Consider *The Day of the Locust.* At first glance it might strike one as simply another exposé of Hollywood, more frenetic and burlesqued, perhaps, than most, but exploiting the familiar vulnerable stereotypes. Tod Hackett, West's young painter and alter ego, comments again on the well-known landscape and observes the habits of the movie world which have been so critically and

*Reprinted by permission from The Hudson Review, Vol. III, No. 4 (Winter 1951). Copyright © 1951 by The Hudson Review, Inc.

uncritically celebrated. But the reader soon discovers that this tale of Hollywood is neither a witty and superficial arraignment of the film colony or Southern California (Evelyn Waugh's *The Loved One*) nor a romantic evocation of Hollywood as epic (F. Scott Fitzgerald's *The Last Tycoon*). Hollywood, West's fantastic "dream dump," is conceived rather as a symbol of despair and unfulfillment.

West had originally planned to call his book "The Cheated." The characters, both major and minor, are not only cheating one another by pretending to be what they are not, but even more significant for West, they have been swindled out of their expectations and illusions. Hollywood, moreover, is not an isolated piece of dreamland or a national joke; it is America carried to its logical conclusion. The tormented, hungry, violent people who end up at the edge of the western ocean and who finally riot in the eerie conclusion of the book are the products of middle-America, the degraded descendents of the Populists, with no further frontiers to conquer. They are the locusts, mindless and numberless, who, like their Biblical namesakes, have turned a once beautiful country into a desert; they are impelled by forces they can neither understand or control. They may even be the instruments of God's wrath. West observes them humorously but also with wonder and fear as they scream imprecations in their "New Thought" temples and swarm aimlessly through the streets waiting for the apocalypse.

The city is unreal where they wander, and the signs of death and sterility are everywhere. Nothing seems really alive in this gaudy paradise except the lizards. The people move jerkily down Vine street, itself a kind of enlarged movie studio, and the dream-like quality is enhanced by the architectural conglomeration—Mexican, Swiss, Tudor, Egyptian—and by the calculated disguises of the pedestrians. As West puts it, "A great many of the people wore sports clothes which were not really sports clothes. Their sweaters, knickers, slacks, blue flannel jackets with brass buttons were fancy dress. The fat lady in the yachting cap was going shopping, not boating; the man in the Norfolk jacket and Tyrolean hat was returning, not from a mountain, but an insurance office; and the girl in slacks and sneaks with a bandanna around her head had just left a switchboard, not a tennis court."

West is charmed by the monstrous masquerade, and there are some fine comic episodes in *The Day of the Locust* which grow out of the incongruity of make-believe and reality. Thus when Tod Hackett visits the set where "Waterloo" is being filmed, he observes that the battle is proceeding briskly. Since neither Wellington nor Napoleon is available, the assistants of the producer, Mr. Grotenstein, take over. "Things looked tough for the British and their allies" until one of the directors bolsters the allied center "with infantry from Brunswick, Welsh foot, Devon yeomanry and Hanoverian light horse." And then, luckily for the British, a man wearing a checked cap repeats Napoleon's classic blunder and orders General Milhaud's cuirassiers to capture Mont St. Jean before the property men have finished their preparation. The whole hill collapses, Napoleon's army is covered with painted cloth, and the insurance company must subsidize the defeat.

Yet the burlesque in *The Day of the Locust* (more subdued here than in his slapstick, *A Cool Million,* which preceded it) finally becomes nightmare, and we know that West is in deadly earnest. Kenneth Burke has remarked that "the grotesque is the cult of incongruity *without* laughter." Certainly the dominating tone of this book is not joyous in spite of its desperate humor. It seems likely that West's image of a tortured demented world grew out of a deep personal anguish and that in the dislocations of society he found the symbols of his private state. Because of his close identification with what he described, his cast of whores, paranoiacs, con-men, and sadists are never presented with the detachment which we expect from the true social castigators who lash out against moral aberration. There is nothing of Juvenal, or of Jonson or Swift or Smollet; nor is there any kindly spoofing. The principal female character, for instance, could properly be the subject for the social satirist: she is witless, if beautiful, and lives in an adolescent trance. But for West, who never presented women sympathetically, this platinum-haired witch with a moon-face and "sword-like legs," is more vicious and destructive than comic. "Her invitation," he writes, "wasn't to pleasure, but to sturggle, hard and sharp, closer to murder than to love. If you threw yourself on her, it would be like throwing yourself from the parapet of a skyscraper. You would do it with a scream."

The apparent objectivity or realism of the book derives, I think, from the extreme clarity with which he projects his scenes of violence, a clarity observable in some surrealist paintings or in a story like Kafka's *The Penal Colony. The Day of the Locust,* starting off almost gaily, becomes very soon a series of sharply focused but disconnected episodes—the showing of an obscene film, a cock-fight in a gargage, several formidable debauches, a crazy riot—which blend his private anxieties with public truths.

It is not really a satisfactory novel, because West never manages to fuse his image of the "dream dump" with the more revealing symbol of the cock-fight. Of all the events in the book, this is the most graphic and relentless and the one which makes clear West's preoccupation with his dippy heroine and the assorted flock of birds who flutter and peck around her. In fact West becomes so absorbed with Faye Greener that he never shows just what relation, if any, exists between her cavortings and the tribulations of Homer Simpson, the yokel from Iowa, in whose garage the cock-fight takes place. Homer, although a central figure, is nothing more than a botched re-working of Sherwood Anderson's grotesque in his story *Hands.* He is intended, I suppose, to be the link between the frustrated Iowans and the raffish movie set, but no conscious idea or metaphor holds this book together. It only succeeds as a kind of baleful commentary on American life and an unhappy record of what Poe once described as "this unfathomable longing of the soul to vex itself."

Collected Novels

◆

Nathanael West: A Particular Kind of Joking

Norman Podhoretz*

The Complete Works of Nathanael West comprises four short novels amounting to only four hundred and twenty-one pages—West was killed in an automobile accident in 1940, at the age of thirty-seven—but it contains some of the best writing that has been produced by an American in this century. During the 30's, West earned the admiration of several important critics, and his two most impressive novels, *Miss Lonelyhearts* and *The Day of the Locust,* are still widely circulated and praised; the others, *The Dream Life of Balso Snell* and *A Cool Million,* have only now been rescued, by the publication of this collected volume, from virtual oblivion. But though West has not exactly been ignored, neither has he been given the close attention he deserves. His name seldom comes up in discussions of modern American literature, and even now it is not clearly realized that, for all the "bitterness" and "savagery" people find in his work, he was first and last a writer of comedy. A year before his death, West complained that his novels were disliked because they fell "between the different schools of writing." He considered himself, he said, on the side of the "radical press," but the radicals objected to his "particular kind of joking," and the "highbrow press" accused him of avoiding the "big, significant things." It is difficult to imagine what the "highbrows" (whoever they were) could have meant; the big, significant things are precisely what West pursued, to

*Reprinted from *Doings and Undoings* (New York: Farrar, Straus & Company, 1964.) Reprinted by permission of Georges Borchardt, Inc. for the author.

greater effect, in my opinion, than Fitzgerald, who lacked West's capacity for intelligent self-criticism, or even Hemingway, whose view of life seems to me rather more limited than West's. But the "radical press" was right in being disturbed by West. Nothing could be further from the spirit of his work than a faith in the power of new social arrangements or economic systems to alleviate the misery of the human condition. West was one of the few novelists of the 30's who succeeded in generalizing the horrors of the depression into a universal image of human suffering. His "particular kind of joking" has profoundly unpolitical implications; it is a way of saying that the universe is always rigged against us and that our efforts to contend with it invariably lead to absurdity. This sort of laughter—which, paradoxically, has the most intimate connection with compassion—is rarely heard in American literature, for it is not only anti-"radical" but almost un-American in its refusal to admit the possibility of improvement, amelioration, or cure.

Yet West was also capable of lesser kinds of joking. His first novel, *The Dream Life of Balso Snell*—written mainly during a two-year stay in Paris, when he was in his early twenties, but not published until 1931—is a brilliantly insane surrealist fantasy that tries very hard to mock Western culture out of existence. Balso, who seems sometimes to represent the naïve romantic poet and sometimes the philistine American, comes upon the Trojan horse while wandering on the plains of Troy and literally gets inside Western culture by entering the horse (which is, of course, a symbol of that culture) through "the posterior opening of the alimentary canal." He meets a series of strange characters who inhabit the horse's innards, and each encounter is an occasion for West to deride art, religion, or civilization itself in the most shocking terms he can think of. There is, for example, Maloney the Areopagite, "naked except for a derby in which thorns were sticking" and "attempting to crucify himself with thumb tacks." Maloney, a mystic, is compiling a biography of St. Puce, "a flea who was born, lived, and died beneath the arm of the Lord." This trick of associating a pious idea with physical images evoking disgust is used generously throughout the novel, which overflows with references to diseased internal organs, mucus, and the like.

But it is all done much too innocently and exuberantly to be as offensive as West seemed to want it to be, and in any case the effort to *épater le bourgeois* is by no means the main purpose of *Balso Snell*. West incorporates into the novel several self-contained short stories that he obviously composed with intense seriousness. The most interesting—the confession of an insane intellectual who has murdered an idiot for what he calls purely "literary" reasons—is a precociously accomplished imitation of Dostoyevsky, and West might well have regarded its extravagant relish of the grotesque and the diseased as a form of deep spiritual insight. Instead, he attributes the story to a twelve-year-old brat named John Raskolnikov Gilson, who informs Balso that he wrote it to seduce his eighth-grade teacher, Miss McGeeney, a great reader of Russian novels. Mocking his own work in this fashion was West's way of telling himself that merely to indulge his feeling for the grotesque and the diseased was morbid sentimentality, that he had to do more with this feeling than take it at face value if he was going to produce mature fiction. The assault on culture in *Balso Snell* is really part of West's assault on himself; he is sneering not so much at Western civilization as at his own ambition to become a part of it. This novel, then, is a battleground on which West the sentimentalist is pitted against West the cynic, each party asserting his claim to superior wisdom and refusing to concede any value to the other. Though the battle ends in a draw, the fighting of it must have helped West achieve the astonishing control over his feelings that makes his second novel, *Miss Lonelyhearts,* one of the masterpieces of modern literature.

Miss Lonelyhearts (West never gives him any other name) is a young newpaperman who conducts a column of advice to the unhappy and confused. At first, his job had seemed a great joke, but after several months—the point at which the novel begins—the letters from his readers begin to trouble him deeply. Brooding over his inability to help the wretched people who turn to him for advice, he decides that love is the only answer; he must bring Christ to them. His colleagues, and particulary the feature editor, Shrike, have a fine time ridiculing this "Christ complex," and his fiancée, Betty, insists on driving him out to the country to cure what she believes is an urban malaise. He himself tries to escape from "the Christ business" through several mechanical ventures into sex and cruelty, but the complex only gets worse. In the end, driven almost insane by his sense of religious mission, he is murdered by one of his correspondents, a cripple whom he had first cuckolded and then attempted to "save."

The letters are the focal point of the book, and a terrifyingly authentic expression of the misery that can be neither cured nor explained away:

> I am 15 years old and [my sister] Gracie is 13 and we live in Brooklyn. Gracie is deaf and dumb and biger than me but not very smart on account of being deaf and dumb. . . . Mother makes her play on the roof because we dont want her to get run over as she aint very smart. Last week a man come on the roof and did something dirty to her. She told me about it and I dont know what to do. . . . If I tell mother she will beat Gracie up awfull because I am the only one who loves her and last time when she tore her dress they loked her in the closet for 2 days and if the boys on the blok hear about it they will say dirty things like they did on Peewee Conors sister the time she got caught in the lots.

The letters make the fact of evil a concrete presence in the novel, and it is in relation to this fact that West forces us to measure the responses of his characters. What we learn is that Miss Lonelyhearts' sentimental spiritualism is no more adequate than Shrike's intellectual cynicism or Betty's naïve unconcern; all three attitudes are equally valid and equally futile, and they constitute, for West, the three possibilities of life in a world whose one ineluctable reality is the letters. And when, in the last chapter, Miss Lonelyhearts rushes feverishly to embrace the cripple who has come to kill him but who he imagines is crying out for salvation, we realize that Miss Lonelyhearts, like Shrike and Betty, suffers in the same degree as "Desperate," "Harold S.," "Catholic mother," "Broken-hearted," "Broad-shoulders," "Sick-of-it-all," "Disillusioned-with-tubercular-husband." That is West's profoundest joke, and it incorporates all the other jokes of the novel.

The formal perfection of *Miss Lonelyhearts*—the spareness and clarity of the style, the tight coherence of the conception, the delicate balance between opposing points of view—is an aesthetic reflection of the harmony that West had established, in the years since the completion of *Balso Snell,* between the conflicting elements of his own character. The tone never falters in *Miss Lonelyhearts,* because the strong-minded, intelligent compassion that emerged from this harmony and that was West's special and most precious quality as a writer gave him a firm perspective from which to judge experience. The impulse toward cynicism that ran wild in *Balso Snell* gets some play in Shrike, but it is now put into its proper place in a comprehensive and complex scheme of things. West regards Shrike's cycnicsm as a stunted form of wisdon, deriving from the recognition that all talk of salvation through love is irrelevant cant beside the reality of the letters, but he also perceives that the price of hiding behind a jeer is an inability to communicate with others—Shrike can neither give nor accept love. By contrast, Miss Lonelyhearts, the embodiment of the morbid sentimentalist in West, does have the power to reach out to others, but West knows that Miss Lonelyhearts' spiritualism also involves a failure of intelligence that drives him to foolishness and ultimately to insanity and death. And the portrait of Betty, whose refusal to be bothered by the letters leads to the frustration of her ambitions for a normal domestic life, can be understood as an assertion by West that his preoccupation with the halt and the sick is not the sign of a decadent or an immature sensiblity but a necessary concern with the problem of evil.

Having accomplished that much, West had earned a vacation. *A Cool Million,* published in 1934, a year after *Miss Lonelyhearts,* seems to me the sort of venture that a novelist who has achieved confidence in his powers feels he can afford to play around with. There are many amusing things in the story of Lemuel Pitkin, who leaves Rat River, Vermont, to make his fortune in another part of the land of opportunity and is dismantled step by step, losing all his teeth, one of his eyes, a leg, even his scalp, and then winds up as the martyred saint of an American fascist movement. But this obvious satire on the Horatio Alger myth, done in mock-heroic prose, must have come right off the top of West's head. And I suspect that he may even have been trying to satisfy the prevailing left-wing *Zeitgeist,* which demanded that a novelist be explicitly political. But that was a mistake for West; what he had to say about

Fascism he said much better in *The Day of the Locust,* his very unpolitical last novel.

The Day of the Locust—written while West was doing screenplays in Hollywood and published in 1939, nineteen months before his death—is a difficult book to get one's bearings in. It lumbers along at a queerly uneven pace, and one is never sure what West is up to. There is also an ambiguity in the treatment of locale and characters, both of which he portrays with meticulous regard for realistic detail while contriving to make them seem unnaturally grotesque. But once we understand that *The Day of the Locust* is intended as high comedy, and once we see that the slight touch of unreality in the narrative is West's method of trying to convey the feel of Hollywood, this apparently weird, disjointed book begins to assume meaningful shape.

A young painter, Tod Hackett, has taken a job at one of the studios as a set and costume designer. Hollywood fascinates him, but not the Hollywood of the big stars and the important producers; he is obsessed with the people on the streets who "loitered on the corners or stood with their backs to the shop windows and stared at everyone who passed. When their stare was returned, their eyes filled with hatred." The only thing Tod knows about these people is that they have "come to California to die." Later, he learns that

> All their lives they had slaved at some kind of dull, heavy labor, behind desks and counters, in the fields and at tedious machines of all sorts, saving their pennies and dreaming of the leisure that would be theirs when they had enough. Finally that day came. . . . Where else should they go but California, the land of sunshine and oranges?
>
> Once there, they discover that sunshine isn't enough. . . . Nothing happens. They don't know what to do with their time. . . . Their boredom becomes more and more terrible. They realize that they've been tricked and burn with resentment. . . . Nothing can ever be violent enough to make taut their slack minds and bodies. They have been cheated and betrayed. They have slaved and slaved for nothing.

These living dead—together with the religious crackpots who worship in all manner of insane churches, venting their rage at the betrayal of their dreams in mad apocalyptic rhetoric—are the people Tod wants to paint. He is planning a painting to be called "The Burning of Los Angeles," in which— anticipating similar fascist outbreaks throughout the country—they gather, like "a holiday crowd," to set the city afire. "He would not satirize them as Hogarth or Daumier might, nor would he pity them. He would paint their fury with respect, appreciating its awful, anarchic power and aware that they had it in them to destroy civilization." And so, indeed, West paints them in *The Day of the Locust.*

So, too, he paints the still living creatures who inhabit Hollywood. The living are tyrannized by dreams, possessed of the same "need for beauty and romance" that once animated the cheated people now waiting for death, but they have not yet acknowledged the futility of their dreams, the inexorability of their betrayal. In another of a series of pictures he calls "The Dancers," they are driven by the stares of the cheated ones "to spin crazily and leap into the air with twisted backs like hooked trout." This is a precise description of the way they look in the novel. Their bodies move uncontrollably, in jerks and spasms, as though refusing to cooperate in their struggle to achieve grace and dignity. They are "hooked" to the most elaborate, most awkward, most obvious of pretenses. Harry Greener, the broken-down old clown whose gestures all come out of an unfunny vaudeville act; his daughter Faye, who wants to be a star but whose affectations are "so completely artificial" that to be with her "was like being backstage during an amateurish, ridiculous play"; Earle Shoop, the cowboy from Arizona, who goes through life giving an unconvincing, incredibly stiff performance of the strong, silent Western hero; Abe Kusich, a pugnacious dwarf who tries to appear big and tough—these sad creatures make up the living populace of Hollywood. Tod, the artist, associates with them, implicated in their antics (he is in love with Faye), aware of their pretenses, but eager to see value and meaning in their grotesque dance of life.

West's Hollywood is a world in which the alternatives are the bitterness of a living death that is consummated in an orgy of destruction, and a convulsive reaching after nobility and grace that culminates in absurdity. There is no escape from these alternatives: Homer Simpson, the bookkeeper from the Midwest to whom nothing has ever happened, whose dreams are suppressed even in sleep, who has been reduced to a subhuman, almost vegetable condition, is finally "hooked" by the dream of love. In the last scene, Homer, maddened by the cruelty and infidelity of Faye, attacks a child who has annoyed him on the street and is mobbed by a crowd waiting outside a theater at a movie première. It is this incident which sets off a riot that finally unleashes the "awful, anarchic power" of the cheated and betrayed of Hollywood.

The Day of the Locust was West's first attempt to explore the implications of the compassionate view of life he had arrived at in *Miss Lonelyhearts*. Gloomy as it seems, this view of life provided a sound basis for writing comedy. *Miss Lonelyhearts* and *The Day of the Locust* are comic novels, not simply because they contain funny passages but because they are about the inability of human beings to be more than human, the absurdity of the human pretense to greatness and nobility. The fact that West has enormous respect for the fury and the hunger behind these pretensions, the fact that he does not demand of people that they surrender their dreams, the fact that he responds to the pathos of their predicament—none of this compromises the comedy. "It is hard," West tells us in *The Day of the Locust,* "to laugh at the need for beauty and romance, no matter how tasteless, even horrible, the results of that need are. But it is easy to sigh. Few things are sadder than the truly monstrous."

This is one of the lessons that comedy teaches—neither to laugh at the need nor to be taken in by the results. It is also the animating principle of true sympathy, which is why West's "particular kind of joking" has so deep a kinship with the particular kind of compassion that is allied to intelligence and is therefore proof against the assaults of both sentimentality and cynicism.

He Might Have Been A Major Novelist

Ralph Russell*

Nathanael West (1903–1940) is one of that long and distinguished line of writers whose success has been posthumous. Since his death in an automobile crash in California when he was thirty-seven, his writings have been taken up by both the critics and the crowd, and various of his works have been reissued, for the intellectuals by New Directions and for the rest of us by the paperback companies. Now all four of his brief, curious novels are published in one not especially bulky volume, with a preface by the British critic Alan Ross, and we have his entire work spread out for us except for a handful of unbought short stories and the scripts of some indifferent-to-good movies.

GRISLY CARICATURES

Time has been kind to West's reputation, and I think justly so, for he was a writer of strong, undiluted purpose and a sort of back-to-the-wall fierceness, who provided a grisly but telling caricature of American life in the Great Depression—a caricature that is all the more telling precisely because it is a caricature and not a slice of heavy realism or a hearty, eye-on-the-future protest in the name of the proletariat.

Except for his first novel, *The Dream Life of Balso Snell,* an unpleasant fantasy about a journey through the intestines of the Trojan horse which makes much of the damper and darker parts of the anatomy, West in each of his novels sets out to illuminate some portion of American life and some set of ideas or preconceptions in the yellowish light of satire and burlesque. Sometimes the humor is ponderous, sometimes it is light; it is, in any case, always there. In *Miss Lonelyhearts,* the scene is New York City—its newspapermen, its speakeasies, and its poor and battered who write in for solace from an advice-for-the-lovelorn columnist, a young man who makes the ultimately fatal mistake of taking seriously his role as comforter. The idea that comes in for West's peculiar brand of destructiveness is the idea of the imitation of Christ, of finding salvation in love for one's fellow men. In *A Cool Million,* the scene is

*Reprinted from the *Reporter* 16 (30 May 1957): 45–46.

practically all America, and the notion to be demolished is that decency and industry are all a young man needs to reach the top of the heap. In *The Day of the Locust,* the scene is Hollywood, and the author's dirty work is, more or less, to demonstrate the vanity of human wishes, the perilous boredom of the mob.

His novels are full of incident, and in all of them West makes his point as rapidly and vividly as a movie would make it if movies were the vehicles of anti-sentimentality instead of the opposite. In each case, the chief characters are either boldly drawn or lightly sketched—in the flat, though, not the round—and make their way through a host of generally gruesome and pitiful bit players.

West's favorites are cripples, dwarfs, down-and-outers, sinister Orientals, plausible crooks, and bullies. The action is generally episodic, and capriciously so—it is possible to imagine any of the novels achieving pretty much the same effects with a different set of episodes—and the method seems to be derived from the picaresque novel. *A Cool Million,* whose hero, a guileless young man named Lemuel Pitkin, sets out for the big city to save his mother from a mean mortgager, is reminiscent of *Candide,* as the young man loses his teeth, an eye, his scalp, and eventually his life, only to be canonized as the hero of a fascist movement that stands for everything his own trusting nature has seemed to stand against.

Too Easy a Hatred

In this and the two better-known novels, then, West's message seems to be that everything is empty and dreadful. Friendship is pretty much a fraud. Such sex as there is—and there isn't much, apart from sexual day-dreams and connivings—is, at best, faintly repellent. The landscape is crowded with people, and the people are uniformly unlovely: deformed, dried up, slovenly, sweaty. They jostle you, they shove their faces into yours, and the faces are rank with suffering and hatred. Even the pretty girls are anatomized to a point where they seem disagreeable. The architecture—especially that of Hollywood, which is splendidly portrayed in *The Day of the Locust*—is incongruous, make-shift, and ghastly; it infects the people, as the people infect it.

Escape from this mess, as Miss Lonelyhearts discovers, is impossible. His editor and guide through hell, Shrike, ticks off the possible escapes—religion, the South Seas, back-to-the-soil, etc.—and effortlessly pulverizes each. Tod Hackett, an artist through whose eyes Hollywood is seen in *The Day of the Locust,* reaches the peak of his power in envisioning an apocalyptic mob scene in Hollywood, which he sees as a dream dump; the book ends as his vision materializes. Nobody gets what he is after, and nobody could imaginably get what he is after. Tod doesn't get the girl. The girl does not get to be a film

star. Miss Lonelyhearts doesn't get to imitate Christ—not for long, anyway—
and Miss Lonelyhearts' clients don't get comfort.

It is a pity that West did not live to write more. As it stands, his despair
seems, to me at least, only a couple of removes from the theatrical despair of
the young aesthete—particulary the young aesthete of the 1930's, who had
to cope not with the syrupy sanctimony of our day but with the grimmer, if
cleaner, realities of a civilization that simply was not performing its most basic
functions. What saves these grotesque novels from being merely a youthful
yawp of tedium and anguish is that West could see and feel and write. For
all his cynicism, his portrait of suffering people in New York and Hollywood
is deeply heartbreakingly sympathetic and for all his grief, his writing is in
places magnificently comic. Emotionally, in his refusal to be comforted, he
appeared to be at a dead end. Perhaps he would have remained there; one of
his merits certainly was the very absoluteness of his disillusionment—his
rejection of all easy appeals to the brighter side, even the slightly brighter side.

But West's talent seemed to be growing, and one may surmise that had
he lived he might have gone far beyond the merely grotesque, the merely
disgusting, the merely hopeless.

The Great Despiser

Anonymous*

"After such knowledge, what forgiveness?" asked T. S. Eliot as he entered the dry season of 1920. At about the same time, another American writer who devoted his life to illuminating this bleakly ruthless question was growing up. Manhattan-born Nathan Weinstein, who later went by the name of Nathanael West, was a knowledgeable man, and nothing he knew induced him to forgive anything. In his brief life (he died in 1940, aged, 37), West wrote only four brief novels, but they were a full life's work. He wrote during that great interlude of negation, the Depression, when the "System" seemed to be breaking down—but among the whimpers of the jilted bachelors of arts of that drab time, West raised a man's voice in savage rage against the general condition of man.

As their titles suggest, the novels are a queer quartet: *The Dream Life of Balso Snell* (1931), *Miss Lonelyhearts* (1933), *A Cool Million* (1934), and *The Day of the Locust* (1939). During his lifetime, West's books were virtually ignored, but for some readers they have long been collector's items. In the bland climate of U. S. letters, true satire rarely flourishes, but the chilling ferocity of West's satirical attack would be rare anywhere. It involves not only a total rejection of common American ideals, but a Swiftian loathing for the texture of life itself. In his earliest work West recognized this of himself, in the character of a Cultured Fiend who says: "I was completely the mad poet. I was one of those 'great despisers' whom Nietzsche loved because 'they are the great adorers; they are arrows of longing for the other shore.'"

Laugh at the Laugh

When West first started to bat about with his phosgene-filled clown's bladder, he was an expatriate *boulevardier* in Paris, sporting umbrella and plaid overcoat among the beards and corduroy of the lost generation. *The Dream Life of Balso Snell* seems on the surface like one of those near-sophomoric, painfully private japes played for the semiprivate public of a little magazine. It concerns the dream adventures of Balso Snell, a poet, who enters a Trojan Horse from the

*Reprinted from *Time* 69 (17 June 1957): 102, 104, 106.

rear end ("Anus Mirabilis!"), and encounters a number of symbolic characters in the murky interior scenery.

Art, religion, and hope itself are derided in the mad figures inhabiting the horse. One is a naked but derby-hatted fellow named Maloney the Areopagite, who is writing the life of Saint Puce, a flea that was born in Christ's armpit. Another is John Raskolnikov Gilson, an eighth-grade schoolboy who wants to sleep with Miss McGeeney, his English teacher. In order to make his views known ("How sick I am of literary bitches. But they're the only kind that'll have me"), the boy has written a pamphlet that sounds very like West's own credo: "I always find it necessary to burlesque the mystery of feeling at its source; I must laugh at myself and if the laugh is 'bitter,' I must laugh at the laugh. The ritual feeling demands burlesque . . ."

AMERICAN CANDIDE

In *A Cool Million,* West burlesqued American optimism of the Horatio Alger type. The book tells of Lemuel Pitkin, who was born in a "humble dwelling much the worse for wear . . . owing to the straitened circumstances of the little family." Like Candide, Lemuel lives out the advice of a philosopher. His is the creed of Nathan "Shagpoke" Whipple, president of the Rat River National Bank and former President of the U. S. In the course of behaving well, *e. g.,* rescuing girls with rich fathers from bolting horses, Lemuel goes to jail, loses a leg, all his teeth and an eye, is robbed of his savings, and is finally martyred by an assassin. On Pitkin's Birthday, a national holiday, the vile Whipple addresses a mob of American fascists wearing coonskin caps: "Jail is his first reward. Poverty his second. Violence is his third. Death is his last." Shagpoke's youthful followers roar "Hail, Lemuel Pitkin! All hail, the American Boy!"

What distinguishes all this from other purposeful literary nightmares that professed to see the ghost of fascism on the American scene during the '30s is that West brought enough invention to one page for most novelists to spread thin over a book, and a style as lean and resourceful as a hungry wildcat. Above all West was not parochial, did not advocate political or social systems. He was one of those men in whom pity must take the form of anger, but his anger was not anything as simple as Anti-American or anti-Babbitt; it was anti-human nature.

TOMTOMFOOLERY

From Horatio Alger Satirist West moved on to Hollywood where he had worked as a script writer. Apart from the usual film-colony grotesques, *The*

Day of the Locust parades witless cowboys, actors, emotional cripples, dwarfs and a memorably mindless chrome-pated sexpot. It ends in madness and violence, like the others—a mob at a Hollywood première tramples an artist who is carried offstage screaming.

West's other work seems like mere tomtomfoolery compared to the drumfire on the nerves in *Miss Lonelyhearts*.

Its hero is a newspaperman—"Miss Lonelyhearts" is his only name known to the reader—who writes the lovelorn column for the New York *Post-Dispatch*. He is one of West's quasi-religious figures: "A beard would become him, would accent his Old Testament look. To the millions without emotional refuge," says one character sardonically, "the Miss Lonelyhearts are the priests of twentieth-century America." The mail brings the daily semiliterate confessions of horror "Dear Miss Lonelyhearts," one letter begins: "I am sixteen years old now—I dont know what to do . . . When I was a little girl it was not so bad because I got used to the kids on the block making fun of me, but now I would like to have boy friends like the other girls and go out Saturday nites, but no boy will take me because I was born without a nose—although I am a good dancer and have a pretty nice shape and my father buys me pretty clothes."

DAMNED ASPIRIN

This sort of thing, signed "Sincerely yours. Desperate," nudges Miss Lonelyhearts to the brink of madness. He is helped along the way by his diabolical editor, a man named Shrike. Coached by Shrike, his newspaper colleagues sneer at his pity for his letter writers and for humanity in general. "A leper licker," they call him in Delahanty's speakeasy. Of himself, Miss Lonelyhearts says to the girl who loves him: "As soon as anyone acts viciously, you say he's sick. Wife-torturers, rapers of small children, according to you they're all sick. No morality, only medicine. Well, I'm not sick. I don't need any of your damned aspirin. I've got a Christ complex. Humanity . . . I'm a humanity lover." As Shrike puts it mockingly, Miss Lonelyhearts is "he of the singing heart—a still more swollen Mussolini of the soul."

In terms of his own self-parody, Miss Lonelyhearts enacts a series of dramas with the hallucinatory clarity of an obscene nightmare. In a dream scene, a lamb is clumsily sacrificed. Miss Lonelyhearts makes love to a maudlin monster of a woman whom he does not want—like most of West's characters, he suffers sex like a dreadful, joyless compulsion. The woman has a crippled husband, and so each succeeding scene of the inhuman triangle is frozen in horror, like a movie still, until the last episode, where, after "accepting" God, Miss Lonelyhearts rushes to meet the husband with his arms outspread in brotherhood. In panic at the other's enveloping pity, the husband accidentally shoots him dead.

What West seems to be saying in spite of himself through all his quirky and relentless blasphemy is religious: that if Christ really is the Incarnate God, life is tolerable: but if mercy is merely embodied in the destructive and sentimental pity of a Miss Lonelyhearts, life is a foul joke.

West's voice—an octave higher than most ears—will make its reverberant echoes heard for a long time. His portrait of the U. S. and of mankind is like a great caricature that remains in the mind long after the loved or hated face itself has been blurred in the memory. A hard man is good to find, and such a one was West.

[An Implacable Vision]

SIMON RAVEN*

Nathanael West deals with power of a very different kind—the power of a hostile universe to reduce mankind to mere waste-bags of lechery and absurdity. West was killed in 1940, and this rather notable book is a reprint of the four short novels he left. *Miss Lonelyhearts,* the story of a reporter who does the personal problems column and goes mad with misery and frustration, and *The Day of the Locust,* which is about hopeless and obscene hangers-on in Hollywood, are probably the best. But all four have two things in common—laconic and viciously hard writing, and an implacable vision of a pagan world from which all the traiditional pagan consolations have been removed. Sex, for example, is either disastrous or farcical, while the liquor always seems to have come straight from somebody's cracked bath-tub.

*First printed in the *Spectator*: (6 December, 1957.) Reprinted by permission.

Miss Lonelyhearts

V. S. Pritchett*

Nathanael West is one of the novelists of the break down of the American dream in the Thirties. His real name was Nathan Weinstein, he moved in fashionable literary society, became a script writer in Hollywood after the success of *Miss Lonelyhearts* and was killed in a motor accident at the age of 37. Two of his novels, *Miss Lonelyhearts*—which is very well known—and *The Day of the Locust* show that a very original talent was cut short. He was preoccupied with hysteria as the price paid for accepting the sentimentalities of the national dream. He feared hysteria in himself, he was morbidly conscious of it in his people; he was attracted and repelled by its false dreams as one might be by a more poisonous way of mixing gin. West did not feel that life was tragic, for the sense of tragedy was lost in the moral collapse of the period he lived in. Like Chekhov—but only in this respect—he was appalled by the banality of city civilisation. Instead of being tragic life was terrible, meaningless and without dignity. Mr. Alan Ross, in a warm, if sometimes difficult, introduction to a volume containing all four of West's novels, makes this point and suggests that while the English writers of the Thirties reached their conclusions "through a series of well-bred intellectual convictions," Americans like West were thrown helplessly among the brute economic facts. For them the experience was emotional and even theatrically so, because hysterical violence is very near the surface in American life.

West's resources were Art—he learned from the surrealists—and compassion. Except in his satire, *A Cool Million,* which is an American *Candide* done in the manner of a parody too obvious and prolonged, he was not a political writer in the literal sense. He explored the illness behind the political situation. Human beings have always fought misery with dreams, Miss Lonelyhearts observes; the dreams and its ignoble deceits, the panic, anger and frustration these deceits expose, gave him his material. In *The Day of the Locust,* his mature novel, it is the boredom exposed by the failure of the Californian dream of an earthly Paradise that puts an expression of hate and destructiveness on the faces of the weary middle-aged population who have retired to Los Angeles. As they pour in to gape at the stars arriving for some world premiere, they have the look of lynchers. Lynch, in fact, they do and for no reason.

*Reprinted, with permission, from *New Statesman and Society*, (7 December 1957): 791–92

This does not covey that West is a comic writer. He has freakishness, wit and a taste for the absurd from the surrealists, also their sophistication in parody and styles, but moved quietly away from their gratuitous and perverse humour. He became comic and humane. *Miss Lonelyhearts* is a potent and orderly distillation of all the attitudes to human suffering. Miss Lonelyhearts himself is the drunken writer of an Advice Column in a newspaper who begins running it as a joke, a sort of sobbing *Americana*, and ends by becoming overwhelmed by the weight of human misery and by his inability to do anything about it. The office gambits sicken him. Christ, Art, the Karamazov line, the Value of Suffering, back to Nature, on to Hedonism and so on have been taped long ago by Shrike, the editor with the deadpan face, an expert in "how to play it." Shrike is one of West's many attacks on the dream-generators of the mass-media—an attack in the sense of one of those unholy recognitions that lie at the centre of the comic view of life:

> "I am a great saint," Shrike cried. "I can walk on my own water. Haven't you heard of Shrike's passion in the Luncheonette, or the Agony in the Soda Fountain? Then I compared the wounds in Christ's body to the mouths of a miraculous purse in which we deposit the small change of our sins. It is an excellent conceit. But now let us consider the holes in our own bodies and into what these congenital wounds open. Under the skin of a man is a wondrous jungle where veins like lush tropical growths hang along overripe organs and weed-like entrails writhe in squirming tangles of red and yellow. In this jungle, flitting from rock grey lungs to golden intestines, from liver to lights and back to liver again, lives a bird called the soul."

In the vulgar, exhausted way of the mass-media, dead-pan Shrike is an aesthete. His jaunty little face looks like a paralysed scream of fright. His remarks are pictorial, but without relation to any meaning. Miss Lonelyhearts is muddled by Shrike's cleverness. He would like to be able to believe in the efficacy of Christ, but the name for him has become another word for hysteria, "a snake whose scales are tiny mirrors in which the dead world takes on a semblance of life." He plowters through a series of alcoholic bouts, tries to seduce Shrike's cold and salacious wife, gets into fights in speakeasies, terrorises and tries to torture an old man in a public lavatory; for Miss Lonelyhearts has stong sadistic fantasies, his pity has a strain of cruelty in it and he has begun to hate the sufferers who have the tempting horror of freaks. He is seduced by the nymphomaniac wife of a cripple, tries illness, love on a farm. These struggles are fuddled but heroic; he feels his "great heart" is a bomb that "will wreck the world without rocking it." In the end he has a vision of the love of Christ and rushes to tell his friend the cripple about it; but the cripple shoots him in a fit of jealousy. Christ may not be hysteria, but he is a tale told by an idiot.

This might have been a slushy book, the derelict lot behind James Barrie's hoardings. It is, instead, a selection of hard, diamond-fine miniatures, a true

American fable. West writes very much by the eye and his use of poetic images has a precision which consciously sustains his preoccupation with the human being's infatuation with his dream and inner story. (All his people are spiders living in the webs they spin out of their minds.) Leaves on trees are like thousands of little shields, a woman's breasts are like "pink-tipped thumbs," a thrush sings like a "flute choked with saliva," a cripple limps along "making waste motions, like those of a partially destroyed insect." If we call *Miss Lonelyhearts* a minor star it is because we feel that the Art is stronger than the passion; that, indeed Miss Lonelyhearts himself is capable only of pathos. His advice to the nymphomaniac who is torturing her husband, to let him win once, is just wise old owlishness; her happiness is to accuse and torture, his to drag his loaded foot. West has not considered that human beings overwhelmingly prefer suffering to happiness and that their sobbing letters are part of the sense of the role or drama that keeps them going. Still, as a performance, *Miss Lonelyhearts* is very nearly faultless.

The Day of the Locust is an advance from fable and from fragments of people, to the courageous full statement of the novel. I say "courageous" because in this kind of transition (the writer) has to risk showing the weakness of his hand. The artificial lights of the freak show are off in this book and we see human absurdity as something normal. This is a novel about Hollywood. West worked in the hum of the American dream generators and he chose those people who have done more for American culture than their coevals in Europe have done for theirs; the casualties, the wrecks, the failures, the seedy and the fakes. They are the people to whom the leisureless yea-sayers have said "No." The observer is a painter from the East who is dreamig up what sounds like a very bad picture, a sort of Belshazzar's Feast. (He is a vestige of West, the aesthete.) He has fallen for Faye, a day-dreaming creature who secretly earns money as a call-girl for a "cultured" brothel, and who hopes, like the rest of the people, to get into pictures. She lives among a ramshackle group which includes old stage hangers-on, a ferocious dwarf, a woman who is grooming her son to be a wonder-child of the screen, an absurd, fairly genuine cowboy extra and a pathetic hotel clerk from the Middle West. Fay is carefully observed. She is the complete day-dreamer, insulated to such an extent by the faculty that it acts as an effective alternative to innocence; she is sexually provoking, cold, little-minded and cruel, but puts gaiety into the roles she takes on and has the survival powers of a cork in a storm. If Los Angeles were destroyed by fire she would easily survive, not because she is hard but because she is flimsy. Already, in *Miss Lonelyhearts,* West had been a delicate student of the American bitch.

This Hollywood novel is mature because the compassion has no theatrical pressure; because now West is blocking in a sizeable society, and because his gift for inventing extraordinary scenes has expanded. The novel is dramatised—in Henry James's sense of the word—in every detail, so that each line adds a new glint to the action. His sadistic streak comes out in an astonishing description of an illegal cockfight in a desert lot. His comic powers fill out in the scenes with the angry dwarf and in the pages where the hero gets lost in a film Battle of Waterloo. The psychological entangling is brought to an appalling climax when Faye leaves her exhausted hotel clerk for a Mexican and this leads on to the great final staging of the world premiere, where riot and lynching are sparked off by the wonder boy of the screen and the hate behind the Californian myth comes out:

> Once there, they discover that sunshine is not enough. They get tired of oranges, even of avocado pears and passion fruit. Nothing happens. They haven't the mental equipment for leisure, the money nor the physical equipment for plea-sure. . . . Their boredom becomes more and more terrible. They realise that they have been tricked and burn with resentment. Every day of their lives they read the newspapers and went to the movies. Both fed them on lynchings, murder, sex crimes, explosions, wrecks, love nests, fires, miracles, revolutions, war. This daily diet made sophisticates of them. The sun is a joke. Oranges can't titillate their jaded palates. Nothing can be violent enough to make taut their slack minds and bodies.

It was a warning against Fascism; it makes the witch-hunt understandable; by extension, it is a statement about the nearness of violence in American life.

The Day of the Locust has the defect of insufficient ambition. It calls for a larger treatment and we have a slight suspicion that the painter-observer is slumming. But West had not the breath for full-length works. Script-writing snaps up the clever. His important contribution to the American novel was his polished comedy, which he displayed with the variety of a master and on many levels. If his talent was not sufficeintly appreciated in the moral Thirties, it was because comedy as a world in itself and as a firm rejection of the respected was not understood. West had something of Europe in him, where it is no crime to know too much.

Nathanael West

Julian Symons*

The history of Nathanael West's reputation is sufficiently curious. His adult life was spent, as Mr. Alan Ross tells us in his introduction, on the outskirts of the literary and social movement of the late 1920s and early 1930s, and then in Hollywood. Associate editorship of a literary magazine, marriage to Eileen McKenney (the original of Ruth McKenney's *My Sister Eileen*), work on film scripts in Hollywood, death in a car accident at the age of thirty-seven: the pattern of the bright, literary young man who knows the right people, goes to the right parties, and ends as a script or copywriter, is not unusual on either side of the Atlantic. It is quite usual, also, to find in the pattern a novel or two, a scriptwriter's protest against his occupation, with a whiff of Scott Fitzgerald or perhaps Carl van Vechten about it. (West was killed on Ventura boulevard on the day after Scott Fitzgerald died.) Such was the general contemporary view of Nathanael West at the time of his death. In 1940 the obituaries were brief; few people thought that an interesting, much less an important, writer had died. Mr. Alfred Kazin's comprehensive survey of modern American writing, *On Native Grounds,* published in 1943, does not even mention West's name.

One notable exception to this communal disregard must be mentioned. Mr. Edmund Wilson, as always in this period, had his ear to the ground for native talent, and praised at least two of West's books at the time of their publication. But the real resurrectory note was struck, as one remembers, in *Partisan Review,* and West's fame in the last decade has flourished in a way that would certainly have pleased his sense of comedy. The reasons for the resurrection are interesting. West was not ignored during his lifetime because, as do some writers, he deliberately swam against the stream of fashion. On the contrary, it is because he was so obviously part of the stream that his work received little attention. In a sense he was a more "revolutionary" writer than, say, John Dos Passos and James T. Farrell: what alienated him from other writers, and from a wide audience, in the 1930s was the extreme pessimism of his attitude towards society and its institutions. It is this nihilistic pessimism, the sense that all social institutions are shams and that the act of love is merely "the incandescence that precedes being more lonely than ever," that plays a

*Reprinted by permission from the *Times Literary Supplement* 57 (24 January 1958): 44.

large part in earning respect for West to-day. If this is a decade when intellectuals are without obvious illusions, it is also one when they are without ideals.

The motive power of West's work, from beginning to end, was a fascinated disgust with the processes of the body and an accompanying obsession with physical violence. The limitation of range imposed upon a writer by such a disgust and such an obsession may be compensated by the intensity of his feeling. West's effective social satire, his scabrous wit, his adolescent desire to shock and his sometimes embarrassing self-pity, all spring from the same source.

In *The Dream Life of Balso Snell,* published in 1931 but written some while earlier, the desire to shock is immediately evident. This short fantasy recounts the experiences of the eponymous hero, whose name must surely have some anagrammatic significance, in the rectum of the Trojan Horse. The narrator's exclamatory comment on Balso's entry: "O Anus Mirabilis!" sets the story's tone of fantastic obscenity. Typical incidents concern Maloney the Areopagite, who in the intervals of attempting to crucify himself with thumb-tacks is writing a biography of Saint Puce, a flea who passed his life beneath the armpit of Christ; the diary of a schoolboy murderer "written while smelling the moistened forefinger of my left hand"; a love passage between Balso and a beautiful hunchback, who says that she has been seduced by a man named Beagle Darwin, and carries his child in her hump.

Before making a long nose at *The Dream Life of Balso Snell* as a piece of scatological juvenilia (as even Mr. Ross, who cannot be accused of underestimating West, is inclined to do) one should remember that it was written at a time when literary fantasy of a free-associative surrealistic kind was by no means the commonplace that it is to-day. *Balso Snell* is a work of some originality which contains images, and even scenes, of remarkable power: the schoolboy's murder of an idiot, for instance, or such a paragraph as this one about the idiot's laughter: "My neighbour, the idiot, never smiled, but laughed continually. It must have hurt him to laugh. He fought his laughter as though it were a wild beast. A beast of laughter seemed always struggling to escape from between his teeth."

The Dream Life of Balso Snell does not really stand apart from West's other fiction; rather, it prefigures the virtues and defects of his later writing. The blasphemy, the obscenity, the deep sense of personal anguish about his own life and the condition of the world, they are all in this early fantasy; and with them the insistent self-mockery, the determination to turn the blood and excrement, the suffering and cruelty, into a joke, that weakens so much of West's work. Thus the genuinely horrific schoolboy's confession must be made the subject of a facetious comment by Balso Snell: "Interesting psychologically, but is it art? I'd give you B minus and a good spanking." So also Balso's lovemaking with the hunchback, equally horrific in its way, is interrupted by her asking: "Would you want someone to ask of your sister what you ask of me? So this is why you invited me to dinner? I prefer music."

The theme of *Miss Lonelyhearts* (1933) is by now fairly well known. The hero writes a newspaper column of advice to those in trouble. Their pleas for help in troubles that are by human standards insoluble ("I sit and look at myself all day and cry. I have a big hole in the middle of my face that scares people even myself so I can't blame boys for not wanting to take me out") are the screws of his agony. These screws are turned by his editor Shrike, an incarnation of evil, who takes pleasure in revealing to Miss Lonelyhearts his inescapable fate as a true metropolitan man. Having discussed, and dismissed, the possibilities of escape through the soil, through perfect hedonism and through art, Shrike dictates a letter to Christ, in whose help lies the only possible hope for Miss Lonelyhearts, and by implication for his readers:

Dear Miss Lonelyhearts of Miss Lonelyhearts—
I am twenty-six years old and in the newspaper game. Life for me is a desert empty of comfort. I cannot find pleasure in food, drink, or women—nor do the arts give me joy any longer . . . I feel like hell. How can I believe, how can I have faith in this day and age? Is it true that the greatest scientists believe again in you?
I read your column and like it very much. There you once wrote: "When the salt has lost its savour, who shall savour it again?" Is the answer: "None but the Saviour?"
Thanking you very much for a quick reply, I remain yours truly,
A Regular Subscriber.

The story is told in short episodes which concern Miss Lonelyhearts' feeble, flickering attempts to escape from his fate, chiefly through drink and lovemaking. In spite of Shrike's mockery he also tries life in the country, in the company of a girl who is in love with him. The country cure fails. When Miss Lonelyhearts returns to the Bronx slums he sees what appear to him typical scenes: people with broken hands and torn mouths moving along the streets with "a dream-like violence," a man who seems to be on the verge of death staggering into a cinema to see a film called *Blonde Beauty,* a woman with an enormous goitre picking a love magazine out of a dustbin. In the end Miss Lonelyhearts feels that his identification with God is complete. He attempts to embrace the crippled husband of a woman whom he has seduced, in the belief that "the cripple would be made whole again, even as he, a spiritual cripple, had been made whole"; but the cripple, thinking he is being attacked, shoots Miss Lonelyhearts.

Mr. Ross in his introduction notes the religious strain in West's writing, what he expressively calls "a sort of pessimistic Messianism in whose aura America becomes a glorified Oxford Street, dirty, haphazard, doped," and says that *Miss Lonelyhearts* is "West's greatest book, because it is conceived most purely as a formal work of art, and is flawless within its structure." But really, one cannot accept the book, or indeed West's other books, as formal works of art. Nor does Mr. Dashiell Hammett's observation that "*Miss Lonelyhearts* is the stuff that makes our daily paper—but seen truly and told truly" seem quite on the mark. West's books reflect reality in the distorting mirror of personal pain. They are moving and distasteful, sometimes horrifying, but he never had the control over his material necessary for the production of a formal work of art, and structurally *Miss Lonelyhearts* splits off into a number of brilliant fragments which could be put together again in another order without any very noticeable effect on the story's emotional impact. The book's undeniable power as a morality is diminished by the fact that it is often written in a style of bright impersonal smartness ("Goldsmith smiled, bunching his fat cheeks like twin rolls of smooth pink toilet paper"), and by West's characteristic hesitancy to commit himself to any positive viewpoint. Pity and disgust are there, and they are finely communicated: but there is no indication that West himself believed these feelings to be valid or helpful, except perhaps as a solvent for his personal unhappiness.

In a way West's next book, *A Cool Million* (1934), is the most interesting work he produced. It is, as Mr. Wilson has said, the American success story in reverse. The central character, Lemuel Pitkin, wishes only to make a fortune by employing the honest American virtue of free enterprise, so that he may redeem the mortgage on his old mother's home. "America," that former President of the United States Shagpoke Whipple assures him, "is the land of opportunity. She takes care of the honest and industrious and never fails them as long as they are both." Honest, industrious Lemuel Pitkin is dismantled of his teeth, an eye, a leg and his scalp, during his search for a fortune. At last he is shot by a Communist at a mass meeting and becomes a martyr of the National Revolutionary (Fascist) Party which, headed by Shagpoke Whipple, takes power in the country.

The theme is a magnificent one for a satirist, but in the event this is one of those books which sound like masterpieces when summarized but in the reading prove something of a disappointment. This is partly because West lacked the range of mind to handle satire upon such a grand scale; but *A Cool Million* fails principally because the tale is told in an uncertain pastiche of the style of the American success story. "One late fall evening, Mrs. Pitkin was sitting quietly in her parlour, when a knock was heard on her humble door" is an example, by no means the unhappiest in the book, of this style. As a conscious literary device the style was, inevitably, ineffective; here, as elsewhere, West seems subconsciously to have sought for a way of making farce out of material which, if seriously rendered, must be intolerably painful to him.

The most successful scenes in the book are those in which West expresses quite nakedly his sense of life's cruelty and injustice. In one of these—it is a scene which could have been conceived by no other modern writer—Pitkin, who has been refused work everywhere, is suddenly given a job by the famous comedy team of Riley and Robbins just because he has a wooden leg, a toupee, a glass eye and false teeth. His stage part is a simple one. The comics beat him with rolled-up newspapers until they knock off his toupee or knock out his teeth and eye. The climax of the act is when they hit Pitkin with an enormous mallet labelled "The Works" so that at one blow his toupee flies off, his eye and teeth pop out and his wooden leg is knocked into the audience. "At sight of the wooden leg, the presence of which they had not even suspected, the spectators were convulsed with joy. They laughed heartily until the curtain came down, and for some time afterwards."

The passionate intensity of feeling that marks such scenes is somewhat diminished in *The Day of the Locust* (1939). In the sense that here West attempted to fit his talent into the common form of a novel, and actually achieved a background portrait of Hollywood and its architecture that has a fine, brittle brilliance, the book marks an advance on his previous work: but he paid the price for it—perhaps one should say that it was a price exacted by Hollywood—in a slackening of energy and concentration. The characters are fantastic—a hotel clerk pathologically concerned about his sexual unattractiveness, a furious hydrocephalic dwarf, a Hollywood cowboy, a film-struck girl intently preserving her virginity—but their frustrations are treated with an attempted realism that sits uneasily on West. It should be added that the scene of crowd violence with which the book ends is one of a brilliance equal to anything he ever wrote. A mass of people who have come out to watch the celebrities arriving at a first night are transformed suddenly into a single monster, good humoured and cheerful, but violent by its very nature. West's hero uses this mob scene in a picture called *The Burning of Los Angeles,* and there is a hint of Fascism in his vision of the people in it, "The people who come to California to die . . . all those poor devels who can only be stirred by the promise of miracles and then only to violence"; but, as in *A Cool Million,* the political and social points are never pushed very far.

Four books, adding up to 400 pages in one rather vulgarly produced volume: what other kind of sum do they make? West was underestimated in his lifetime, but his work has surely been grossly over-praised in recent years. "In his books there are no echoes of other men's books," Mr. Dashiell Hammett has said, and Mr. Wilson somewhat make the same sort of remark; and it is true that he had a rare originality in the choice of a theme, and showed a fantastic imaginative power in the treatment of the themes he chose. His books are always interesting, and even exciting, to read. The finest passages in them are those in which violence, and particularly mob violence, is described and analysed, in which a real attempt is made to give universal significance to personal agonies and fears. But this sad moralist was too often facetious: this careful and even finicky writer never developed a personal style, but relied for the most part on the ready-made conventional smartness of the period. West was by intention a satirist, and the limitations of his work are suggested by a comparison with the most important modern English satirists, George Orwell, Wyndham Lewis, Mr. Evelyn Waugh. Unlike them he has no positive idea to offer, no belief in the values of Socialism or of art or of tradition: beneath the chromium brightness of its surface his work suggests only a self-corrosive despair.

A Period Piece

GRAHAM HOUGH*

I find it hard to regard the Nathanael West omnibus as much more than a period piece, an impression which is confirmed by the appalling typography of the title-page. It is made up of four short novels. Of these "Miss Lonelyhearts" has had a justified minor celebrity. (The claim that West is one of the greatest of the American writers of this century is surely absurd?) This horrifying nouvelle of an agony-column writer, who becomes so deeply involved with the hopeless misery of his correspondents that he comes to make a hysterical identification of himself with Christ, succeeds in capturing a mood of megalopolitan despair with great power. Written during the depression, it reflects something of the truth about its period, and perhaps something that is a general truth (one general truth among many) about American big-city life. But for all the hero's messianic delusions, it is nausea rather than charity that remains as the final flavour of the book. Of the rest, "The Dream Life of Balso Snell" is a piece of juvenile surrealism, better left buried. Part of it concerns the life of Saint Puce, a flea who lived in the armpit of Christ, and part the diary of an insane schoolboy. The setting, I forgot to say, is in the rectal passages of the Trojan Horse. "A Cool Million" is a sort of American *Candide,* not very much on the mark in its social criticism, and told in a parody best-seller style inapt for sustained irony. The worst of doing a whole tale in a parody of a despised manner is that it can hardly avoid reproducing many of the defects of the original. "The Day of the Locust," written in 1939, makes a more serious attempt to grapple with the realities of the situation it presents. It is the fruit of West's sojourn in Hollywood, and shows a squalid and pointless life in a tone of half-fascinated horror. There are scenes of considerable force; but the continual nerveless acquiescence of people who are beaten before they start is a hopeless theme for any but a very narrow kind of success. Reading these revivals one feels a strange contrast with the general tone of reassurance breathed by current American letters.

*Reprinted from *Encounter* 10 (February 1958): 86.

Prophet of Black Humour

Martin Seymour-Smith*

Nathan Weinstein felt that to be Jewish was irrelevant. Perhaps this more than anything else explains why American critics have neglected him in his *persona* as Nathanael West, novelist. For the contemporary American novel, although profoundly anticipated by West, is certainly self-consciously Jewish. Alfred Kazin's *On Native Grounds,* an unusually thorough and intelligent survey published in 1942, does not even mention him. And although he is now discussed in every survey of American fiction, he has still received nothing like his due.

Not much is publicly known about West's life. Although an American critical study—not a very adequate one—has recently appeared, there is no biography. He was born in 1903, and educated at Brown University. He edited *Contact* with William Carlos Williams, ran a hotel, and spent the last six or seven years of his life in Hollywood. His sister married S. J. Perelman, and he married Eileen McKenney, who was the original of the book *My Sister Eileen,* which was later successfully dramatised, by Ruth McKenney. In 1940 both he and his wife were killed in a car accident.

West was not only original in his own right, he was also the original black comedian, the prophet of the Jewish American novel of the 'fifties and 'sixties and apparently the only writer of his time to assimilate Kafka (but he had not read him). None of his four books is perfect, but each—excepting the first, which is 'prentice work—is, in its way, a masterpiece. It is high time that he was read extensively.

West spent some time in Paris, and his first and most inconsiderable book, *The Dream Life of Balso Snell,* reflects this. It is a perfect *Transition* piece, though bursting with talent, in which the obscenely named hero discovers, while walking "in the tall grass that has sprung up around the city of Troy," Homer's "ancient song"; he decides to enter the wooden horse, and discovers the "posterior opening of the alimentary canal," by which he enters it, "O Anus Mirabilis!"

The rest of the book is better than its dismal, too clever opening; but undiluted surrealism did not prove to be a right method for West's genius. As one can see from the difficulties he encountered in finishing *The Dream Life*

*Reprinted by permission from *The Spectator* 22 (19 July 1968): 94–95.

of Balso Snell, he needed no procedures superior to those of a straightforward realist.

His next novel, *Miss Lonelyhearts* (1933), is the one by which he is most widely known. It is not his best book, but because in it he discovered the methods most suitable to his genius, it does sometimes reasonably seem to be. Miss Lonelyhearts, the male Evelyn Home of a popular newpaper (and why doesn't someone, since Miss Home actually exists, ask her opinion of this book?), collapses under the pressure of his job and the cynicism of Shrike, his colleague ("Why don't you give them something new and hopeful? Tell them about art"); he needs to become nothing less than Jesus Christ, and, because he cannot do so, he perishes, the accidental victim of a cripple whose wife he has seduced and whom he too sentimentally wishes to save.

The irony of this novel was already beyond anything that America had ever produced; and possibly no novelist anywhere had exhibited West's capacity for sardonic economy. But apparently only the film world appreciated (if that is the correct word) his genius, for while the literary world remained comparatively silent, Hollywood commissioned—among other work—the script of *Advice to the Lovelorn,* an adaptation of the novel. West's next novel, *A Cool Million, or The Dismantling of Lemuel Pitkin* (1934), was a departure from the realism of *Miss Lonelyhearts.* It has been criticised, and probably underrated, because it adopts a parody of a mock-melodramatic woman's magazine style. This paragraph, from near the beginning, is sufficiently representative of both the advantages and the disadvantages of the method: "Our hero's way home led through a path that ran along the Rat River. As he passed a wooded stretch he cut a stout stick with a thick gnarled top. He was twirling this, as a bandmaster does his baton, when he was startled by a young girl's shriek. Turning his head, he saw a terrified figure pursued by a fierce dog. A moment's glance showed him that it was Betty Prail, a girl with whom he was in love in a boyish way."

As a *tour de force, A Cool Million* comes off. No one had ever dared to try such a thing before. It remains exquisitely readable, even when the posturing melodrama of its prose becomes too much of a good thing; and there are nuances, cruelly aware nuances, in its parody that go well beyond mere criticism of bad, superficial narrative. Consider, for example, the significance of the "stout" stick in the passage quoted above: it is only a slight reminiscence of the kind of prose that boys are told to admire at school, but the effect of these subtle touches is cumulative.

A Cool Million is entirely successful as satire. There is still no more devastatingly contemptuous exposure of naïve "Americansim" and capitalist optimism than this story of the honourable, trusting and parodically innocent Lemuel Pitkin, who loses an eye, his teeth, his scalp and his leg, and after being jailed and used as a tool for both communist and fascist conspiracies, is killed and becomes a martyr in the fascist cause. It disappoints only because it fails to transcend its immediate object and become a major work of imagination. The precedent for this is, of course, *Gulliver's Travels,* of which West was clearly actutely aware, since his hero's Christian name is Lemuel.

For Pitkin, besides serving as a butt, very nearly comes to life, and serves to represent something much more than just the idiotic Horatio Alger-American. Has anyone noticed the resemblance between West's satire and John Crowe Ransom's famous poem, 'Captain Carpenter'? Carpenter, as will be remembered, is just such an honourable innocent as Pitkin: he rides out, and is systematically shorn of his eyes, ears, limbs and life. But, whereas Ransom's poem is deliberately archaic and unmodern, West's novel is as slickly sick as his fundamentally poetic imagination would allow it to be. Nevertheless, there is enough promise in *A Cool Million* to suggest that had West lived he might have produced books that would have made such admirably ambitious but literary-egg-bound fowls as *Giles Goatboy* look contrived and even silly.

But his finest book, written directly out of his long Hollywood experience, was his last: *The Day of the Locust* (1939). This was composed in a straightforwardly realistic style, with the greatest economy of effect that West had yet achieved. He has not yet been equalled in this respect. But despite its total refusal to compromise facts of situation or character with sentiment or, indeed, with emotion of any kind, and despite the air of despair which pervades it, *The Day of the Locust* is redolent with pity and understanding. It is an extraordinary achievement, and remains one of the best short novels (in length it is hardly more than a *novella*) of the century.

For although West might fairly be said to have invented 'sick' humour, and to have been a prophet of doom, and although his stylistic economy functions as a kind of hardness, he always displays a poet's awareness of the existence, in his victims, of truly human standards. However outrageous the events he depicts, he nurses their vitality, sadly celebrating it.

West's decade was that of Jean Harlow, who initiated a line of sex-symbols that culminated in Marilyn Monroe. In the character of Faye Greener in *The Day of the Locust* he showed a more perfect understanding of the type, and what it represents, than any writer since. What would his wry, cruel and yet compassionate genius have made of the Miller-Monroe marriage, in which the intellectual—however briefly—'caught' the dream-girl? His description of the relationship between his intelligent chief protagonist, the painter Tod Hackett—certainly the nearest he came to representing himself in a book—and Faye Greener suggests an answer. Tod knows what Faye is, but she captivates him. He will do anything to possess her honourably, but has qualms about approaching her as a client when she is working in a brothel. He travels hundreds of miles in order to see her misperform brief scenes in movies that she has made. 'Her invitation wasn't to pleasure,' West writes in one of his profoundest passages.

If *The Day of the Locust* just fails to be a masterpiece, this is only because it is not quite substantial enough. Its neglect can only be explained by the fact that its sharpness is uncomfortable. Such truthfulness needs to wait years before it is heeded. "It is hard to laugh at the need for beauty and romance," as West said in *The Day of the Locust,* "no matter how tasteless, even horrible, the results of that need are. But it is easy to sigh. Few things are sadder than the truly monstrous." This sums up the essentially poetic feeling that pervades his work: he relentlessly depicted the truly monstrous but he also expressed the exact and human quality of its sadness.

Postscript: *The Boys in the Back Room*

EDMUND WILSON*

These notes were first written during the fall and early winter of 1940. Since then several events have occurred which require a few words of postscript.

On December 21, F. Scott Fitzgerald suddenly died in Hollywood; and the day after Nathanael West was killed in a motor accident on the Ventura boulevard. Both had for some years been working in Hollywood, and both had been occupied in writing novels about the movies.

The development of West as a writer had taken place largely outside the tradition to which the other novelists of Hollywood belong. He derived rather from those post-war French writers who had specialized, with a certain preciosity, in the delirious and diabolic fantasy that had in turn come out of Rimbaud and Lautréamont. Beginning with *The Dream Life of Balso Snell*, a not very successful exercise in this vein of phantasmagoria, he produced, after many revisions, an excellent short novel called *Miss Lonelyhearts*. This story of a newspaper hack who conducts an "advice to the lovelorn" department and is eventually destroyed by taking seriously the sorrows and misfortunes of his clients, had a poetic-philosophic point of view and a polish and feeling for phrase which made it seem rather European than American. It was followed by *A Cool Million*, a less ambitious book, which, following the pattern of *Candide*, parodied Horatio Alger by throwing the American success story into reverse; and, later, by *The Days of the Locust*, of which it is appropriate to add here, with apologies for repetition of ideas I have already expressed above, a notice written in 1939 at the time the book appeared:

> Nathanael West, the brilliant author of *Miss Lonelyhearts*, went to Holly-
> wood several years ago, and his silence had been causing his readers alarm lest
> he might have faded out on the Coast as so many of his fellows have done. But
> Mr. West, as this new book happily proves, is still alive beyond the mountains,
> and can still tell what he feels and sees—has still, in short, remained an artist.
> His new novel, *The Day of the Locust*, deals with the nondescript characters on
> the edges of the Hollywood studios: an old comic who sells shoe polish and
> his film-struck daughter; a quarrelsome dwarf; a cock-fighting Mexican; a

*From Edmund Wilson, *The Boys in the Back Room* (San Francisco: The Colt Press, 1941): 67–72. Reprinted with the permission of Farrar, Straus & Giroux, Inc.

Hollywood cowboy and a Hollywood Indian; and an undeveloped hotel clerk from Iowa, who has come to the Coast to enjoy his savings—together with a sophisticated screen-writer, who lives in a big house that is an exact reproduction of the old Dupuy mansion near Biloxi, Mississippi." And these people have been painted as precisely and polished up as brightly as the figures in Persian miniatures. Their speech has been distilled with a sense of the flavorsome and the characteristic which makes John O'Hara seem pedestrian. Mr. West has footed a precarious way and has not slipped at any point into relying on the Hollywood values in describing the Hollywood people. The landscapes, the architecture and the interior decoration of Beverly Hills and vicinity have been handled with equal distinction. Everyone who has ever been in Los Angeles knows how the mere aspect of things is likely to paralyze the esthetic faculty in providing it with no *point d'appui* from which to exercise its discrimination, if it does not actually stun the sensory apparatus itself, so that accurate reporting becomes impossible. But Mr. West has stalked and caught some fine specimens of these Hollywood lepidoptera and impaled them on fastidious pins. Here are Hollywood restaurants, apartment houses, funeral churches, brothels, evangelical temples and studios—in this latter connection, an extremely amusing episode of a man getting nightmarishly lost in the Battle of Waterloo. Mr. West's *surréaliste* beginnings have stood him in good stead on the Coast.

The doings of these people are bizarre, but they are also sordid and senseless. Mr. West has caught the emptiness of Hollywood; and he is, as far as I know, the first writer to make this emptiness horrible. The most impressive thing in the book is his picture of the people from the Middle West who have passed on from their meager working lives to the sunlit leisure of the Coast, wanting something more than they have had but not knowing what they want, with no capacity for the enjoyment of anything except gaping at movie stars and listening to Aimée McPherson's sermons. In the last episode, a crowd of these people, who have come out to see the celebrities at an opening, is set off by an insane act of violence on the part of the cretinous hotel clerk, and gives way to an outburst of mob mania. The America of the murders and rapes which fill the Los Angeles papers is only the obverse side of the America of the inanities of the movies. Such people—Mr. West seems to say—dissatisfied, yet with no ideas, no objectives and no interest in anything vital, may in the mass be capable of anything. The fantasies purveyed by Hollywood, the romances that in the movies can be counted on to have slid around all obstacles and disposed of all "menaces" by the end of two or three hours but which their audiences do not find in life, only cheat them and exacerbate their frustration. Of such mobs are the followings of fascism made.

I think that the book itself suffers a little from the lack of a center of the community which it describes. It has less concentration than *Miss Lonelyhearts*. Mr. West has introduced a young Yale man who, as an educated and healthy human being, is supposed to provide a normal point of view from which the deformities of Hollywood may be criticized; but it is precisely one of the points of the story that this young man should find himself swirling around in the same aimless eddies as the others. I am not sure that it is really possible to do anything substantial with Hollywood except by making it, as Dos Passos did in *The Big Money*, a part of a larger picture which has its center in a larger world. But in the meantime Nathanael West has survived to write another remarkable book—in its peculiar combination of amenity of surface and felicity of form and style with ugly subject matter and somber feeling, quite unlike— as *Miss Lonelyhearts* was—the books of anyone else.

Scott Fitzgerald, who at the time of his death had published only short stories about the movies, had been working for some time on a novel (to be brought out in its unfinished form) in which he had tackled the central figure of the industry: the successful Hollywood producer. This subject has also been attempted, with sharp observation and much humor, by Mr. Budd Schulberg, Jr., whose novel *What Makes Sammy Run* has been published since my articles were written. But Mr. Schulberg is still a beginner, and his book does not get beyond the plane of a George Kaufman with more sincerity and more feeling. Scott Fitzgerald, at his best an accomplished artist, had written a substantial part of what promised to be by all odds the best novel ever devoted to Hollywood.

Here you see the society and the business of the movies, no longer from the point of view of the outsider to whom everything is glamorous or ridiculous, but from the point of view of people who have grown up or spent most of their lives in Hollywood and to whom its laws and values are their natural habit of life. These are criticized by higher standards and in the knowledge of wider horizons, but the criticism is implicit in the story; and in the meantime, Fitzgerald, by bringing us inside and making us take things for granted like insiders, is able to create a kind of interest in the mixed fate of his Jewish producer which lifts the book quite out of the class of this specialized Hollywood fiction and attaches it to the story of man in all times and all places.

Both West and Fitzgerald were writers of a conscience and with natural gifts rare enough in America or anywhere; and their failure to get the best out of their best years may certainly be laid partly to Hollywood, with its already appalling record of talent depraved and wasted.

"The Truly Monstrous":
A Note on Nathanael West

DANIEL AARON*

Mr. Cyril Connolly in his essay, "The Novel-Addict's Cupboard," mentions a class of novels "that one feels are little known or underrated, that are never followed by a successor, or whose effect on people is unpredictable and subversive." Among them he lists Nathanael West's *Miss Lonelyhearts*, a "defiant masterpiece of futility." Although New Directions has recently re-issued *Miss Lonelyhearts*, it still belongs to the category of "neglected books." A small group of West devotees continues to cherish the novel and the memory of its author, but it has neither been popular among those who enjoy bad novels nor known to enough people who like good ones. Mr. Alfred Kazin does not mention West's name in his study of recent American literature; he can't be located in Fred B. Millett's *Contemporary American Authors*. In preparing this note I have found practically no critical treatment of West save for a handful of reviews, most of them hurried and inadequate. Only one critic, Edmund Wilson, has dealt with West at length (*The Boys in the Back Room*), recognizing his strange and remarkable talent.

When Nathanael West died after an automobile accident in 1940, he was thirty-seven years old. Aside from the fact that he was married to Eileen McKenney, lived in Hollywood after 1935, and wrote screen plays (*I Stole a Million*, *Born to be Wed*, *Men Against the Sky*, etc.) I have been able to discover only the following information about his life.

He was born Nathan Wallenstein Weinstein. He graduated from Brown University in 1924. The college yearbook described "Pep" at this time as "an easygoing, genial fellow" who introduced his classmates to *Jurgen* and "passed his time in drawing exotic pictures" or "quoting strange and fanciful poetry." I do not know what he did after graduation, but some time during this period he worked as a manager of a residential hotel. His first novel, *The Dream Life of Balso Snell* (Contact Editions), was published in 1931 and *Miss Lonelyhearts* came two years later. *A Cool Million* (Covici-Friede, 1934)—dedicated to his brother-in-law S. J. Perelman, whom he had known at Brown—followed, and

*From *Partisan Review*, 14 (January–February 1947): 98–106. Reprinted with the permission of the author and *Partisan Review*.

his last novel, *The Day of the Locust* (Random House), appeared a year before his death, in 1939.

In August of 1933, during the interval between the publication of his first and second novel, West became one of the associate editors of *Americana*, a satirical magazine which the *Nation* aptly characterized as a "symbol and symptom" of the depression. The tone of the magazine can best be illustrated by quoting the conclusion of its opening manifesto: "We are Americans who believe that our civilization exudes a miasmic stench and that we had better prepare to give it a decent but rapid burial. We are the laughing morticians of the present." It featured the drawings of George Grosz (the other associate editor), the burlesques of E. E. Cummings and S. J. Perelman, essays by Gilbert Seldes, M. R. Werner, and Lawrence Dennis, and the work of several brilliant and savage cartoonists. West had nothing to do with the first numbers of *Americana*, and it was discontinued shortly after he had joined the staff, but his connection with it is important. Some of its raucous and Dadaist quality is caught in his subsequent novels, together with its bitterness and cynicism and rage born of breadlines and national skullduggery.

West's earliest work, *The Dream Life of Balso Snell*, excerpts of which appeared later in *Americana*, was a privately printed little exercise that never should have been printed at all. Self-conscious, arty, full of quips and learned allusions and painstakingly shocking, it possesses few of the merits of the other novels, and yet it reveals certain characteristically Westian touches that reappear in his later writing. It is savage, iconoclastic, uterine (it begins in the anus of the Wooden Horse and ends with the dreamer's orgasm)—and most typical of all it illustrates West's predilection for the perverse and the grotesque. We meet in these pages the first of the monstrosities who are to be more artistically and credibly presented in the later books. West is obviously experimenting in style and technique as well as subject matter. The book is a composite of satirical rhapsodies, lewdly pedantic speculations, and parodies reminiscent of S. J. Perelman in his less subtle moments. Scatological and pretentiously wise, the book is novel without being original.

Somewhere in *Balso Snell* appears the following reflection: "An intelligent man finds it easy to laugh at himself, but his laughter is not sincere if it is thorough. If I could be Hamlet, or even a clown with a breaking heart 'neath his jester's motley, the role would be tolerable. But I always find it necessary to burlesque the mystery of feeling at its source; I must laugh at myself, and if the laugh is 'bitter,' I must laugh at the laugh. The ritual of feeling demands burlesque and, whether the burlesque is successful or not, a laugh. . . ." In *Miss Lonelyhearts* West burlesques "the mystery of feeling at its source." The hero, a newspaper reporter conducting a Beatrix Fairfax column for "Sick-of-it-all," "Desperate," and "Disillusioned-with-tubercular-husband" begins to take seriously what he undertook as a joke. He is inundated with misery, develops a Christ complex (thereby becoming a *grotesque* in the Sherwood Anderson sense) and dies after experiencing the full measure of frustration which West invariably reserves for his bedeviled protagonists. All of Miss L.'s misadventures are carried on in a surrealist atmosphere of newspaper offices, speakeasies, and bedrooms, and we are never permitted to forget the ineffectualness of this neurotic Charlie Chaplin, this two-bit Dostoevsky.

One of the spokesmen for West's Mephistophelian commentary on man's desperation is Miss L.'s boss, Shrike, who first appeared as Beagle Darwin in *Balso Snell*. Shirke, another damned soul, is a grotesque parallel of Mallachi Mulligan or one of Aldous Huxley's articulate cynics, but he stifles his despair with furious humor and destructive rhetoric. It is the satanic Shrike who mockingly holds up the possibilities of escape to Miss L.—the rural life, the South Sea idyll, the cultivation of the senses, art—and then rejects them. No, Shrike concludes, "God alone is our escape. The church is our only hope, the First Church of Christ Dentist, where He is worshipped as Preventer of Decay. The church whose symbol is the trinity new-style: Father, Son, and Wire-haired Fox Terrier. . . ." Robert Cantwell was right when he called *Miss Lonelyhearts* a "modernized, faithless, *Pilgrim's Progess*."

The world of *Miss Lonelyhearts* is less fantastic than the insides of the Trojan Horse, for West became increasingly objective, but it is still an intensely personal world, a wasteland, where, as far as Miss L. could discover, "there were no signs of spring. The decay that covered the surface of matted ground was not the kind which life generates. Last year, he remembered, May had failed to quicken these soiled fields. It had taken all the brutality of July to torture a few green spikes through the exhausted dirt." Here too in New York, "crowds of people moved throughout the street with a dreamlike violence," and "the gray sky looked as if it had been rubbed with a soiled eraser. It held no angels, flaming crosses, olive-bearing doves, wheels within wheels. Only a newspaper struggled in the air like a kite with a broken spine." No fructifying rains relieve the drought, and at the end of the novel, the Fisher King still sits desolate by a dry canal. *Miss Lonelyhearts* must be read against a background of crashing banks, breadlines, and the WPA; it is symptomatic of economic as well as of moral stagnation. George Grosz—if he did not help to inspire it—might have drawn the illustrations.

That West himself was thinking about social portents and latent revolution is made clear in this third novel, *A Cool Million* or *The Dismantling of Lemuel Pitkin*, a kind of inverted mock-heroic *It Can't Happen Here*. The American success code had lost some of its magic by 1934, and the prestige of the businessman, enormously inflated during the twenties, had come down a little with the Market. West administered a *coup-de-grâce* to the Alger myth and incidentally wrote the first of the postdepression fictional anticipations of American fascism.

The hero of *A Cool Million*, Lemuel Pitkin, is a modern Phil the Fiddler who follows the advice of Nathan "Shagpoke" Whipple, ex-President, Vermont sage, and future Führer, and is slowly "dismantled" for his pains. Imbued with business folklore and rigidly adhering to the success code, Pitkin successively loses his teeth, eye, leg, and scalp. At the end of the book and prior to becoming a Yankee Horst Wessel for the Leathershirts, he is earning his living as a stooge for a couple of comedians who punctuate their patter by beating him with newspapers: "For a final curtain, they brought out an enormous wooden mallet labeled, 'The Works' and with it completely demolished our hero. His toupee flew off, his eye and teeth popped out, and his wooden leg was knocked into the audience."

A Cool Million, in spite of its heavy facetiousness and sophomoric insolence, seemed mildly funny in 1934; it is not hilarious reading now. At first glance it appears to be a departure from the two previous novels and his last one, and yet the characteristic themes persist. Lemuel the Stooge, like Miss L. gets lost in his quest for certainty, and the plight of his sweetheart, Betty Prail— ravished by an endless procession of men while Lemuel is snatched away by the Third International or languishes in a bear trap—might symbolize the rape of Columbia by resolute hordes of 100 per cent Americans. But West's unpleasantly genial parody is only a weak tour de force which is hardly saved by its serious undertones and occasional insights.

With *The Day of the Locust*, however, we return again to a more significant level of writing. Although it lacks the concentration and focus of *Miss Lone-lyhearts*—the stories of Homer Simpson, the Iowa hotel clerk, and Tod Hackett, West's Yale man observer-hero, are not sufficiently fused—it nevertheless shows a detachment, a curious and penetrating discernment that makes it, as Edmund Wilson has said, one of the most satisfying books about Hollywood. The plot is negligible. Tod Hackett finds himself involved with a typical collection of queeries and degenerates: a moronic but disturbing Venus after whom the hero unsuccessfully lusts, her batty ex-comic father, her cowboy paramour, a vindictive and swashbuckling dwarf, and a Sherwood Anderson grotesque named Homer. The author's chief concern, however, is not with the roisterings of these infantile adults but with the *Walpurgisnacht* which is Hollywood.

West's notations on the Hollywood flora and fauna are brilliant enough. He writes amusingly and with an air of wonder about the architecture, dress, and lingo (one character remarks: "How silly, batting an inoffensive ball across something that ought to be used to catch fish on account of millions are starving for a bite of herring"). But the tension of the novel comes, as in West's other books, from his recognition of the ineluctable discontent of the masses. In *Miss Lonelyhearts* he lifted up the board to show grubby things writhing in urban darkness; he described a people devoured by personal anguish. *The Day of the Locust* is also a season in hell which erupts at the end with a middle-class riot precipitated by a movie premiere.

West sees in the Hollywood mob a people brutalized by leisure, cheated by phony illusions. And like his painter-hero (later to catch the spirit of this thwarted host of sideline lookers in his canvas, "The Burning of Los Angeles") he dramatizes "the contrast between their drained-out, feeble bodies and their wild, disordered minds." Lured to California by sunlight and orange juice and stupefied by a maddeningly blank climate, these Iowa picnickers are "stirred only by the promise of miracles and then only to violence." They suffer from a cosmic ennui which only lynchings and love-nests can mitigate. "It is hard to laugh at the need for beauty and romance," West observes, "no matter how tasteless, even horrible, the results of that need are. But is easy to sigh. Few things are sadder than the truly monstrous."

Any moral conclusions about New York or Hollywood or American life in general are never stated explicitly in West's novels, and his anger is seldom obvious. He resembles his friend Perelman in this respect or the successful screen writer in *The Day of the Locust*—"a master of the involved comic rhetoric that permitted him to express his moral indignation and still keep his reputation for worldliness and wit." That he had values and standards and a social philosophy is perfectly plain, however, even though he was not a social realist who celebrated brawny proletarians.

The books of West deal with the obsessions and behavior of grotesques, but they are none the less political. They tell us more about the fascist mentality and the coming cataclysm than most class-conscious novels of the thirties, because West was able to feel, as well as to picture in his impressionistic way, the emptiness and ugliness of the times. His books are a kind of feverish preview of the sadistic and irrational forties.

Other novelists among his contemporaries actually gave a more faithful presentation of a country on the skids; West's novels do not begin to approximate the colorful and violent documentations of Dos Passos or the grim tracts of Farrell. But they do give us in an arresting and sometimes poetic way, a glimpse of a mindless people doped by the pulps, the tabloids, and the cinema, a people ripe for catastrophe.

West was cut off just at the moment when he seemed to be developing into a novelist of more than ordinary proportions, and it is of course fruitless to speculate about what he might have become had he lived. *Miss Lonelyhearts* will possibly remain a "minor classic," and West may come to rate a footnote in the histories of the academicians. But he will always appeal to readers with a taste for the bizarre, who can respond to his delirious vision and find some meaning in his fantastic realism.

Interlude: West's Disease

W. H. Auden*

Nathanael West is not, strictly speaking, a novelist; that is to say, he does not attempt an accurate description either of the social scene or of the subjective life of the mind. For his first book, he adopted the dream convention, but neither the incidents nor the language are credible as a transcription of a real dream. For his other three, he adopted the convention of a social narrative; his characters need real food, drink and money, and live in recognizable places like New York or Hollywood, but, taken as feigned history, they are absurd. Newspapers do, certainly, have Miss Lonelyhearts columns; but in real life these are written by sensible, not very sensitive, people who conscientiously give the best advice they can, but do not take the woes of their correspondents home with them from the office, people, in fact, like Betty of whom Mr. West's hero says scornfully: "Her world was not the world and could never include the readers of his column. Her sureness was based on the power to limit experience arbitrarily. Moreover, his confusion was significant, while her order was not." On Mr. West's paper, the column is entrusted to a man the walls of whose room

> were bare except for an ivory Christ that hung opposite the foot of the bed. He had removed the figure from the cross to which it had been fastened and had nailed it to the walls with large spikes. . . . As a boy in his father's church, he had discovered that something stirred in him when he shouted the name of Christ, something secret and enormously powerful. He had played with this thing, but had never allowed it to come alive. He knew now what this thing was—hysteria, a snake whose scales were tiny mirrors in which the dead world takes on a semblance of life, and how dead the world is . . . a world of doorknobs.

It is impossible to believe that such a character would ever apply for a Miss Lonelyhearts job (in the hope, apparently, of using it as a stepping-stone to a gossip column), or that, if by freak chance he did, any editor would hire him.

Again, the occupational vice of the editors one meets is an overestimation of the social and moral value of what a newspaper does. Mr. West's editor,

Shrike, is a Mephisto who spends all his time exposing to his employees the meaninglessness of journalism: "Miss Lonelyhearts, my friend, I advise you to give your readers stones. When they ask for bread don't give them crackers as does the Church, and don't, like the State, tell them to eat cake. Explain that man cannot live by bread alone and give them stones. Teach them to pray each morning: 'Give us this day our daily stone.'" Such a man, surely, would not be a Feature Editor long.

A writer may concern himself with a very limited area of life and still convince us that he is describing the real world, but one becomes suspicious when, as in West's case, whatever world he claims to be describing, the dream life of a highbrow, lowbrow existence in Hollywood, or the American political scene, all these worlds share the same peculiar traits—no married couples have children, no child has more than one parent, a high percentage of the inhabitants are cripples, and the only kind of personal relation is the sadomasochistic.

There is, too, a curious resemblance among the endings of his four books.

> His body broke free of the bard. It took on a life of its own; a life that knew nothing of the poet Balso. Only to death can this release be likened—the mechanics of decay. After death the body takes command; it performs the manual of disintegration with a marvelous certainty. So now, his body performed the evolutions of love with a like sureness. In this activity, Home and Duty, Love and Art were forgotten. . . . His body screamed and shouted as it marched and uncoiled; then with one heaving shout of triumph, it fell back quiet.

> He was running to succor them with love. The cripple turned to escape, but he was too slow and Miss Lonelyhearts caught him. . . . The gun inside the package exploded and Miss Lonelyhearts fell, dragging the cripple with him. They both rolled part of the way down stairs.

> "I am a clown," he began, "but there are times when even clowns must grow serious. This is such a time. I . . ." Lem got no further. A shot rang out and he fell dead, drilled through the heart by an assassin's bullet.

> He was carried through the exit to the back street and lifted into a police car. The siren began to scream and at first he thought he was making the noise himself. He felt his lips with his hands. They were clamped tight. He knew then it was the siren. For some reason this made him laugh and he began to imitate the siren as loud as he could.

An orgasm, two sudden deaths by violence, a surrender to madness, are presented by West as different means for securing the same and desirable end, escape from the conscious Ego and its make-believe. Consciousness, it would seem, does not mean freedom to choose, but freedom to play a fantastic role, an unreality from which a man can only be delivered by some physical or mental explosion outside his voluntary control.

There are many admirable and extremely funny satirical passages in his books, but West is not a satirist. Satire presupposes conscience and reason as the judges between the true and the false, the moral and the immoral, to which it appeals, but for West these faculties are themselves the creators of unreality.

His books should, I think, be classified as Cautionary Tales, parables about a Kingdom of Hell whose ruler is not so much the Father of Lies as the Father of Wishes. Shakespeare gives a glimpse of this hell in *Hamlet*, and Dostoievsky has a lengthy description in *Notes from the Underground*, but they were interested in many hells and heavens. Compared with them, West has the advantages and disadvantages of the specialist who knows everything about one disease and nothing about any other. He was a sophisticated and highly skilled literary craftsman, but what gives all his books such a powerful and distrubing fascination, even *A Cool Million*, which must, I think, be judged a failure, owes nothing to calculation. West's descriptions of Inferno have the authenticity of first-hand experience: he has certainly been there, and the reader has the uncomfortable feeling that his was not a short visit.

All his main characters suffer from the same spiritual disease which, in honor of the man who devoted his life to studying it, we may call West's Disease. This is a disease of consciousness which renders it incapable of converting wishes into desires. A lie is false; what it asserts is not the case. A wish is fantastic; it knows what is the case but refuses to accept it. All wishes, whatever their apparent content, have the same and unvarying meaning: "I refuse to be what I am." A wish, therefore, is either innocent and frivolous, a kind of play, or a serious expression of guilt and despair, a hatred of oneself and every being one holds responsible for oneself.

Our subconscious life is a world ruled by wish but, since it is not a world of action, this is harmless; even nightmare is playful, but it is the task of consciousness to translate wish into desire. If, for whatever reason, self-hatred or self-pity, it fails to do this, it dooms a human being to a peculiar and horrid fate. To begin with, he cannot desire anything, for the present state of the self is the ground of every desire, and that is precisely what the wisher rejects. Nor can he believe anything, for a wish is not a belief; whatever he wishes he cannot help knowing that he could have wished something else. At first he may be content with switching from one wish to another:

> She would get some music on the radio, then lie down on her bed and shut her eyes. She had a large assortment of stories to choose from. After getting herself in the right mood, she would go over them in her mind as though they were a pack of cards, discarding one after another until she found one that suited. On some days she would run through the whole pack without making a choice. When that happened, she would either go down to Fine Street for an ice-cream soda or, if she were broke, thumb over the pack again and force herself to choose.

While she admitted that her method was too mechanical for the best results and that it was better to slip into a dream naturally, she said that any dream was better than none and beggars couldn't be choosers.

But in time, this ceases to amuse, and the wisher is left with the despair which is the cause of all of them:

When not keeping house, he sat in the back yard, called the patio by the real estate agent, in a broken down deck chair. In one of the closets he had found a tattered book and he held it in his lap without looking at it. There was a much better view to be had in any direction other than the one he faced. By moving his chair in a quarter circle he could have seen a large part of the canyon twisting down to the city below. He never thought of making this shift. From where he sat, he saw the closed door of the garage and a patch of its shabby, tarpaper roof.

A sufferer from West's Disease is not selfish but absolutely self-centered. A selfish man is one who satisfies his desires at other people's expense; for this reason, he tries to see what others are really like and often sees them extremely accurately in order that he may make use of them. But, to the self-centered man, other people only exist as images either of what he is or of what he is not, his feelings towards them are projections of the pity or the hatred he feels for himself and anything he does to them is really done to himself. Hence the inconsistent and unpredictable behavior of a sufferer from West's Disease: he may kiss your feet one moment and kick you in the jaw the next and, if you were to ask him why, he could not tell you.

In its final stages, the disease reduces itself to a craving for violent physical pain—this craving, unfortunately, can be projected onto others—for only violent pain can put an end to wishing *for* something and produce the real wish of necessity, the cry "Stop!"

All West's books contain cripples. A cripple is unfortunate and his misfortune is both singular and incurable. Hunchbacks, girls without noses, dwarfs, etc., are not sufficiently common in real life to appear as members of an unfortunate class, like the very poor. Each one makes the impression of a unique case. Further, the nature of the misfortune, a physical deformity, makes the victim repellent to the senses of the typical and normal, and there is nothing the cripple or others can do to change his condition. What attitude towards his own body can he have then but hatred? As used by West, the cripple is, I believe, a symbolic projection of the state of wishful self-despair, the state of those who will not accept themselves in order to change themselves into what they would or should become, and justify their refusal by thinking that being what they are is uniquely horrible and uncurable. To look at, Faye Greener is a pretty but not remarkable girl; in the eyes of Faye Greener, she is an exceptionally hideous spirit.

In saying that cripples have this significance in West's writing, I do not mean to say that he was necessarily aware of it. Indeed, I am inclined to think he was not. I suspect that, consciously, he thought pity and compassion were the same thing, but what the behavior of his "tender" characters shows is that all pity is self-pity and that he who pities others is incapable of compassion. Ruthlessly as he exposes his dreamers, he seems to believe that the only alternative to despair is to become a crook. Wishes may be unreal, but at least they are not, like all desires, wicked: "His friends would go on telling such stories until they were too drunk to talk. They were aware of their childishness, but did not know how else to revenge themselves. At college, and perhaps for a year afterwards, they had believed in Beauty and in personal expression as an absolute end. When they lost this belief, they lost everything. Money and fame meant nothing to them. They were not worldly men." The use of the word *worldly* is significant. West comes very near to accepting the doctrine of the Marquis de Sade—there are many resemblances between *A Cool Million* and *Justine*—to believing, that is, that the creation is essentially evil and that goodness is contrary to its laws, but his moral sense revolted against Sade's logical conclusion that it was therefore a man's duty to be as evil as possible. All West's "worldly" characters are bad men, most of them grotesquely bad, but here again his artistic instinct seems at times to contradict his conscious intentions. I do not think, for example, that he meant to make Wu Fong, the brothel-keeper, more sympathetic and worthy of respect than, say, Miss Lonelyhearts or Homer Simpson, but that is what he does:

> Wu Fong was a very shrewd man and a student of fashion. He saw that the trend was in the direction of home industry and home talent and when the Hearst papers began their "Buy American" campaign, he decided to get rid of all the foreigners in his employ and turn his establishment into a hundred percentum American place. He engaged Mr. Asa Goldstein to redecorate the house and that worthy designed a Pennsylvania Dutch, Old South, Log Cabin Pioneer, Victorian New York, Western Cattle Days, Californian Monterey, Indian and Modern Girl series of interiors. . . .
>
> He was as painstaking as a great artist and in order to be consistent as one he did away with the French cuisine and wines traditional to his business. Instead, he substituted an American kitchen and cellar. When a client visited Lena Haubengruber, it was possible for him to eat roast groundhog and drink Sam Thompson rye. While with Alice Sweethorne, he was served sow belly with grits and bourbon. In Mary Judkins' rooms he received, if he so desired, fried squirrel and corn liquor. In the suite occupied by Patricia Van Riis, lobster and champagne were the rule. The patrons of Powder River Rose usually ordered mountain oysters and washed them down with forty rod. And so on down the list. . . .

After so many self-centered despairers who cry in their baths or bare their souls in barrooms, a selfish man like this, who takes pride in doing something really well, even if it is running a brothel, seems almost a good man.

There have, no doubt, always been cases of West's Disease, but the chances of infection in a democratic and mechanized society like our own are much greater than in the more static and poorer societies of earlier times.

When, for most people, their work, their company, even their marriages, were determined, not by personal choice or ability, but by the class into which they were born, the individual was less tempted to develop a personal grudge against Fate; his fate was not his own but that of everyone around him.

But the greater the equality of opportunity in a society becomes, the more obvious becomes the inequality of the talent and character among individuals, and the more bitter and personal it must be to fail, particuarly for those who have some talent but not enough to win them second or third place.

In societies with fewer opportunities for amusement, it was also easier to tell a mere wish from a real desire. If, in order to hear some music, a man has to wait for six months and then walk twenty miles, it is easy to tell whether the words, "I should like to hear some music," mean what they appear to mean, or merely, "At this moment I should like to forget myself." When all he has to do is press a switch, it is more difficult. He may easily come to believe that wishes can come true. This is the first symptom of West's Disease; the later symptoms are less pleasant, but nobody who has read Nathanael West can say that he wasn't warned.

Development and Frustration

LESLIE A. FIEDLER*

It is fitting that the most memorable and terrible woman in an American novel of the '30's is a portrait of the blond movie actress, Jean Harlowe as shabby extra and call-girl. She is, of course, the Faye Greener of Nathanael West's *Day of the Locust*, and her very name is a fitting climax to the series we have been tracing through the history of our fiction: Charlotte Temple to Temple Drake, Daisy Miller to Daisy Fay to Faye Greener.

In West's earliest fiction, there are traces of queasiness before woman's surrender of her traditional role, her usurpation of male privileges which so disturbed Faulkner. In *The Dream Life of Balso Snell* (1931), this is projected as a fantasy in which the female turns, at the moment of possession, into something disturbingly like a male. "Throwing his arms about her, Balso interrupted her recitation by sticking his tongue into her mouth. But when he closed his eyes to heighten the fun, he felt that he was embracing tweed. He opened them and saw that what he held in his arms was a middleaged woman dressed in a mannish suit and wearing hornrimmed glasses." To such a betrayal, in which the erotic object becomes at once something mannish and schoolmarmish, there is only one answer: "By this time, Balso had gotten one of his hands free. He hit Miss McGeeney a terrific blow in the gut and hove her into the fountain."

The rest of West's fiction contains a series of precisely such blows in the female gut: travesties of the teasers and betrayers and lady rapists who assault and torment his male protagonists, baffle them in their search for a love which is more than desire. Even the most submissive of Good Girls only succeeds in enraging West, as the Betty of *Miss Lonelyhearts* enrages her lover. "She was like a kitten," he thinks, "whose soft helplessness makes one ache to hurt it." And taking her nipple between his fingers, " 'Let me pluck this rose,' he said, giving a sharp tug. 'I want to wear it in my buttonhole.' " It is in *A Cool Million*, however, that the Good Good Girl, again called Betty, gets her full comeuppance, raped with appalling regularity from the time she is twelve, pursued by mad dogs, bullies and corrupt politicians, she fulfills her destiny as the final adornment of the Colonial American Room of Wu Fong's whorehouse,

---

*From Leslie A. Fiedler, *Love and Death in the American Novel* (New York: Criterion Books, 1960): 316–18, 461–67. Reprinted with the permission of the author.

where she blends admirably into a background of "antimacassars, ships in bottles, carved whale bone, hooked rugs."

Betty is still the Good Good Girl, even as an unsuccessful prostitute, an American Justine, which is to say, a victim. But Faye Greener is the blond bitch in all her archetypal purity, a woman willing at last to take up the role that old Rappaccini had once vainly dreamed for his daughter: "to be endowed with marvellous gifts against which no power and strength could avail an enemy . . . to be as terrible as . . . beautiful." Like Temple Drake before her, Faye does her destroying on the run; pursued by everyone, possessed by anyone with the price, she is somehow unattainable still—certainly to the artist-narrator, Tod, who has seen her pawed by a seedy cowboy actor and a brutal Mexican hanger-on, but cannot quite bring himself to buy her. "If only he had the courage to throw himself on her. Nothing less violent than rape would do. The sensation he felt was like that he got when holding an egg in his hand. Not that she was fragile or even seemed fragile. It wasn't that. It was her completeness, her egg-like self-sufficiency, that made him want to touch her." But she cannot really be touched, for she is the dream dreamed by all of America, the dream of a love which is death; and in a strange sense she remains virginal as death is virginal: the immaculate, degraded *anima* of a nation, her realest existence on the screen.

It is because West's book is about Hollywood, and because he knows that Hollywood is where all America comes to die, that Faye is its proper center, dispensing what the bored hinterlanders do not quite know that they desire, as they press against the restraining ropes at a gala preview: a *Gotterdämmerung*, an orgy of destruction. Precisely because she is a phantom bride, she is also a child, epitome of the quest for eternal youth which is the obverse of the lust for death: "Although she was seventeen, she was dressed like a child of twelve in a white cotton dress with a blue sailor collar. Her long legs were bare and she had blue sandals on her feet." The long legs are a further clue: those improbable legs which America has bred onto the naturally short-legged female form to symbolize castrating power. "She was a tall girl," West tells us of Faye, "with wide, straight shoulders and long, sword-like legs." The rest is conventional enough: the long neck, the full face, the widely divided breasts, the platinum hair tied back with a blue ribbon, the sailor suit of a small girl; but it is the sword-legs which give away the game: Annabel Lee elevated on stilts, which are also weapons dealing death!

"Her invitation wasn't to pleasure," West explains, "but to struggle, hard and sharp, closer to murder than to love. If you threw yourself on her, it would be like throwing yourself from the parapet of a skyscraper. You would do it with a scream. You wouldn't expect to rise again. Your teeth would be driven into your skull like nails into a pine board and your back would be broken. You wouldn't even have time to sweat or close your eyes." It is a peculiarly American version of love, a peculiarly American view of woman, surviving even in an age of social consciousness and "proletarian" fiction. Only the fantasies of post–World War I Germany have relfected (in films like *The Blue Angel*) comparable excesses of male masochism; and Marlene Dietrich, who embodied the cruel woman of those fantasies, soon emigrated to the United States which appreciated even more than Germany the delicious threat of her million-dollar legs. But it is not male masochism alone which creates and acclaims images of the castrating bitch; there is a corresponding female sadism which greets such images and collaborates in their fabrication. . . .

. . . .

If Nathanael West appears to us from our present vantage point the chief neglected talent of the age, this is largely because he was immune to the self-deceit which afflicted his contemporaries; he knew what he was doing. Despite his own left-wing political sympathies and the pressures of friends more committed than he, he refused to subscribe to the program for proletarian fiction laid down by the official theoreticians and critics of the Communist movement. And he turned unashamedly to the business of rendering the naked anguish he felt, rather than projecting the commitment to action and faith it was assumed he should feel. Even more importantly he rejected the concept of realism-naturalism, refused to play the game (variously connived at by Dos Passos and Steinbeck and Farrell) of pretending to create documents rather than poetry. He returned, despite the immediate example of three decades of falsely "scientific" writing, which sought to replace imagination with sociology, the symbol with the case report, to the instinctive realization of the classic American fictionists that literary truth is not synonymous with fact. West's novels are a deliberate assault on the common man's notion of reality; for violence is not only his subject matter, but also his technique.

His apprenticeship was served in Europe, in the world of the Left Bank, where from the Surrealists he learned (his finger-exercises are to be found in his first book, *The Dream Life of Balso Snell*) a kind of humor expressed almost entirely in terms of the grotesque, that is to say, on a perilous border-line between jest and horror. Yet his Surrealist-inspired techniques—the violent conjunctions; the discords at the sensitive places where squeamishness demands harmony; the atrocious belly-laughs that shade off into hysteria—are not very different, after all, from the devices of *Pudd'n-head Wilson* or *Gordon Pym*. Surrealism is only a late European development of the same gothic themes, the same commitment to atrocity, the same dedication to mocking the bourgeoisie which helped form the work of Poe; and, indeed, it is through Poe that the tradition descends to the Surrealists themselves. West is, in a sense, then, only reclaiming our own; yet, in another, he is introducing into the main line of American fiction a kind of sophistication, a view of the nature of art, of which our literature was badly in need.

It is possible for an American, of course, to find in his native sources, his native scene and his American self cues for the special kind of horror-comedy which characterizes West's novels. The uneducated Twain once did precisely that, and the half-educated Faulkner has pretended at least to follow his example. Yet in Twain everywhere, and in Faulkner more and more as the years go by, there is evident a presumptuous, home-made quality, which mars their work whenever they pass from the realm of myth to that of ideas. Nothing is more bald and thin than the back-porch atheism of Twain's *The Mysterious Stranger*, except perhaps the red-neck Protestantism of Faulkner's *A Fable.* . . . [B]oth Faulkner and Twain . . . are driven compulsively toward religious themes, but dissolve them into easy rationalism or sentimental piety.

The religious dimension to which they aspire, West attains in part because he is aware of a European tradition in thought and art, out of which Kafka, so like him in certain ways, had earlier emerged. It is not accidental that both these anguish-ridden comedians, as uncompromisingly secular as they are profoundly religious, should be Jews; for Jews seem not only peculiarly apt at projecting images of numinous power for the unchurched, but are skillful, too, at creating myths of urban alienation and terror. The '30's, not only in America (where Daniel Fuchs and Henry Roth—the latter in a single astonishing book, *Call It Sleep*—are outstanding figures) but everywhere, is a period especially favorable for the Jewish writer bent on universalizing his own experience into a symbol of life in the Western world. More and more it has seemed to such writers that what they in their exile and urbanization have long been, Western man in general is becoming. This is, presumably, the claim implicit in West's name (he was originally called Nathan Wallenstein Weinstein), his boast that he is an American Everyman; though surely to none does the epigram of C. M. Doughty apply more tellingly than to West, who quotes it in *Balso Snell*: "The Semites are like to a man sitting in a cloaca to the eyes, and whose brows touch heaven."

Yet West is a peculiarly American case, too. In one of his few published critical notes he declares: "In America violence is idiomatic, in America violence is daily." And it is possible to see him as just another of our professional tough guys, one of the "boys in the backroom" (the phrase is applied by Edmund Wilson, in a little study of our fiction, to West along with John O'Hara). This is not to deny, though West himself tried to, that West is, in some meaningful sense, a Jew. He is enough the child of a long tradition of nonviolence to be racked by guilt in the face of violence, shocked and tormented every day in a world where violence is, of course, daily and most men are not at all disturbed. In *Miss Lonelyhearts*, he creates the portrait of a character, all nerves and no skin, the fool of pity, whom the quite ordinary horror of ordinary life lacerates to the point of madness. His protagonist is given the job of answering "letters to the lovelorn" on a daily newspaper; and he finds in this job, a joke to others (he must pretend in his column to be a woman, for only women presumably suffer and sympathize), a revelation of human misery too acute for him to hear. It is the final modern turn of the gothic screw: the realization that not the supernatural, the extraordinary, but the ordinary, the everyday are the terrors that constrict the heart.

Dear Miss Lonelyhearts—

... I would like to have boy friends like other girls and go out on Saturday
nites, but no boy will take me because I was born without a nose—although
I am a good dancer and have a nice shape and my father buys me pretty clothes.

I sit and look at myself all day and cry. I have a big hole in the middle of
my face that scares people even myself so I can't blame the boys for not wanting
to take me out ...

What did I do to deserve such a terrible bad fate? I asked Papa and he says
he doesnt know, but that maybe I did something in the other world before I
was born or that maybe I was being punished for his sins. I dont believe that
because he is a very nice man. Ought I commit suicide?

Sincerely yours,

Desperate

Miss Lonelyhearts is, finally, the comic butt who takes upon himself the
sins of the world: the *schlemiel* as Everyman, the skeptical and unbelieved-in
Christ of a faithless age. But such a role of absurd Christ is West's analogue
for the function of the writer, whom he considers obliged unremittingly to
regard a suffering he is too sensitive to abide; and in no writer is there so
absolute a sense of the misery of being human, though he also believes that
such misery is a more proper occasion for laughter than tears. He is child
enough of his time to envision an apocalypse; but his apocalypse is a defeat
for everyone. The protagonist of *Miss Lonelyhearts* is shot reaching out in love
toward a man he has unwillingly offended; while the hero-*schlemiel* of the more
deliberately farcical *A Cool Million: or The Dismantling of Lemuel Pitkin* (in theme
and style a parody of Horatio Alger) staggers from one ridiculous, anti-heroic
disaster to another, becoming after his death the idol of an American fascist
movement. But the true horror-climax of his life and the book comes when,
utterly maimed, he stands on the stage between two corny comedians, who
wallop him with rolled-up newspapers in time to their jokes, until his wig
comes off (he has been at one point scalped), his glass eye pops out, and his
wooden leg falls away; after which, they provide him with new artificial aids
and begin again.

It is not until *The Day of the Locust*, however, which is West's last book,
and the only novel on Hollywood not somehow trivialized by its subject, that
one gets the final version of the Apocalypse according to Nathanael West. At
the end of the book, a painter, caught in a rioting mob of fans at a Hollywood
première, dreams, as he is being crushed by the rioters, the phantasmagoric
masterpiece he has never finished painting, "The Burning of Los Angeles."
West does not seem finally a really achieved writer; certainly, no one of his
books is thoroughly satisfactory, though there are astonishing local successes
in all of them. His greatness lies like a promise just beyond his last novel, and
is frustrated by his early death; but he is the inventor of a peculiar kind of
book, in which the most fruitful strain of American fiction is joined to the
European tradition of avant-garde, anti-bourgeois art, native symbolism to

imported *symbolisme*. The Westian or neo-gothic novel has opened up possibilities, unavailable to both the naturalistic semi-documentary and the over-refined novel of sensibility, possibilities of capturing the quality of experience in a mass society—rather than retreating to the meaningless retailing of fact or the pointless elaboration of private responses to irrelevant sensations. Putting down a book by West, a reader is not sure whether he has been presented with a nightmare endowed with the conviction of actuality or with actuality distorted into the semblance of a nightmare; but in either case, he has the sense that he has been presented with a view of a world in which, incredibly, he lives!

In West, there emerges, side by side with an intent to move American literature back into the mainstream of European modernism, a willingness to reinterpret the formulae of gothicism in the light of Freudian psychology. The first gothic novelists had written at a time when the sole name for the unconscious was "hell"; and only their intuition had served them as a guide in their infernal descent. By the twentieth century, however, psychoanalysis had begun to work out a science of the irrational, a lexicon of the dream symbols, which the earlier tale of terror had exploited without a real sense of their ultimate meanings. The Freudian world-view suggested, in addition, new grounds upon which to base the artist's attack on the moral codes and taboos of the bourgeoisie; and along with Marxism, it helped define the contemporary intellectual's view of himself as an enemy of society. Such a view was generally associated in the '30's, however, with an espousal of realistic modes in fiction; and it is the special contribution of Nathanael West to have demonstrated the superiority of gothicism for projecting a denial of middle-class values and the analysis of the secret soul of the bourgeoisie.

Yet the importance of West's work was scarcely realized in his own day; and it would be misleading even now to speak of his general influence. Though his novels continued to move younger writers, and though the last few years have witnessed not only a growing critical acclaim, but attempts to extend his audience by stage adaptations and moving-picture versions, West is still more admired than directly emulated. S. J. Perelman, who is West's brother-in-law and was a contributor to the little magazine *Contact*, which West helped edit, has been conducting a strange experiment, whose end is the transformation of Surrealist gallows humor into commercial entertainment. It is all part of an extraordinary process, which begins for literature in the columns of *The New Yorker*, and for art in the cartoons of the same magazine, as well as in certain shop-windows decorated by Salvador Dali—but whose end is not yet in sight. The avant-garde images of twenty-five years ago and the grotesquerie which distinguished the short-lived *Contact* have become now the common property of gifte shoppes and greeting-card racks, fall as stereotypes from the lips of hip twelve-year-olds. "Hate cards" and ashtrays adorned with "Nebbishes" (the surreal, Jewish sad sack of West reduced to the level of *kitsch*) spread now the self-contempt, the anti-bourgeois virulence, the contempt for home,

mother, birthdays, and Christmas, once the exclusive stock-in-trade of bohemi-
ans; and the "sick" joke popularizes the nauseated giggle before violence,
which not so long ago belonged only to books like *Miss Lonelyhearts*. "Can
Johnny come out to play, Mrs. Jones?" "You know Johnny has no arms and
legs!" "We don't want players. We need bases."

It is not only a matter, however, of neo-gothicism becoming a prevailing
mode on the level of popular culture; on more serious levels, too, the mode
of West, if not his example, is evident. The alienated *schlemiel*-heroes of Saul
Bellow surely owe something to West's protagonists whose anguish never
quite overbalances their absurdity; and everywhere in the Jewish American
novelists of the last two decades, West's influence is felt, if only as a temptation
toward sheer terror rejected in favor of sentimentality or some abstract espousal
of love. Though lonely in his own time, West was not really alone in his
attempt to redeem French horror for the American soul, as Poe had once
redeemed that of Germany; Djuna Barnes (whom he probably did not even
know) had made a similar, even less popular assay in *Nightwood* (1937). The
dislocated lyricism, hallucinated vision and oddly skewed language of Miss
Barnes's black little book were improbably introduced to the United States
by T. S. Eliot, with a rather unconvincing assurance of their ultimately religious
import. In his preface, Eliot argues, at any rate, that the homosexual ambience
of *Nightwood*, its ecstatic evocations of disease and death reflect a genuine
concern with the problem of evil and not just an obsession with the properties
of decadent gothicism. Linguistically, *Nightwood* is too complex, and thematically, it is too little concerned with the experience of America to achieve even
the belated and limited success of West's work; it lives now chiefly in the minds
of a limited number of admirers and in quotations included in anthologies of
modern verse.

"He Charts Our World"

VICTOR COMERCHERO*

West's originality and modernity are only now beginning to be appreciated. It is difficult to understand why previous readers lagged in this respect. Perhaps his small output, a too realistic reading by his readers, and his melancholy insistence on suffering and defeat all militated against him. Moreover, though there is much ingenuity in West's novels, ultimately there is little variety. He did not have great range. Troubled by a vision of a civilization going under, he sounded but one note, and that a half-warning, half-despairing cry.

In his two masterpieces, West, like many another modern artist, sought out a mythic lens through which to view his age and to compare its contemporary distortions against a backdrop of eternity. Viewed from such a mythic distance, the aberrations of the time are grotesque; but they are recognizable.

The victim of this age is Westian man, distillation of the modern malaise. A psychological abstraction exaggerated beyond reality, Westian man is nevertheless a powerful, suggestive, and disturbing character. He seems to be an objectification of each reader at his most unsympathetic and pathetic moments. Perhaps much of the hostility directed at him is a defense against the faintly sickening self-pity he arouses.

An archetypal neurotic, Westian man is more complex than he appears. Much of his complexity, as well as that of the novels, is the result of West's method, a fusion of Baudelaire's and Freud's. From Baudelaire West probably derived his belief in the autonomy of the imagination:

> For Baudelaire, the work of art is essentially a work of the imagination and yet it is true and real at the same time. This is perhaps the best way of defining what is meant by the sincerity of a work of art: the fidelity with which it adheres to the imagination of the artist. Additionally, for Baudelaire, a work of the imagination comes from a very real kind of anguish. No so much the impermanent and transitory anguish of daily living, of insecurity, of war and love, as the inner and deeply permanent anguish of man which is usually repressed and covered over with willful forgetfulness. As in the treatment of psychoanalysis, the poet has to go very far down into his past, into the significance of his childhood. . . . Baudelaire's self-discovery in his anguish and his self-revelation in

*From Victor Comerchero, *Nathanael West: The Ironic Prophet* (Syracuse: Syracuse University Press, 1964): 167–71. Reprinted by permission of the publisher.

his writing were archetypal. . . . All literature is to some degree psychoanalytic. Baudelaire went so deeply into psychoanalytic exploration that he passed beyond personal reminiscence into the universal.[1]

From Freud West borrowed his myths and many of his symbols. Beneath West's novels there is a Freudian psychoanalytic vein that cannot be ignored. West's use of this symbolic vein is something new and startling in American literature. By using simple images and symbols to suggest the psychological state of his characters, West in his two major works transcends the limits set by their dated references applicable to the American thirties. It is this added psychological dimension that makes Miss Lonelyhearts such an unforgettable character. To a large extent, it is what makes the characters so enormously suggestive and what makes them seem to speak so intimately to the reader. The characters are not deep, but they are vivid; like Sophocles' personages, they seem to burn themselves indelibly into one's mind. Ultimately, it is this psychological method that allows such broad generalization about the characters. They are, to paraphrase West, case studies raised to a mythic level.

The author's interest in Westian man, however, is not merely personal or psychological; it is sociological. In this sociological concern, West bridges the gap between the literature of sensibility, wherein the writer turns inward upon himself in order to unfold his own malaise, and the literature of naturalistic social protest, in which the artist unfolds the working of society upon the individual. West must have sensed, quite clearly, that his personal estrangement was shared by the society at large, for despite the subjective nature of his inspiration, he suggests the collective tragedy.

West brings home the full horror of his characters' tragedy by assigning these perverted souls religious, mythic roles. Miss Lonelyhearts playing Christ or Percival cuts a comic and pathetic figure; and Tod, musing on a fancied rape of Faye Greener, or shouting "at her like a Y. M. C. A. lecturer on sex hygiene" (*The Day of the Locust*, p. 90), is an inept Jeremiah. The calculated incongruity is grotesquely comic, but there is genuine despair in it as well.

Miss Lonelyhearts and Tod, indeed Westian man, are peculiarly modern figures in their introspection, their schizoid temperament. They represent the new hero, "the unadaptable man, the wanderer or the dreamer or the perpetrator of illogical action."[2] In creating this type, West has not only translated the traditional great myths—the quest, the scapegoat, and the holy fool—into present-day forms, he has exploited some of the newer "pervasive myths or patterns of symbolic statement . . . in contemporary literature . . . the Myth of the Isolato, the Myth of Hell, the Myth of Voyage, and the Myth of Sanctity."[3] These myths are played out on the streets of the city, that most recurrent of modern symbols, which in West and so many other modern novelists is "an image of despair, as it is in Isaiah and Jeremiah."[4]

The mythic conception is obscured by the novels' garish landscapes. The very gift which allowed West to seize upon stark, vivid images worked against him by masking the subsurface meaning. The narrative logic and grotesque texture of his two masterpieces convey their own limited reality. He had a poet's eye and a sociologist's understanding; and whether he was dramatizing Miss Lonelyhearts' searing conflict, or merely satirizing American funeral customs, the density of his created world is sufficient to hold his reader's attention. But West's world was always a half-world; his desire was imaginatively to seize upon a deeper reality. Like so many other modern writers, he "often felt it necessary to use violence and melodrama as instruments for awakening his age out of its lethargies, for destroying its specious securities and revealing its underlying nightmare and tragedy."[5]

Perhaps it is the very violence of his novels, their stridency, and their brilliance which have resulted in so widespread a realistic reading of his work. West's world will never come alive as it should under such a reading. If *Miss Lonelyhearts* is ever to be staged again, it must never be played realistically; it must be played in the new style of Genet, Pinter, and Albee—the style of the absurd.

This is not to represent West as merely a novelist of the absurd; he is more than that. But his work contains elements of the absurd; just how many can be seen by some passages from an essay on Edward Albee. They describe West so well one would think he was a dramatist of the fifties and sixties rather than a novelist of the thirties:

> Both the American and English rebels were in sympathy with those dramatists in Paris (Beckett, Ionesco, Genet) who found that the world, bereft of confidence in traditional values, no longer made sense, was in fact "absurd." Language and ideologies were a currency with nothing in the bank! Substance had dissolved; everything was in fission. Even tragedy was unreal. Despair took on the airs of farce. As Saul Bellow put it, "Things had gotten all mixed up somewhere between laughter and insanity."
>
> These . . . trends . . . struck many observers as nihilistic if not nuts. But it has become increasingly evident that most of the dramatists who wrote these plays were deeply troubled and that what impelled them was not sport or jest but protest. To be sure it was not protest with a program or a "solution" (they no longer knew where to seek one); their plays were jeers, imprecations, outcries of agony—frequently masked as ribald jokes.[6]

Although these remarks do not sum up West, they are suggestive. Ultimately, West's strength is that he is too unique to be classifiable; and perhaps this strength has been, paradoxically, the reason why even now he has failed to capture the critical imagination. It is difficult to find the perspective (realistic? mythic? psychoanalytic?) by which to approach his novels. The works are prismatic, and perspective is important. We are beginning to have that perspective. For West, like Lawrence, "has made it possible for those who read him critically to understand aesthetically, to grasp in the mode of immediate apprehension aspects of our contemporary world that, had he left them uninformed, would have remained for us mere threatening, oppressive chaos. He charts our world. Without him and the other poets who also chart it, we would be likely to be blind to the specific process of disintegration of which we are victims."[7]

West was one of those rare American phenomena, a visionary, and *Miss Lonelyhearts* and *The Day of the Locust* are his visionary nightmares. They appeal to the deepest wellsprings of man's being, calling up hidden, nameless terrors. They exist in a nightmare world of unreality, and when the reader has left the fictional nightmare, he experiences, as he does in life, that afterglow, that twilight panic and dawning relief which beset the spirit. In West, however, the afterglow is an enduring one.

It may be argued that four short novels, only two of which are likely to endure, do not make a great impression on the literary scene. But if the ability to scar a reader, to leave an indelible impression on a reader's mind, is a mark of achievement, West left that mark the way few other writers do. It is a narrow scar, but a very deep one.

Notes

1. Wallace Fowlie, *Age of Surrealism* (Bloomington: Indiana University Press, 1950), p. 26.

2. *Ibid.*, p. 18.

3. Nathan A. Scott, "Religious Symbolism in Contemporary Literature," in *Religious Symbolism*, ed. by F. Ernest Johnson (New York: The Institute for Religious and Social Studies, 1955), pp. 168–69. The four myths are the myth of moral isolation, of man as part of the mass of "homeless derelicts in search of self-definition and the Mystery of Being" (p. 170); the myth of the wasteland, of the distance of God; the myth of the quest; and the myth of beatitude.

4. *Ibid.*, p. 170. Scott, in his discussion of the city and the modern mythic characters who populate it, makes the following remark about Kafka—a remark so applicable to West that we need only substitute his name for Kafka's: "It is perhaps in the novels of Franz Kafka . . . that we get the most archetypal presentation of the contemporary hero. His is the religious consciousness of our age. . . . I mean that Kafka's is 'a mind which contains the terrors and nightmares of the age which most of us can't face.' What is perhaps first to be remarked upon is the atmosphere of isolation that pervades his books, enveloping and conditioning the destiny of his hero. . . . At the center of his novels there is always the single individual, the lonely and uprooted 'isolato,' for whom there is no fixed abode and who, in becoming a kind of clown, grows 'more conscious of his center, of his distance from God, of the mechanical awkwardness of his gestures, of the dizzying somersaults his spirit performs before the revolving universe and the eternal peace of God.'" (pp. 170–71)

5. *Ibid.*, p. 176.

6. Harold Clurman, "Edward Albee in the American Theatre," program notes to *Who's Afraid of Virginia Woolf* by Edward Albee (Columbia Records), pp. 4–5.

7. Eliseo Vivas, *D. H. Lawrence: The Failure and the Triumph of Art* (Evanston: Northwestern University Press, 1960), pp. 271–72.

Days of Wrath and Laughter

R. W. B. LEWIS*

We might well begin with Faulkner's *The Hamlet* (1940), where the unmistakable figure of Satan unloosed is named Flem Snopes, where the victory of the Antichrist over the novel's world is virtually complete, and where laughter is indeed a major instrument for coping with the awfulness. But this antipastoral masterpiece has such a variety of fictional tones and narrative modes that an effective analysis of it would pull us off course. We will do better to begin with Nathanael West's *The Day of the Locust*, and its hardminded comic portrait of the imminent destruction of America by a holocaust of hate. The Satanic character in West's novel, the harnesser of all that hatred, goes in fact unnamed; but we know that he will be an even greater scoundrel, making even wilder promises, than the lesser demagogues we have seen throughout the book serving the bitter frustrations of the aging California citizenry. He will be a successor as well to West's earlier Antichrists, the editor Shrike in *Miss Lonelyhearts* (1933) and Shagpoke Whipple in *A Cool Million* (1934). The realm of the California super-promiser, however, seems larger than that of Shrike and Shagpoke; for if there is not, unarguably, an increase in West's imaginative power from *Miss Lonelyhearts* to *The Day of the Locust*, there is an observable increase in the range of the horror always comically explored.

The world of *Miss Lonelyhearts* is an airlessly tight little island—Manhattan Island, in fact, plus a short stretch of countryside; a world so narrowed, in a novella so compressed, that its rhythms and tensions (which themselves are eschatological in nature and have to do with the last things) are well-nigh uncontainable. The novella moves unfalteringly between nightmare and actuality, its tone between horror and jesting; which is West's exemplary way of apprehending *our* world as under the dominion of a contemporary Antichrist. The human condition thus apprehended is characterized by a sort of absolute dis-order, by a dislocation observable pre-eminently in the relations of love, in almost every heterosexual and homosexual variety; but also a dislocation in man's other crucial relations—his relation to things, to words, to the rituals of life, to his own perennial aspirations. Human life, as depicted in *Miss*

*Reprinted, with permission, from R. W. B. Lewis, *Trials of the Word: Essays in American Literature and the Humanistic Tradition* (New Haven: Yale University Press, 1965): 212–18. Copyright © Yale University Press, 1965.

Lonelyhearts, has become a grotesque parody of itself; and the name of the book's Antichrist, Shrike, has the merit not only of meaning a toothbeaked bird of prey, but also of being as it were a parody of the name Christ, or Christ almost spelled backward. It is Shrike who rules over and preys upon an urban scene composed of the heartless, the violent, and the wretched. And it is Shrike who pits himself against the would-be imitator of Christ, the hapless columnist we know only by his pen name Miss Lonelyhearts, and whom Shrike torments in particular by spoken parodies of the Eucharist—that holy *communion* after which Miss Lonelyhearts so yearns. The central image of the novella, indeed, is a parody of the Gospel encounter between Christ and the Devil—in this case between a man, on the one hand, whose soul is sickened by a human misery he cannot assuage; and, on the other, the spokesman of an ice-cold and yet witty and intellectually brilliant inhumanity. In speech after speech, Shrike tempts and taunts Miss Lonelyhearts with vistas of grandeur, channels of escape, resources of compensation; until he drives the columnist to attempting the final absurd miracle. In a ludicrously ill-timed and ferverish effort to embrace and hence to redeem by love at least one individual human victim— a crippled homosexual named Pete Doyle—Miss Lonelyhearts is accidentally shot and killed; and in the abrasively ironic eschatology of this novella, the field is left to the further machinations of the Antichrist. But Shrike, consummate satirist through he be, is at the same time an object of satire—that is, of West's satire—and the field of his triumph is no more than a frozen chaos.

The enlargement of setting in *A Cool Million* is suggested by this: that Miss Lonelyhearts is shot (in an obscure rooming house) not even by a man but, as though in its supreme revolt, by a thing, by the freakish explosion of a gun wrapped in a newspaper; while Lemuel Pitkin, whose gradual "dismantling" is half of the theme of *A Cool Million*, is shot by a hired assassin, "Operative 6348XM," during a huge political rally staged in New York by the National Revolutionary Party. The satire in *A Cool Million* is cruder and broader than in *Miss Lonelyhearts*; and West is not himself implicated in that which he satirizes, as he had been earlier. Still, while *A Cool Million* plays comical havoc with the Horatio Alger tradition and the American daydream of the easy surge upward to fame and fortune, it is also this country's most vigorous narrative vision of the political apocalypse—far more penetrating, for example, than the rather hastily contrived image which appeared the following year in Sinclair Lewis' *It Can't Happen Here*. The devil as the editor Shrike is succeeded in *A Cool Million* by the devil as national political Fuehrer: by Shagpoke Whipple, a more ambitious and amiable and even more completely fraudulent figure than his predecessor. The "mantling" of Shagpoke, former President and future dictator of the United States, is the other half of the book's theme; his loudmouthed and evidently interminable reign is just beginning as the story ends. On the national holiday commemorating young Lemuel's assassination, Whipple spells out his triumphant program to shouting thousands at a Fifth Avenue parade: "The National Revolutionary Party [has] triumphed, and by that triumph this country was delivered from sophistication, Marxism and International Capitalism. Through the National Revolution its people were purged of alien diseases and America became again America."

This is a fine example of what Richard Hofstadter has defined as the paranoid style in American politics: a style historically based, as Mr. Hofstadter points out, on a most intensive apocalyptic outlook—a belief in some evil worldwide conspiracy, an identification of a wild conglomeration of elements as agencies of the Antichrist (communism, eastern capitalism, intellectual sophistication, and so on), a conviction of approaching disaster unless counteraction is swiftly taken.[1] West's complex achievement in *A Cool Million* is to satirize this apocalyptic temper in such a way as to show that it is itself the source of the potential catastrophe. But Mr. Hofstadter was talking primarily not about the political debaucheries of the 1930s, the actual scene of *A Cool Million,* but about the presidential campaign of 1964; and it is because that phenomenon is still so close to us that one finds it harder to laugh at Shagpoke's speech or at Shagpoke than it used to be. Yet, even as we are once again astonished at the capacity of life to follow slavishly in the wake of art, and as our admiration for West's prophetic power deepens into downright awe, we also become aware that the perspective in *A Cool Million* is exactly right. For in West's perspective of rough-hewn satire, the squalid reality of American fascism—the absurdities that pervade its spurious nostalgia and its venomous racism, its radical ignorance and contradictory assortment of fears—gets utterly exposed. What passes among the brutalized citizenry as the New Jerusalem is revealed to be a catastrophic vulgarity. And the very real menace, even as it is uncovered and defined, is in part overcome (insofar as a work of art can ever overcome anything) through the restoration of sanity by laughter.

But *The Day of the Locust,* as I have already said, is West's supreme Book of Revelations. This beautifully composed novel makes dreadfully and hilariously evident in the superb dance of its elements a threat beyond that of *A Cool Million:* a threat to the very roots of life in America, a threat as it were to the human nature of American humanity. It is a threat incarnate in a certain mass of people—bored, frustrated, vindictive, and moribund—who have come to California impelled by a dream of their own obscene millennium, by a sterile lust for some experience of violence that might exhilarate and revivify. They are disappointed—"nothing [could] ever be violent enough to make taut their slack minds and bodies"—and with a devouring sense of having been betrayed, they await the summons to provide out of themselves the violence denied. The summons begins to be audible in the animal roaring of a mob rioting outside a Hollywood theater as the novel ends.

Against that tremendous force of hatred—and for West, since love is the sign of spiritual grace, hatred, its polar opposite, is the defining quality of apostasy and damnation—West poses the allied powers of art and comedy. His hero is a young painter named Tod Hackett, presently employed as a set designer in Hollywood; a tougher-spirited Miss Lonelyhearts and a more self-protective Lemuel Pitkin. It is Tod who takes to studying the dead ferocity of the invaders, seeking them out in odd nooks and corners of the city, driven by a profound fascination with their "awful anarchic power" and determined to represent them on canvas. He finds them gathered, more than anywhere else, in the temples and churches, the lunatic-fringe cults of California; for one of the most terrible of the truths and prophecies disclosed in *The Day of the Locust* is the organic connection in America between radical religiosity, an extreme Protestantism gone finally insane, and the organized impulse of hatred and destruction. "As [Tod] watched these people writhe on the hard seats of their churches, he thought of how well Alessandro Magnasco would dramatize the contrast between their drained-out feeble bodies and their wild disordered minds. He would not satirize them as Hogarth and Daumier might, nor would he pity them. He would paint their fury with respect, appreciating its awful, anarchic power, and aware that they had it in them to destroy civilization." Nathanael West does not precisely satirize them either; despite its carefully wrought poetic intensity, *The Day of the Locust* stays closer to a palpable historical reality than his other fictions. The tone and movement of the novel are comic, nonetheless, and both are suited to a world in which, due to the utter instability of its outward forms, everything is on the verge of giving way.

The scene upon which the locusts descend is a scene made up of masqueraders and impostors; of movie actors dressed up as French and British generals and of ordinary citizens dressed up as Tyrolean hunters. Even plants and natural phenomena are fictitious: cactus plants are made of rubber and cork; a hill on a movie set, as it collapses, spills the nails and rips the canvas of which it is composed. A world so grotesquely insubstantial is ripe for conquest; and yet within its atmosphere, the wrath to come can be contemplated with just that drunken and hazily amused equanimity that Tod Hackett expresses when, lying on his back in a clump of wild mustard, he thinks about the invasion of California by "the cream of America's madmen" and feels certain that "the milk from which it had been skimmed was just as rich in violence. The Angelenos would be first, but their comrades all over the country would follow. There would be civil war." That antic Armageddon, however, takes place not quite in the actual rioting and lynching and sexual assaults of the final scene; but, rather, in an interpretive work of art, in the painting (and it is to be a great painting, West clearly wants us to believe) Tod Hackett is meticulously projecting on the last page, even as he is being mauled and half-crushed by the frenzied mob.

Thus superimposed in thought above the actual disorders, the painting— it will be called "The Burning of Los Angeles"—will eventually explain and comment upon the apocalypse it describes by the patterned juxtaposition of its elements. It will show a "mob carrying baseball bats and torches" down a long hill street, a mob that includes "the cultists of all sorts" whom Tod had been observing—"all those poor devils who can only be stirred by the promise of miracles, and then only to violence." Now, "no longer bored, they sang and danced joyously in the red light of the flames," following the leader who "had made the necessary promise"; "they were marching behind his banner in a great united front of screwballs and screwboxes to purify the land." Elsewhere on the canvas, various postures suggest various responses to that savage absurd Puritanism: a girl running naked in smiling mindless panic; a man named Claude turning to thumb his nose; Tod himself pausing to throw stones at the mob like a small boy. Nose thumbing and stone throwing are commendable acts of derision; but Tod's major response is of course his painting, just as West's major response is the novel that contains it. And both painting and novel fulfill their purpose by portraying these maddened humans, whirling forward in their orgiastic dance, as devils who are yet poor devils, seized by a fury of hatred which is as silly as it is explosive.

Notes

1. *Harper's Magazine,* November, 1964.

[Comic Writers and Extreme Violence]

John Hawkes *

Nathanael West, I think, did make use of a kind of sick joke, but I think he uses the sick joke always so that you feel behind it the idealism, the need for innocence and purity, truth, strength and so on. This is at least implied. Now, it may be implied very faintly, or let's put it that the sick joke is saved by a kind of deperate joke, a larger desperate joke, that is in, say, West's work. Nathanael West, Joseph Heller, Flannery O'Connor. All of these are, I think, comic writers dealing in extreme violence. Bernard Malamud is, it seems to me, is—they call him—a magic realist; his humor, his comedy, is perhaps more obviously saving—I think that Malamud is a writer of extraordinary imaginative ability. I think his fiction is filled with something—I hesitate to use the word "grace" because it has special meaning or connotations—but his fiction lives out of a concern for humanity. I think all, I think any fiction that I would be interested in, would live out of that concern. Comedy works in two ways, say in my own work and in West, Flannery O'Connor, and in Heller, the comedy almost seems a self-inflicting affair, it is also a saving, a saving attitude. If something is pathetically humorous or grotesquely humorous, it seems to pull us back into the realm, not of mere conventional values but of the lasting values, the one or two really deep permanent human values. I think any writer of worth is concerned with these things.

*Reprinted, with permission, from *The Massachusetts Review* 7 (Summer 1966): 461. © 1966 The Massachusetts Review, Inc.

Nathanael West's "Desperate Detachment"

MAX F. SCHULZ *

Nathanael West is reputed to have remained detached from the grotesqueries of Hollywood during the many years he worked there and from the follies of the human world for the thirty-seven years he lived in it.[1] Yet West's novels make it clear that in the deeper reaches of his mind he was obsessed with man's nightmarish dual nature: his neurotic isolation and his social impulse, his self-deception and his self-mockery. Unlike Singer, and so many of the current Jewish-American writers, West was unable to rest content in the human suspension between heavenly aspirations and earthly limitations, belief and skepticism, order and disorder. He portrays life in his novels as a conflict of inadequate imperatives offered to man by society and culture as guides to live by. Conflict supposes not equipoise between codeterminants but supremacy of one over another. In that sense each novel, despite its basic satirical intention, represents a search for absolutes. "Reality! Reality! If I could only discover the Real," John Gilson calls for in his "journal." "A Real that I could know with my senses."[2] In the astringent disillusionment of West's hope of finding something real to believe in—"A Real that would wait for me to inspect it as a dog inspects a dead rabbit [p. 14]"—each novel ends as a mocking denunciation of a false dream: the bardic dream (*The Dream Life of Balso Snell*), the Christ dream (*Miss Lonelyhearts*), The Horatio Alger dream (*A Cool Million*), and the Hollywood dream (*The Day of the Locust*). West's bitter cognizance of betrayal is pervasive. The thoroughgoing nature of his sense of the fraudulence and destructiveness of life is brilliantly, almost excessively, portrayed by the Trojan Horse correlative in *The Dream Life of Balso Snell*. Synonymous in Western thought with falsity and the end of a civilization, the wooden horse— specifically its alimentary canal—becomes the hallucinatory terrain over which Balso Snell wanders. Thus West clearly identifies man's dream world with sham and *fin de siècle*. He uneasily describes its death rattle, while trying desperately to dissociate himself with a comic ploy from emotional involvement in its agony. Unfortunately for the complete success of his stories, he was unable to control his own sense of outrage and despair. His shriek of laughter, as Victor Comerchero notes, "keeps breaking into a sob."[3]

*Reprinted, with permission, from Max F. Schulz, *Radical Sophistication: Studies in Jewish-American Novelists* (Athens: Ohio University Press, 1969): 36–55.

The first work of a writer is more likely to rely on literary analogues than later works which draw directly on experience for their substance. Such is the case with the four novels of West. *The Dream Life of Balso Snell* satirizes the ineffectuality of the imagination by way of an inexhaustible stream of allusions to and parodies of English writers from Dryden to Joyce, and from Dostoevsky to the French Symbolists and Dadaists, as well as much miscellaneous Western thought. The novel is a book perversely bent on proclaiming the illusoriness of books. West is reported to have told Liebling "that he had written Balso as a protest against writing books."[4] That is ostensibly its general satirical aim. In fact, the novel strikes out thematically in a variety of directions, foreshadowing most of the preoccupations of West in his subsequent novels.[5] Of these I wish to look at one to demonstrate West's ambivalent involvement in the despairing world that he depicts.

An essential thematic antithesis in the story pits romantic love against the procreative instinct. Like the nympholeptic shepherd-king in Keats's *Endymion* (and like Samuel Perkins, the subject of a biography by Mary McGeeney), Balso Snell swoons in and out of a dream within his dream as he mentally pursues Miss McGeeney, his thoughts struggling "to make the circle of his sensory experience approach the infinite [p. 36]." The prevailing situation is one of incompatibility. Lust encounters conditions of courtly love, and sacred love the wiles of the seducer. "Oh, I loved a girl once," Balso Snell laments: "All day she did nothing but place bits of meat on the petals of flowers. She choked the rose with butter and cake crumbs, soiling the crispness of its dainty petals with gravy and cheese. She wanted to attract flies, not butterflies or bees" [p. 57]. This perverse merger of the fleshly and the ethereal becomes inextricably ambiguous in the witty biography of Saint Puce, the flea "who was born, lived, and died, beneath the arm of our Lord" [p. 11]. In his daily sensations of supping on Christ, whose body provided him with both meat and drink, Saint Puce enacted perpetual Holy Communion.

As the ironic tone of these two examples indicates, West will not allow the mystery of the "Two-become-One" to remain intact. For him the contraries reconciled are always coming undone. Like Fra Lippo Lippi he forever sees "the garden and God there / A-making man's wife"; and this lesson of "The value and significance of flesh" he "can't unlearn ten minutes afterward."[6]

If the spiritual connot exist without the incarnate, through substance then must we confirm our substancelessness. Thus West fashions his own infernal mystery. The ideal vanishes into solid flesh. "Who among us can boast that he was born three times, as was Dionysius?" B. Hamlet Darwin asks caustically.

> Or who can say, like Christ, that he was born of a virgin?. . . Alas! none of us. . . . You who were born from the womb, covered with slime and foul blood, 'midst cries of anguish and suffering.
> At your birth, instead of the Three Kings, the Dove, the Star of Bethlehem,

there was only old Doctor Haasenschweitz who wore rubber gloves and carried a towel over his arm like a waiter.

And how did the lover, your father, come to his beloved?. . . Did he come in the shape of a swan, a bull, or a shower of gold? No! But with his pants unsupported by braces, came he from the bathroom. [p. 55]

Unfortunately for West's peace of mind, as the savage despair of the passage suggests, he found no satisfaction in this reduction of the infinite into the corporeal either. In an acrid satire of fleshly desire the story (and dream) concludes with Balso having a nocturnal emission. (The entire story represents the strenuously intellectual efforts of Balso's body to have a wet dream.) Even sex, the urge to procreate, ends as a pointless solo exercise in release of tension, likened to "the mechanics of decay" [p. 61]. At the instant of emission, West exultantly informs us that Balso's "body broke free of the bard" and "took on a life of its own" "that knew nothing of the poet Balso" [p. 61]. Despite this freedom from the false constraints of the categorizing imagination, not life, not the organic, but death and the mechanical describe the evolutions of the body. The basic metaphor used is that of an army performing "the manual of disintegration," maneuvering automatically "with the confidence and training of chemicals acting under the stimulus of a catalytic agent" [p.6]. Release is described in terms of a mortally wounded soldier: "His body screamed and shouted as it marched . . . then with one heaving shout of triumph, it fell back quiet . . . victorious." Thus the "miracle was made manifest" in the One, West says sardonically. "The One that is all things and yet no one of them: the priest and the god, the immolation, the sacrificial rite, the libation offered to ancestors, the incantation, the sacrificial egg, the altar, the ego and the alter ego, as well as the father, the child, and the grandfather of the universe, the mystic doctrine, the purification, the syllable 'Om,' the path, the master, the witness, the receptacle, the Spirit of Public School 186, the last ferry that leaves for Weehawken at seven" [pp. 61–62]. In the diminishing manner of the burlesque stanzas of Byron's *Don Juan,* this catalogue of the body's regality ("the Spirit of Public School 186"!) underscores the skepticism with which West assents to the enthronement of matter.

Worse, yet, mind returns in the form of false literary sentiment to adulterate further the autonomous reality of the body. In a brilliant analysis of its style, Victor Comerchero [pp. 57–61] shows how Balso's imagined copulation with Mary McGeeney is a parody of the melting, swooning seduction of eighteenth-century sentimental literature, of the stereotype passion of pulp fiction, of the hard-boiled back-seat wrestle of the realistic school, of the decadent *fin de siècle* dreams of encounters with an oriental *femme fatale,* and of the Molly Bloom monologue at the conclusion of Joyce's *Ulysses.* Saturninely, if comically, West reveals that even Balso's "dreams have been corrupted by literature. When he dreams even a wet dreams, it is a literary one."[7] Driven by sexual desire, Balso Snell in his dream exploration of the nature of mind and matter may have discovered complacently that the body reigns supreme; but West's interpretation of the same event is less optimistic. In acrid disillusionment he concludes (corroborated by the dream context of the narrative) that Balso's solution to the hopeless bifurcation of life is as chimerical as the empty constructs of the mind, which man fools himself into believing are a pledge of meaningful order in the world.

"If there is a vision of love" in West's fiction, Josephine Herbst has remarked, "it is etched in the acid of what love is not."[8] *The Dream Life of Balso Snell* presents a satyr's conception of love, *Miss Lonelyhearts* that of the whorehouse madam turned church-choir mistress. From cynical exploiter of his correspondents' cries for help, Miss Lonelyhearts metamorphoses into a Christlike savior of these lost and lonely souls of modern civilization.

West's point of view, however, is more subtle and complex in *Miss Lonelyhearts* than in his other three novels. His virulent skepticism is forever testing the validity of a thought and seeking the motive behind an action. Thus, he constantly and ambivalently undercuts his effort to find a pattern in existence. The horrifying lives of Miss Lonelyhearts' readers unquestionably moves the columnist to sincere desire to succor them. But his conversion from hard-boiled columnist to soft-souled evangelist is compromised at every turn. The psychology of sex—the twentieth-century substitute for previous centuries' religious faith—is the instrument of his betrayal of others as well as of himself. More often than not he is depicted as selfishly demanding rather than selflessly giving of his love. His impulse toward the Divine Love of man and "all God's creation" [p. 75] advocated by Father Zossima in *The Brothers Karamazov*, which he has been reading, manifests itself in sexual cruelty, self-loathing seduction, latent homosexuality, and religious hysteria. Like infernal stations of the cross in his outrageous progress toward saintly love of humanity, he bloodily bungles (in a dream) the sacrifice of a lamb, viciously tugs at the nipples of his fiancée's breasts, brutally twists the arm of an old homosexual, calculatingly attempts to seduce his boss's wife, distastefully submits to the sexual advances of a correspondent, ardently holds hands with her crippled husband, eventually strikes the housewife seductress in the face again and again, and finally achieves union with Christ while in a fever.

Throughout this inverse way of the pilgrim, religious ardor is confused with sexual desire, love with lust, and lust with violence and destruction. Miss Lonelyhearts' addresses of love to Betty, Mary Shrike, and Mrs. Doyle are associated with a Mexican War obelisk that like a giant phallus "lengthening in rapid jerks," and "red and swollen in the dying sun," seems "about to spout a load of granite seed" of death [p. 89]. The arm of the "clean old man" [p. 85], who was pulled from the stall of a public restroom and accused by Miss Lonelyhearts of being a pervert, become "the arm of all the sick and miserable, broken and betrayed, inarticulate and impotent . . . of Desperate, Broken-hearted, Sick-of-it-all, Disillusioned-with-tubercular-husband" [p. 88]. In its effort to create order out of the entropy about him, Miss Lonelyhearts' sensibility, ill from its encounter with Fay Doyle, nightmarishly grapples with the contents of a pawnshop window, "the paraphernalia of suffering." Out of this jumble of articles it attempts to construct a phallus. Failing in this, it works to form the paraphernalia into a gigantic cross on the shore of an ocean, but "every wave added to his stock faster than he could lengthen its arms. His labors were enormous. He staggered from the last wave line to his work, loaded down with marine refuse—bottles, shells, chunks of cork, fish heads, pieces of net" [pp. 104–105]. The linkage of Christ with the sea has strong libidinous overtones (cf. pp. 75–76, 138–139, where Christ and a phallic snake and Christ and a fish are also joined). The prior encounter with Fay Doyle is described in marine terms. Her undressing in the dark is heard by Miss Lonelyhearts as "sea sounds": "Something flapped like a sail; there was the creak of ropes; then he heard the wave-against-a-wharf smack of rubber on flesh. Her call to him to hurry was a sea-moan, and when he lay beside her, she heaved, tidal, moon-driven." And in language that foreshadows his subsequent building of the cross, he staggers out of bed fifteen minutes later "like an exhausted swimmer leaving the surf" [p. 101]. In short, moved by the inadequacy of sex to steady his nerves and allay his self-hatred, he sublimates his eroticism in Christian humility, as a complementary form of therapy.

West could not formulate the ambivalence of his hope for a religious solution to life more clearly. As if the condemnation of *agapé* is not vehement enough, Miss Lonelyhearts' religious conversion, as Victor Comerchero demonstrates conclusively, has a homosexual origin, further underlining West's "mythic, mocking, agonizing" suspicion that "true compassion" is unendurable in this decaying world.[9] In the plight of Miss Lonelyhearts West portrays a devastating debasement of the Ulysses and Sirens motif. And the blasphemously blind universe that he envisions, in which "the Miss Lonelyhearts are the priests of twentieth-century America" [p. 122], receives full confirmation when Miss Lonelyhearts interprets his fever as a religious experience and climbs out of bed to embrace the crippled Doyle, whom he believes "God had sent him so that Miss Lonelyhearts could perform a miracle and be certain of his conversion" [p. 139]. But West in his heart of hearts knew that God was dead. Miss Lonelyhearts never quite qualifies for membership in Graham Greene's pantheon of tainted saints. West's faith is at once too strong of desire and too weak of belief. Miss Lonelyhearts' need for a confirmatory miracle italicizes this profound skepticism. And the consequences of his desire for certainty are ironically devastating on both the sacramental and psychological levels of the narrative. He rushes to embrace the cripple and heal his leg. Doyle, however, is terrified by Miss Lonelyhearts' mad charge and by Betty's sudden appearance at the bottom of the stairs. As they grapple, a pistol Doyle is carrying accidentally fires, killing Miss Lonelyhearts. Locked in each other's arms they roll down the stairs. The symbolic union of the two men at the end is no doubt on one level expressive of Miss Lonelyheart's spiritual yearnings; but their embrace, as Stanley Edgar Hyman observes, is also homosexual, the one ironically penetrating "the body of the other with a bullet," "while the woman stands helplessly by."[10] The disparity in the novel between the simple narrative affirmation of religious faith and the underlying metaphoric insinuation of Oedipal obscenities adumbrates the tortured ambiguity of West's imagination—its attraction to a Christ dream that it could not believe in.

In *A Cool Million* and *The Day of the Locust*, West explores the *Zeitgeist* of the cheaters and the cheated on native grounds. The dreams are now distinctly the homegrown variety found sprouting in the land of opportunity. "America takes care of the honest and industrious and never fails them as long as they are both," Nathan "Shagpoke" Whipple expounds from his perch on a cracker barrel. "The story of Rockefeller and of Ford is the story of every great American," he tells Lemuel Pitkin, "and you should strive to make it your story. Like them, you were born poor and on a farm. Like them, by honesty and industry, you cannot fail to succeed" [p. 150]. The rest of *A Cool Million* is West's saturnine retort. Not from rags to riches but to the same old shirtsleeves, not from log cabin to White House but to the same old mortgaged farm house—this is the just reward of the barefoot, but honest and industrious, American boy. With acrid irony West equates business enterprise with the imagination, foresight, and aggressiveness of Wu Fong's white slavery emporium; and economic success with unapprehended chicanery and thievery. The American capitalistic system is posited on the productive ideal that the building of a better mousetrap is always good for the community. West's answer is to demonstrate that the folklore of Horatio Alger is more likely to be destructive of the individual than to be beneficial to society. And so he gives us the allegory of Lemuel's inexorable dismemberment on the barricades of capitalism: *sans* teeth, eye, thumb, scalp, and leg. To the memory of this derelict of the American way of life, the fascistic "Leather Shirt" followers of Shagpoke Whipple shout at the conclusion in a national holiday celebration of Lemuel's birthday, "All hail, the American Boy!" [ch. 31].

Victor Comerchero contends that because of the broadly comic tone of *A Cool Million*, a reversion to the tone of *The Dream Life of Balso Snell*, it fails to engage the reader. Consequently one tends to miss the serious point of the novel; "one is so amused by America as West presents it that one is neither frightened nor angered by it" [p. 118]. In his effort to set up a critical issue, a straw man, so to speak, Comerchero exaggerates the difficulty posed by the blurred focus of the book's tone. The plain fact is that few readers (critical commentators, that is) have missed the central warning of the novel. Comerchero's observation, however, about the strange refusal of the story to take itself seriously is penetrating. The "personal involvement" that he suggests as an explanation has more than a grain of truth in it, as this essay, I hope, makes clear. But Comerchero does not, unfortunately, make anything more of this insight.

With what in the story is West involved? One cannot see the temperament and agony of West in either Lemuel Pitkin or Shagpoke Whipple, as one can in Balso Snell, Miss Lonelyhearts, and Tod Hackett. Hence the disturbing reserve of the story, by way of its excessiveness, does not derive from West's effort to dissociate himself from the central characters. Closer to the simple truth, probably, is that West, like his great predecessor Swift, is engaged in a lover's quarrel with a world that does not live up to his expectations. The broadly vulgar style in which he tells the story is, of course, on one level a parody of the crass, didactic prose of the Horatio Alger tale. Not so much the economic system, however, as the noisome aura of sanctity which enshrouds it is the object of his attack. After all, in writing his books, West himself hoped to turn an honest dollar. That hope was appropriately enough strongest with *A Cool Million*.[11] The pious cant of a Shagpoke Whipple celebrates the manufacturing process and the pursuit of gain as the golden ends of human activity. The result is that the manufactured article deteriorates into a by-product and man is lost sight of altogether, transformed into a helpless ministrant to his own inexorable dehumanization. In the "Chamber of American Horrors, Animate and Inanimate Hideosities," West brilliantly pictures the debasement of taste and of sensibility produced by this carnival atmosphere. Here the flotsam of an industrial civilization buttressed by a false ethic is accorded the revered permanence of museum exhibits. Man's Hippocratic ideal is enshrined in the patent medicine offerings of the drugstore: in a "Hercules wearing a small, compact truss" and in "a copy of Power's 'Greek Slave' with elastic bandages on all her joints." Technical know-how is displayed in the cheap imitative tricks of paper "made to look like wood, wood like rubber, rubber like steel, steel like cheese, cheese like glass, and, finally, glass like paper" [ch. 28]. So the inconstant and the deceptive are memorialized with sneaking admiration as a tribute to American technological genius.

In Greenfield Village, Henry Ford's monument to Americana, there is an ash heap meticulously encased and labeled as having come from behind Thomas Edison's Menlo Park laboratory. Gazing at this dump pile, one can never be quite sure of the degree of fetish worship and, contrariwise, of sly humor that it represents. Nor can one categorically isolate West's attitude in *A Cool Million*. Shagpoke Whipple, the homespun American philosopher, wins our sufferance: but Shagpoke the politician, the America-firster, terrifies us. Lemuel, the innocent pawn, evokes our pity; but Lemuel the fool, the classic rube, equally arouses our derision. The names that West chooses for his characters are invariably witty wordplays, adding an extra dimension to our understanding of that person. Lemuel Pitkin's last name is close in sound to pipkin. Whether we are right to associate pipkin with Lemuel, we cannot avoid the scathing sense of the diminutive in his name; hence in comparison to his namesake Lemuel Gulliver, his misfortunes are seen as a diminuendo echo of the Brobdingnag gulling suffered by Gulliver on *his* Whittingtonian travels in search of fame and fortune.

The big lie is certain. Less evident is the source of the lie: the ideals of the American Way of Life? the naïveté of such simpletons as Lemuel? the "sophisticated aliens" [ch. 31] decried by Whipple? or the ingrained evil of an economic system? The tone of *A Cool Million* reflects West's own uncertainty of what to finger. For all his pessimism he was not a little bitten with the American dream of a new Eden in the wilderness, as Betty's and Miss Lonelyhearts' nostalgic interlude on the farm in Connecticut hints—a surprising performance for seemingly so confirmed an urban novelist. There is also his love of the Bucks County countryside and of hunting and fishing. And there is the prophet's fervent need to believe in something, which in West is strung taut by the contrary pull of the cynical side of his nature. It is no wonder in his daily life that he strove to divorce himself from the furious indignation which drove his artistic vision.

With *The Day of the Locust*, West's view of life approaches Swift's in the fourth book of *Gulliver's Travels*. Spectators and performers alike feel the lash of his derision. Attracted by its semblance of life, Midwesterners come to Hollywood only to be tricked into death by a diet of sophisticate sex. They gyrate from movie premiere to movie premiere, as much automatons as the celluloid celebrities they push and shove to glimpse. The cinematic promise of ripe love and of a richer, fuller life never materializes. Faye Greener is a pathetic imitation of the Hollywood sex goddess, her thoughts and mannerisms a pastiche of Grade B movies. Both Homer Simpson and Tod Hackett (note the puns on death and havoc in the latter's name) discover in her ever fresh lure of sexuality a fey, receding will-o-the-wisp. Her appearance promises love, but it proves no more rewarding than the suggestive accents and movements of a screenland heroine. Each one's desire for renewal of person is eventually betrayed by her beauty, "whose invitation wasn't to pleasure, but to struggle, hard and sharp, closer to murder than to love" [p. 271]. The mechanically destructive recoil of the mob at the end of the novel reflects West's view of what happens to man when his hopes end as tattered scarecrows of reality. The adulatory pursuit of celebrities blurs sinisterly into the sexual violence that underlies emotional hunger. Spasms surge periodically through the crowd. Smutty remarks pass freely from stranger to stranger. Men hug passing complacent women. With such senseless eroticism, the mob apes the dark underside of the lives of its screen heroes and heroines. Death is inextricably linked to love. Human energy is easily diverted from a life instinct to a death impulse. Thus the adoration of the premiere mob is manifested as the blight of locusts, just as the alteration of the primordial hills of southern California into travesties of exotic architecture is another manifestation of the locust's presence.

The Westian novel is concerned at its center with the instability of existence, which derives basically from a metaphysical reaction to the modern world picture of everything being in flux. What more frighteningly askew world of metamorphosis can one imagine than the one of architecture, aesthetics, music, and mathematics Miss McGeeney tells us that Samel Perkins discovered "in the odors of a woman's body" [p. 36]. In these terms the Hollywood setting of *The Day of the Locust* provides West with the most perfect of the correlatives he has used to set forth his vision of life. As is proper in the city dedicated to the making of movies—to the creation of shapes that alter before one's eyes—the guises and gestures of the celluloid world of shadowy change, of make-believe, become the status quo. A fat lady in yachting cap converts into a housewife going shopping; a man in Norfolk jacket and Tyrolean hat, an insurance agent returning from his office; and a girl in slacks and sneakers with a bandanna around her head, a receptionist leaving a switchboard. The painted canvas, plaster, and lath sets on the back lots of the film studios reappear as the Mexican ranch houses, Samoan huts, Mediterranean villas, Egyptian and Japanese temples, Swiss chalets, and Tudor cottages that line Pinyon Canyon at the end of Vine Street. Repeatedly the Westian man transmutes into a woman. John Gilson as Raskolnikov, after murdering a dishwasher, caresses his breasts "like a young girl who has suddenly become conscious of her body on a hot afternoon." He imitates "the mannered walk of a girl showing off before a group of boys," flirts with some sailors, going "through all the postures of a desperate prostitute," and "camping" for all it is worth [p. 22]. Lemuel is transformed momently into a male prostitute in Wu Fong's establishment. And Miss Lonelyhearts exhibits more than one symptom of the homosexual. The many periods in history endlessly shift their outlines. Searching for Faye, who has a bit part in the movie "Waterloo," Tod Hackett wanders through a kaleidoscope of time and place and of the artifices of civilization:

> The only bit of shade he could find was under an ocean liner made of painted canvas with real lifeboats hanging from its davits. He stood in its narrow shadow for a while, then went on toward a great forty-foot papier mâché sphinx that loomed up in the distance. He had to cross a desert to reach it, a desert that was continually being made larger by a fleet of trucks dumping white sand. . . .
>
> He skirted the desert, making a wide turn to the right, and came to a western street with a plank sidewalk. On the porch of the "Last Chance Saloon" was a rocking chair. He sat down on it and lit a cigarette.
>
> From there he could see a jungle compound with a water buffalo tethered to the side of a conical grass hut. Every few seconds the animal groaned musically. Suddenly an Arab charged by on a white stallion. He shouted at the man, but got no answer. A little while later he saw a truck with a load of snow and several malamute dogs. He shouted again. The driver shouted something back, but didn't stop.
>
> Throwing away his cigarette, he went through the swinging doors of the saloon. There was no back to the building and he found himself in a Paris street. He followed it to its end, coming out in a Romanesque courtyard. He heard voices a short distance away and went toward them. On a lawn of fiber, a group of men and women in riding costume were picnicking. They were eating cardboard food in front of a cellophane waterfall. [p. 351]

Faye Greener and her father, Harry, have maintained their theatrical poses of movie siren and vaudeville clown so long that, in the words of Comerchero, each "has been dispossessed of his personality—of his identity—through disuse" [p. 138].

West's obsession with flux is a central controlling force in *The Dream Life of Balso Snell*. In keeping with the protean nature of a dream, shapes are forever altering before Balso's eyes. His first sight of Miss McGeeney is of a slim young girl "standing naked before him . . . washing her hidden charms in a public fountain." She calls to him in the erotically charged language of the Romance. "Throwing his arms around her, Balso interrupted her recitation sticking his tongue into her mouth. But when he closed his eyes to heighten the fun, he felt that he was embracing tweed. He opened them and saw that what he held in his arms was a middle aged woman dressed in a mannish suit and wearing hornrimmed glasses" [pp. 31–32]. Balso's orgasm at the end of the book, while dreaming of having sexual intercourse with Miss McGeeney (changed again, "alas! but with much of the old Mary left, particularly about the eyes," p. 57), enacts not only the completion of his own desire but also the wish fulfillment of John Gilson's schoolboy dream of sleeping with her. Dreams figure in all the novels except *A Cool Million*—where the dream is conceived of as a nationwide and patriotic preoccupation with the getting and keeping of money. Critics have made much of the Freudian and Surrealistic impulse in West's frequent resort to dreams, and rightly so; but their significance for West is not restricted to the psychological and aesthetic. In their reflection of a volatile universe, they also have a strong metaphysical import.

Another instance of West's preoccupation with the metamorphosis of things is the recurrence in his novels of performers and of the blurring of distinction between performer and spectator. In one way or another almost all his characters pursue an occupation, usually as writer or actor or painter, which transforms one kind of reality into another kind. The poet Balso discovers to his dismay that the wooden horse "was inhabited solely by writers in search of an audience" [p. 37]. Instead of writing he finds himself involuntarily reading the work of others. *Miss Lonelyhearts* is a story about a nameless man writing the daily "agony column" for a newspaper, answering letters, written under pseudonyms by the afflicted, for the entertainment of the majority of its readers. Here columnist and correspondent blur together in their dual categories of writer and reader. Even Lemuel Pitkin ends as a human prop at the Bijou Theater, dismantled nightly of his toupee, false teeth, glass eye, and wooden leg by the comedy team of Riley and Robbins. The complete symbiosis of performer and spectator occurs in *The Day of the Locust,* when the surrealistic actions of the mob become confused in Tod's mind with his painting of "The Burning of Los Angeles," which depicts such a mob savagely chasing the objects of their adulation. Here participant and observer (not to mention the actual and the fanciful) fuse indistinguishably into a macabre dance of death, celebrating the impermanance of all things.

The despair implicit in this obsession with change cannot be exaggerated. West's Jeremiahlike search for permanent values was forever overturning proof of the transiency of things. "West's brilliance" as a novelist, Comerchero observes, "proceeds with his ability to generalize frustration" [p. 163]. West's vision of frustration stems from his metaphysical sense of the helplessness of man trapped in an unstable universe.

"If I could be Hamlet, or even a clown with a breaking heart 'neath this jester's motley," the writer of The Pamphlet exclaims, "the role [of being man] would be tolerable. But I must always find it necessary to burlesque the mystery of feeling at its source; I must laugh at myself, and if the laugh is 'bitter,' I must laugh at the laugh" [p. 27]. These lines are often quoted as expressive of the strenuous effort of West to dissociate himself from the horrors of his age. In his novels he tried to realize distance by treating his fictional characters with extreme objectivity. But the cold malice with which he analyzes their faults, like the excessive scatology or sexual and bodily nausea found in all his writing, reveals the radical nature of his revulsion, and the extremity of his reaction, to the frustrated aspirations of his protagonists—which were also (with the exception of homosexuality) his own frustrations. The Westian man is an early species on the evolutionary scale of *genus victima.* Like the Neanderthal man, as compared to present-day *Homo sapiens,* he excites our morbid interest and disgust more than our sympathy or love. West's involvement with him is that of the prophet. He has the reformer's instinct. He wishes reality to be different from what it is and people from what they are. He hates what will not heed his jeremiads, unlike a Malamud or a Bellow, who can love their fictional *schlemiels* without feeling a strong urge to reform them. In this fact lies one of the fundamental differences between the idealistic naïveté of West and his generation and the radical sophistication of the Jewish-American writers of the fifties and sixties.

Strong overtones of antifascism and anticapitalism characterize West's novels as sincere expressions of their time. As Josephine Herbst remembers him, "The horror of this age was in West's nerves, in his blood."[12] In his passionate search for something to believe in, West exhibits the desperate commitment of the thirties; but in his bitter sense of betrayal by ideas, he suffers the anguished disillusionment of the liberal of the thirties in the decades that followed. His need for detachment was intense; but the age and his background made that well nigh impossible for him to realize. At a time when most of his Jewish contemporaries were still writing realistically of the Jewish experience in America, West was attempting to define symbolistically the larger American experience. His vocabulary necessarily relied heavily on literary fashion. His vision of American life was inevitably narrow and limited. His insecure control of his material, despite his inventiveness and his expenditure of incredible labor on his stories, foredoomed the results to shakiness of form, uncertainty of tone, inconstancy and occasional vulgarity of language, and finickiness of output. His passionate involvement in ideas led to his quasi-identification with the search for values of his central characters. Unfortunately, such identification with his fictional creations also inhibited his judgment of their quest. His stories are more heated and polemical than is good for them. He too often lost what a later generation would call his cool. Yet in his exploration of the meaning of Hollywood and in his probe of the psychic blows suffered by being American, he courageously homesteaded forty acres on which Mailer, Bellow, Fiedler, and the other contemporary Jewish-American novelists are currently building a Levittown.

Notes

1. Cf. James F. Light, *Nathanael West: An Interpretative Study* (Evanston, Ill.: Northwestern University Press, 1961), pp. 151–152.

2. *The Dream Life of Balso Snell* (1931) in *The Complete Works of Nathanael West,* edited with an introduction by Alan Ross (New York: Farrar, Straus and Cudahy, 1957), p. 14. All references to this and the other novels—*Miss Lonelyhearts* (1933), *A Cool Million* (1934), and *The Day of the Locust* (1939)—cite this edition.

3. Victor Comerchero, *Nathanael West: The Ironic Prophet* (Syracuse, N.Y.: Syracuse University Press, 1964), p. 71. [Reprinted in part in this volume.]

4. Quoted by Richard B. Gehman in the introduction to *The Day of the Locust* (New York: New Directions, 1950), p. xv.

5. Cf. James F. Light, *Nathanael West* (Evanston, Ill.: Northwestern University Press, 1961), who considers the basic theme to be "the struggle between the spirit and the flesh" [p. 46]; Victor Comerchero, *Nathanael West* (Syracuse, N. Y.: Syracuse University Press, 1964), who defines its central theme to be "literary falseness versus the truth of reality" [p. 52], and its variants "the sexual origins of human behavior" [p. 64], and "the disparity between men's spiritual aspirations and their physical reality" [p. 70]; and V. L. Lokke, "A Side Glance at Medusa: Hollywood, the Literature Boys, and Nathanael West," *Southwest Review,* XLVI (1961), who reads the book as a denunciation of "the dreams of the creators of *avant-garde* art as well as the fantasy world of the middle-brow intellectuals who consume the product" [p. 36].

6. Robert Browning, *Fra Lippo Lippi,* 11. 266–269.

7. Victor Comerchero, *Nathanael West* (Syracuse, N. Y.: Syracuse University Press, 1964), p. 60.

8. Josephine Herbst, "Nathanael West," *Kenyon Review,* XXIII (1961), 611.

9. Victor Comerchero, *Nathanael West* (Syracuse, N. Y.: Syracuse University Press, 1964), pp. 95–102.

10. Stanley Edgar Hyman, *Nathanael West* (Minneapolis, Minn.: University of Minnesota Press, 1962), pp. 22–23.

11. Cf. James F. Light, *Nathanael West* (Evanston, Ill.: Northwestern University Press, 1961), p. 128.

12. Josephine Herbst, "Nathanael West," *Kenyon Review,* XXIII (1961), 611.

Approaches to the Novels

Irving Malin*

Nathanael West is an important American novelist. His four novels—*The Dream Life of Balso Snell; Miss Lonelyhearts; A Cool Million;* and *The Day of the Locust*—take up less than 450 pages in the one-volume edition published by Farrar, Straus in 1957; but they have already compelled many critics to study them seriously. There are three critical studies—*Nathanael West: An Interpretative Study* by James F. Light (1961); *Nathanael West: The Ironic Prophet* by Victor Comerchero (1964); *The Fiction of Nathanael West: No Redeemer, No Promised Land* by Randall Reid (1967)—a critical biography—*Nathanael West: The Art of His Life* by Jay Martin (1970)—and a pamphlet in the University of Minnesota series, *Nathanael West* by Stanley Edgar Hyman (1962). At least fifty articles have been devoted to his novels.

Although there has been so much written, no critical study attempts to read the novels in a chronological way, from the opening chapter to the end. We are offered discussions of sources—Dostoevsky, William James, the French symbolists, Freud—and although these are valuable comparativist studies— I am especially impressed by Randall Reid's work—they somehow overwhelm the novels and disrupt the reading experience.[1] They assume that the text is not the last word. I believe that this is a dangerous procedure. I concentrate, therefore, upon the explication of texts, perhaps giving them more attention (especially *A Cool Million*) than they deserve.

The novels are constructed tightly. *Miss Lonelyhearts* and *The Day of the Locust,* the best ones, demand that we explore intensively images, metaphors, and symbols because they are the heart of the matter. The symbols are as important, if not more important, than characterization and theme. They incarnate the latter elements. The novels are formal designs which create their powerful effects by the accumulation of significant recurring details. They are perfectly suited to explication.

I am interested in West because he is so ambivalent. Although he creates his art with great care, as I hope to demonstrate, he does not possess a closed mind. He gives us no final solutions. When we read the last sentence of any of his novels, we are not completely relieved of the tensions and ambivalences

*Reprinted, with permission, from Irving Malin, *Nathanael West's Novels* (Carbondale: Southern Illinois University Press, 1972): 1–10. Copyright © 1972 by Southern Illinois University Press.

preceding it. *Miss Lonelyhearts,* for example, concludes with: "They both rolled part of the way down the stairs." I underline "part of the way"—it symbolizes his refusal to write an easy conclusion, fixing guilt and offering rewards. Miss Lonelyhearts, Peter Doyle, and Betty are implicated in the violence—they share responsibility; they are all on the stairs. The novels reverberate with such ambiguities.

Some critics have tried to capture the sources of West's ambivalence. James F. Light claims that "the reason West's novels are involved in the Quest is his rejection of a heritage both familial and racial, that burdened West just as Joyce's heritage weighed on that great nay sayer."[2] He maintains that West is tormented by his Jewishness and his need to rebel against it. Surely Light is correct in a general way. We cannot read *The Dream Life of Balso Snell* or, for that matter, any of the other novels, without noticing the crude slurs directed toward Jewish merchants. Their names, manners, and clothing are ridiculed. But Light is simplistic in his sociological analysis. He links West, Salinger, Bellow on one page as raging for order. Although he admits that "the rage for order is hardly a Jewish monopoly," he, nevertheless, believes that he has found the key.[3]

Max F. Schulz is a better reader of Jewishness. He realizes that it lies in West's inability to "rest content in the human suspension between heavenly aspirations and earthly limitations, belief and skepticism, order and disorder. He portrays life in his novels as a conflict of inadequate imperatives offered to man by society and culture as guides to live by."[4] He views him as a religious writer seeking answers outside of the faith he knew as a child. I think that Schulz does not go far enough. He does not have the space—his chapter on West is followed by chapters on Malamud, Mailer, Salinger, et al.—to define the Jewish experience as more than "radical sophistication." He does not make much of the elements of exile, family life, head and heart, and transcendence in traditional Jewish experience.[5] He does not isolate the use of irony, parable, or dream by Jews in their art. Schulz is, however, on the right path.

The problem with reading the novels for their Jewish (or anti-Jewish?) themes and characterization is that they tend then to become sermons or texts for sermons. They are made to carry unnecessary burdens. Their careful, literary designs are partially neglected.

Several critics make them carry other burdens. They see West's ambivalence resulting from his sexual tensions. Comerchero suggests that "For West, sex was such a primary motivating force that it shaped, if it did not determine, most human behavior. At the same time, it was a force as inexplicable as any other one might choose, and also one which concretely dramatized forces beyond man's control."[6] He searches for and discovers castration, homosexuality, and Oedipal guilt in the novels (especially in *Miss Lonelyhearts*), citing many phallic details. Comerchero, following Stanley Edgar Hyman (whom he praises for his tidy reading),[7] becomes obsessive about Freudianism, and neglects to observe that psychosexual overtones are not the final clue to *Miss*

Lonelyhearts. He does not heed the advice that he offers in his opening chapter: "The vague uneasiness we feel when reading West is often due to our subliminal perception of this Freudian dimension."[8] Comerchero is so conscious of the perception that he kills it. The novels are, in the end, more than case histories. Randall Reid puts the matter concisely: "The homosexual interpretation is, then, so weak that it requires us to ignore many of [*Miss Lonelyhearts'*] details and invent others. It is also quite irrelevant to the novel's issues. Nothing in the diagnosis explains the fact of mass suffering or the reasons for Miss Lonelyhearts' response to that suffering or the ultimate failure of his mission."[9]

There is no doubt that we can read the novels psychologically, but we must remember West's own notes on *Miss Lonelyhearts:* "Psychology has nothing to do with reality nor should it be used as motivation. The novelist is no longer a psychologist. Psychology can become something much more important. The great body of case histories can be used in the way the ancient writers used their myths. Freud is your Bulfinch; you can not learn from him."[10] These notes are frequently quoted, but they remain tantalizingly obscure. West is as ambivalent toward Freud as he is toward the Jew. (He does not realize that Freudianism itself is largely Jewish in content and form.)[11] I interpret his remarks to mean that novels should take psychology for granted—it is an axiom, a given myth which is not the answer but merely the beginning. He goes beyond psychology. He refuses to give us the childhoods of Lemuel Pitkin, Balso Snell, Tod Hackett, and Miss Lonelyhearts. His heroes may remember a few incidents from their pasts, but they never stop to analyze their parents or their traumas. They exist in a kind of vacuum; their present condition is all that matters—and this condition has as much to do with religious transcendence as violent sex.

It is, of course, interesting to compare the reactions of West's heroes (much more interesting than to relate these reactions to the writer himself), but we should be tentative. I believe that narcissism is closer to the missing source of their reactions than homosexuality, castration etc.; it predates the latter. The heroes are fascinated with their bodies in such a way that they cannot cope with reality. They keep thinking about holes, wounds, deformities, and even beauties. Their bodies become totemic, holding secret and mysterious power. Their narcissism is strikingly ambiguous. They are in love-and-hate with their physical being; they would like to surrender it or, to use West's word, "dismantle it," but they cannot let go. Thus they are caught in a vicious cycle. They hate what they need to live with. This psychological phenomenon is the novelistic axiom.

West stops here. He does not inform us where the narcissism began; he omits parental training, childhood rituals of excretion, Oedipal romance. He destroys the past. At the same time he makes his heroes act strangely toward other people. Women are usually maternal (see Betty and Fay in *Miss Lonelyhearts*; Mrs. Pitkin in *A Cool Million;* or Miss McGeeney in one of her transformations in *The Dream Life of Balso Snell*) or destructive creatures (see

Faye Greener in *The Day of the Locust*). Men are threatening authorities (Shrike in *Miss Lonelyhearts,* the various guides in *The Dream Life of Balso Snell,* and the police and judges in *A Cool Million*). The heroes are out of place in the adult world. Wherever they turn for comfort and instruction, they find danger. It is no wonder that they retreat into their beds (or shells or enclosures), preferring to play mentally with their own bodies. Perhaps this is the secret of the novels' endings. A wet dream (*Balso Snell*); a shooting and falling down the stairs (*Miss Lonelyhearts*); a final dismantling and martyrdom (*A Cool Million*); a hysterical laugh (*The Day of the Locust*)—these various endings rehearse the flight into sleep, dreams, the womb of self.

West's novels are childish. Although they are written with great authority, they lapse into silliness (*A Cool Million*) and exhibitionism (*The Dream Life of Balso Snell*). These lapses are often noted—what critic could neglect them?—but they are usually dismissed without analyzing their sources. I suggest that they are the clue to the shaping spirit behind all the novels. The novels deal with the fears (and rages) that an innocent child feels in the adult world; heroes vent their feelings in primitive ways—they have fits or tantrums when they discover that their bodies are mere objects to others. The fact that *The Dream Life of Balso Snell* is a closed dreamworld should alert us to this narcissistic quality.

Closed dreamworld! The phrase, once we think of it, applies to the underlying structure of all the novels. *Balso Snell* is a series of dreams-within-dreams, centering in the hero's unconscious desires for sexual fulfillment. Despite the many episodes, it returns to the adolescent wet dream as the source of the preceding art. *Miss Lonelyhearts* has many more realistic characters than the first novel, but they seem to be extreme projections of the hero; they are aspects of his tormented personality. It is impossible at times to separate Miss Lonelyhearts from Shrike or Peter Doyle. There is a dreamlike quality because events and characters are melodramatic, stylized, and self-serving. *A Cool Million* describes the American dream (the freedom to gain success), but behind this dream lies the same narcissistic desires and attitudes we have seen. Mr. Whipple, Jake Raven, Wu Fong, and Lemuel Pitkin are drawn in heavy strokes as a child would portray them. *The Day of the Locust* is set in the closed dreamworld of Hollywood. Here childish feelings are given professional status because they are the creative forces behind our movies. The novel opens with an army marching with "the jangle of iron"; the entire scene emphasizes the unreal, primitive nature.

West's novels are "on the edge." They begin with quest (or, better yet, wish-fulfillment) and end with nightmarish failure. Balso Snell dreams of completion as an artist (and man); Miss Lonelyhearts wants to save the world; Lemuel Pitkin, on a lower level of aspiration, travels extensively to find money for his mother's house; and Tod Hackett hopes to paint "The Burning of Los Angeles." These heroes are defeated. They are overwhelmed by dark violence (bred of frustration). West is shrewd enough to underline the dreams of his heroes by writing dreams-within-the-basic-dream. His novels are full of dreams—to the point that it becomes difficult to separate or define clearly the waking state. By emphasizing dreams, he compels us to realize that rationalism, sanity, and daylight thinking are less important (and creative) than the irrational dreams we share.

I believe that West writes about compulsive designs. His heroes try to plot their lives to reach the goals they have set for themselves, but they act obsessively. The do not see much of reality—only those aspects which fit or mirror their needs. Is there any difference betweeen Miss Lonelyhearts and Ahab or John Marcher in "The Beast in the Jungle"? These three heroes— not to mention a Thomas Sutpen or William Wilson—are similar because they refuse to acknowledge the demands of others. They cannot be fully human (or grown up) insisting as they do upon their self-centered dreams of glory. West's novels are very American in their portrayal of these designs.

They resemble the romances described by Richard Chase.[12] They shy away from the full-bodied, substantial materials used by George Eliot or Jane Austen. They are flat, stylized, and nocturnal. Their very strength lies in such qualities. They refuse to accept the world as it is; they rage against it as they cry for more—for more wisdom and goodness. They want to believe in the values of everyday life—as the English novel does—but they know that such values cannot exist with certainty in a world of illusion, deception, and violence. The oddity, the narrowness, the intensity—aren't these, finally, the only clear method to capture the American experience?

West is often praised by our contemporary writers. I am thinking especially of Flannery O'Connor and John Hawkes. Hawkes's essay, "Flannery O'Connor's Devil," is an important document not only for its shrewd analysis of Miss O'Connor but for its comparison of her novels with those of West.[13] It establishes the bonds between West and new American Gothic represented by her and Hawkes himself (and Purdy).[14]

Hawkes makes several significant points: "I would propose that West and Flannery O'Connor are very nearly alone today in their employment of the devil's voice as vehicle for their satire or for what we may call their true (or accurate) vision of our godless actuality."[15] He believes that although the sources of their aesthetic authority are different, both writers demolish man's pretensions to rationality. They refuse to compromise with their respective faiths (Miss O'Connor as orthodox believer; West as atheist); they attack the prevailing softness of our culture. Hawkes affirms their devilish power; he suggests that they are half in love with the violence and immortality they portray. They are curiously ambivalent.

Hawkes makes one more point. He underlines the comic vision of both writers—this vision violates "anticipated, familiar reality" and creates a new, strange, independent reality which is, ironically, for him a more valid one. He insists, therefore, on their literary designs.

The essay must be read by anyone interested in contemporary American fiction. It tells us that West's influence is great because his novels represent a tense, artistic attempt to redeem our culture (and personalities) through extreme patterns. These patterns, as I have maintained, must be viewed in literary terms. They go beyond Freudian reductionism (although they begin with narcissistic axioms) because they are shaped by West's consciously symbolist imagination.

I find in rereading my first chapter of *New American Gothic* that almost everything I say there can apply to West. I refer specifically to my comments on the dreamlike nature of Gothic. West employs many opposing symbols—the house and the voyage (or "field-trip"—to use his word); the actor and the spectator; the real and the unreal, et al. These couples establish the frame of reference for his narcissistic heroes. Because Miss Lonelyhearts or Tod Hackett cannot solve his religious-psychological problems (who can?), he tends to have double vision. He is unable to see reality clearly; he tends to view it as a set of ambivalent forces. The objects which surround him (aside from his body) become terrifying. Thus Miss Lonelyhearts cannot merely accept his room and forget about it. It gets out of control; it suddenly becomes imbued with all sorts of meaning (enclosure, womb, tomb), and these meanings shake him because he cannot take a stand. He cannot commit himself to one meaning. His ambivalence, of course, is much greater when he has to cope with various metaphysical symbols. Christ disturbs him more than his room, but the two externals share this perplexing quality.

Rooms: the "horse" in *The Dream Life of Balso Snell;* the newspaper office in *Miss Lonelyhearts;* the interior decoration in *A Cool Million;* the frame-devices in *The Day of the Locust.* These basic rooms are echoed in so many other symbolic structures that West almost gives us the "other voices, other rooms" of Capote. The important thing is that they are all haunted. Balso feels trapped (as he is in his own body), and he cannot get out. When he journeys forth, he is destroyed by violent, frenetic movement.

Voyage: all the novels are built on a journey as the epigraph to *The Dream Life of Balso Snell* would lead us to believe: "After all, my dear fellow, life, Anaxagoras has said, is a journey." But the journey is "to the end of night" because the heroes do not move steadily. Their "pilgrim's progress" is interfered with by repetitions, coincidences, and crowds. Any page of West's novels stresses such unbalanced movement. I need only cite the army "jumbled together in bobbing disorder" at the beginning of *The Day of the Locust* to point the way.

I have compulsively stressed unclear vision of the heroes (not of West who sees clearly and independently). This vision also functions symbolically. Balso perceives "strange foreshortenings" (he is describing the girl cripples) throughout his adventures; Miss Lonelyhearts stares at the crucifix and "it becomes a bright fly"; Lemuel Pitkin has a glass eye; and Tod is a painter who uses fantastic, deformed models to get at reality. The novels are visionary, but like those of new American Gothic, they propose that epiphanies are duplicitous, warped, and somehow unbelievable.

I have mentioned three recurring symbols—there are, of course, many more examples which I will note in my explications—to imply that West is the spiritual father (or brother) of the writers I have discussed in *New American Gothic.* He is important not only as an independent figure but as a traditional, inspirational guide to younger writers.

Now that I have perhaps belabored these various comparisons, I propose to turn directly to West's novels. They stand alone, finally, as powerful, complex works of art.

Notes

1. Cf. Randall Reid, *The Fiction of Nathanael West: No Redeemer, No Promised Land* (Chicago: University of Chicago Press, 1967), pp. 50–60 for a valuable study of the borrowings from Dostoevsky in *Miss Lonelyhearts.* Mr. Reid never relates West to such classic American writers as Poe, Hawthorne, and Henry James. I hint at this connection later in the chapter.

2. James F. Light, *Nathanael West: An Interpretative Study* (Evanston, Ill.: Northwestern University Press, 1961), p. 136. Light could have noted that rebellion against one's heritage partially explains the fiction of Hawthorne, Twain, and Faulkner.

3. Ibid, p. 138. Light does not pursue the great differences between these writers. Certainly Salinger's acceptance (?) of Zen should be contrasted to West's faithlessness and Bellow's hard-earned humanism.

4. Max F. Schulz, *Radical Sophistication: Studies in Contemporary Jewish-American Novelists* (Athens: Ohio University Press, 1969), p. 36. [Reprinted in part in this volume.]

5. Cf. my *Jews and Americans* (Carbondale: Southern Illinois University Press, 1965) for an exploration of traditional themes and literary devices in the work of Bellow, Malamud, Philip Roth, Isaac Rosenfeld, Karl Shapiro, Delmore Schwartz, and Leslie Fiedler.

6. Victor Comerchero, *Nathanael West: The Ironic Prophet* (Syracuse: Syracuse University Press, 1964), p. 163. [Reprinted in part in this volume.]

7. Cf. Stanley Edgar Hyman, *Nathanael West* (Minneapolis: University of Minnesota Press, 1962), pp. 22–24 for a controversial reading of *Miss Lonelyhearts* as a "homosexual novel." Hyman tries to write the "hero's case history before the novel begins"; he offers no real justification for his description of the classic Oedipus complex. His reading, nevertheless, challenges all later critics of West.

8. Comerchero, *Nathanael West: The Ironic Prophet*, p. 3. Even in this paragraph he insists that West "reminds us that our behavior is rooted in sexuality." Cf. the definitive biography by Jay Martin, *Nathanael West: The Art of His Life* (New York: Farrar, Straus and Giroux, 1970) et passim for interesting biographical details about West's sexual attitudes and problems. I stress that these details never completely help us to read the final texts.

9. Reid, *Fiction of Nathanael West*, p. 77.

10. Nathanael West, "Some Notes on Miss Lonelyhearts," *Contempo* 3, May 15, 1933, 2. [Reprinted in this volume.]

11. Cf. David Bakan, *Sigmund Freud and the Jewish Mystical Tradition* (Princeton: D. Van Nostrand Company, 1958), for an intriguing analysis of the relationship between psychoanalysis and *kabbala.* He makes the point that Freud introduced such Jewish devices as secret wordplay and dream-interpretation into psychoanalysis.

12. Cf. Richard Chase, *The American Novel and its Tradition* (New York: Doubleday & Co., Anchor Books, 1957), p. 2, for this representative statement: "Oddity, distortion of

personality, dislocations of normal life, recklessness of behavior, malignancy of motive—these the English novel has included. Yet the profound poetry of disorder we find in the American novel is missing, with rare exceptions, from the English." West surely gives us the "poetry of disorder."

13. John Hawkes, "Flannery O'Connor's Devil," *Sewanee Review* 70 (Summer 1962), 395–407.

14. Cf. my *New American Gothic* (Carbondale: Southern Illinois University Press, 1962) for a complete discussion of Capote, Salinger, Carson McCullers, Purdy, Hawkes, and Flannery O'Connor.

15. Hawkes, "Flannery O'Connor's Devil," p. 406.

Nathanael West's Burlesque Comedy

Jay Martin*

Two of the greatest of all burlesque comedians, Joe Weber and Lew Fields, once wrote about their conception of humor. "An audience," they say, "will laugh loudest at these episodes:

(1) When a man sticks one finger into another man's eye.

(2) When a man sticks two fingers into another man's eyes.

(3) When a man chokes another man and shakes his head from side to side.

(4) When a man kicks another man.

(5) When a man bumps up suddenly against another man and knocks him off his feet.

(6) When a man steps on another man's foot."[1]

W. C. Fields entirely agreed: "I never saw anything funny that wasn't terrible."[2] However, comedy does not proceed from the infliction of pain. When Joe Fields invites Weber to sit down on a chair whereon he has placed a rubber tack, the audience screams with mirth; but a real tack would cause alarm. Let us suspend poor Weber above that tack for a bit, while we see why.

Nathanael West, certainly, was in accord with the Weber-Fields theory of comedy. Though in the context of later writing he has seemed to some to write "black" or surrealist comedy, on its own and in terms of his training in comedy, his work might better be understood as the result of his familiarity with the standard routines, acts, turns, "tabs" and "bits" of the burlesque stage. In some very clear ways he attempted to turn traditional burlesque materials into the very stuff and even the structure of fiction.

West was born during the golden age of burlesque; in 1904 more than forty shows were on the "wheel," or circuit. As early as his teens, West appears to have sought his education more often in the 125th Street burlesque theatres than in DeWitt Clinton High School; soon he was visiting the burlesque and vaudeville houses on the East Side, as far south as St. Marks Place and Houston Street. Very probably, however, until the mid twenties, he did not perceive

*Reprinted, with permission, from *Studies in American Jewish Literature* 2 (Spring 1976): 6–14.

that a connection could exist between serious writing and burlesque. Then, in *The Seven Lively Arts* (1924) Gilbert Seldes declared that the inestimable value of burlesque was "its complete lack of sentimentality in the treatment of emotion and . . . appearance," qualities which Seldes felt were lacking in most contemporary writing. Though scornful of the dull "legitimate" theatrical fare of the day, another prominent critic George Jean Nathan, praised burlesque for its "pure unadulterated and heartwarming old knock 'em down and 'drag 'em out' vitality." In an article appearing in the *New Republic* in 1925, Edmund Wilson spoke of the connection between vulgar buffoonery and "wistfulness and sadness" in burlesque.[4] These and other critics were all rebelling against American gentility, reticence and puritanism, and they liked the burlesque show, its vulgarity, its colorful language, and its frank obscenity. Critical opinion was paralleled by popular approbation in 1927 when the play titled *Burlesque* by George Manker Watters and Arthur Hopkins became a huge success.[5] At this time West was writing *The Dream Life of Balso Snell*, a novel that reveals West's deliberate effort to suffuse fiction with burlesque episodes and burlesque style. In 1931, the year that *Balso Snell* was published, and at about the same time that West was beginning *Miss Lonelyhearts*, he read Bernard Sobel's *Burleycue*, an "Underground History" of burlesque. Most of West's life after 1933 was spent in Hollywood and Los Angeles, where burlesque lasted longer than in any other part of the country, due to the fact that a great many burlesque comedians moved from the stage to motion pictures between 1915 and 1925.[6] West knew several of the old comics, he hung around the bars they frequented, and once, after he brought Melvin Levy to the Los Angeles Follies burlesque, he took Levy backstage to meet the comics, he explained the routines to him, and in "an accurate and scholarly" way he traced burlesque comedy back to Aristophanes. He acknowledged that he regarded himself as "a comic writer," but he complained to George Milburn that few people appreciated the "scheme" or "method" of the comic tradition in which he worked.[7]

From the point of view of physical comedy, the basic element of that tradition was the violence relied on so resolutely by hundreds of burlesque comics. From the point of view of mental comedy, the basic techniques of burlesque were parodic. One of the first great successes of the American burlesque stage was *The Geezer*, a Weber and Fields parody of *The Geisha*, a popular play.[8] Of course, American literary burlesque had a lively tradition, with roots in English parody and exponents like Mark Twain. There is plenty of slapstick comedy in West's novels and a lot of burlesque by-play. West's characters are continually clowning, even as they are struck down by an astonishing variety of implements, from a mallet to a mob. In *The Dream Life of Balso Snell*, Beagle Darwin exits with a "tearjerker" story and then he does a juggling act for an encore. Obviously, this novel is parodic: it is hardly anything else. Joyce, Proust, Dostoevsky, James Branch Cabell, Baudelaire, Huysmans, and numerous other writers are all parodied in Balso's dream.

West's book is well described by the title of one of Bret Harte's burlesque collections: *Condensed Novels*. When he begins by caricaturing Joyce in crying out, "O Beer! O Meyerbeer! O Bach! O Offenbach! Stand me now as ever in good stead," we know we are in for what the burlesque critic would call "the woiks." Again, in *Miss Lonelyhearts*, parodic technique is evident in the mockery of love-lorn columns, psychiatric sessions, and sexual dalliance. *A Cool Million* is hardly anything but slapstick, built upon the formula of Weber and Fields and the less subtle "Knockabout acts" or "Bone Breaking acts" of the Four Mortons, Collins and Hart, Caron and Herbert, and the Brutal Brothers. *A Cool Million* also ends with a description of an actual burlesque performance in which Lem plays the pathetic clown and is "completely demolished." *The Day of the Locust*, of course, includes a washed-up burlesque comedian as one of its leading characters; several other common burlesque types have walk-ons, or brief appearances. The novel even burlesques burlesque when a fake Indian speaks Jack Pearl's famous Baron Munchausen line: "Vas you dere, Sharley?"

In addition to employing slapstick and parody, West drew upon burlesque conventions for characters, situations and patterns. He portrays such familiar characters as the dumb blonde chased by many men (Faye Greener); the rural rube or "jay" (Homer Simpson); the "mis-speaker"—such as the Chinaman who speaks Italian (Wu Fong) or the Indian who speaks Yiddish (Israel Satinpenny); the wiseacre child (Adore Loomis); the deadpan comic (Shrike); the stooge (Lem); the dwarf (Abe Kusich), the cowboy (Earle Shoop), and the female impersonator (Miss Lonelyhearts). Each of these characterizations had been the basis for one or more famous burlesque acts, such as those by Lydia Thompson and the English Blondes, Anita Pines ("Dumb Dora"), Chic Sales, Rube Dickinson, Ben Welch, Harry Puck, Buster Keaton, Singer's midgets, Will Rogers, the Russell Brothers and Julian Eltinge. West consistently uses standard burlesque routines—such as parodies of oratory, outlandishly dressed characters, speed-ups, falls, sexual gestures and risque double entendre, nutty dialogues, bonebreaking sight acts, knockabouts, clowning and acrobatics.[9] He was especially attracted to representations of the absurd and seems to have paid particular attention to the techniques of illogic in what was usually called "nut acts," such as those practiced by Ed Wynn, Bert Fitzgibbon and Duffy and Sweeney. Joe Cook's baseball "bit" was a famous nut act:

> It was in the ninth inning. The score was tied—five to three—in favor of us. We needed six runs to win .... We have four men on base—two men on second, one a little guy the umpire couldn't see .... I says, "Bring me my bat." So Gerry and three other fellows bring my bat over for me. I used a telegraph pole ... in those days. I was very tall at one time but I have been out in the rain. [He hits the ball over the centerfield fence.] ....
> I started for first base ... the fans were cheering, bands playing, the King

and Queen throwing kisses to me. The railroads started running excursions into the park. The crowd started to throw money at me. I picked up over $9,000 on my way to first base alone and put it in an old steamer trunk I always carried on my back when I ran bases.

I light out for second base—third, fourth, fifth, sixth—this was a double-header we were playing—and just as I am sliding home the umpire, Daniel Boone . . . yells out "Foul Ball!" . . . I got off my bicycle and says: "Hey! where do you get off to call that a foul when I hit the ball to centerfield?" And he says, "Yes, but you hit the ball over the center fielder's head."

Of course, he had me there.[10]

Perhaps the nut act was the farthest range of vaudeville, and also the place where West *started* in his treatment of twentieth-century absurdities— not of baseball (though he did write one baseball burlesque), but of modern politics, economics, and social life. Despite the difference in material, West shared the basic conviction of the nut comic that everything was ridiculous. Clifton Fadiman once remarked that the "ethical effect of any Marx Brothers picture on the spectator is to awaken in him bitter doubts as to whether it is worthwhile not to be a fool."[11] Nut comics, from Joe Cook to the Marx Brothers to West, all agree on this fundamental point.

Finally, it seems clear that West learned a good deal about dramatic pacing and structure from burlesque. James Madison, a writer for the burlesque stage in the early part of the century, gave this accurate analysis: "Burlesque does not depend for success upon smoothly joined plot . . . . Since its purpose is to raise uproarious laughter, it does not take time to smooth the changes from one comedy to the next, but one bit follows another swiftly . . . . Finally the burlesque tab comes to an end quickly. It has made use of a plot merely for the purpose of stringing on comedy bits . . . ."[12] This also perfectly describes the general structure of all of West's novels, with their loose assemblage of turns. Both George Milburn and Edmund Wilson compared *The Day of the Locust* to film montage; but its form is far closer to the structure of the burlesque show: it begins and ends with ensembles (the film of the Battle of Waterloo and the movie premiere), between which are solos (Tod's meditation), duets (Tod and Faye, Tod and Homer), group scenes, slapstick, scenes of sexual joking and a risque episode, dancing, female impersonation, scenes involving props (the rubber horse, the backlot sets) and animals (the cock fight). The burlesque show was a melange of comic turns—often, it was called a "stew"—and its liveliness was only increased by its disjointed rapidity and astonishing variety. Clearly, West learned from the total structure of the burlesque show how to assemble his materials.

Like the burlesque show, West repudiated the assumption that experience can be presented under the guise of rationality: improvisation is the rule since experience is only provisional. Irving Kristol has said that the belief that absurdity is more true to experience than rationality is the essence of Jewish jokes.[13] And certainly, a considerable part of what I have been calling "Burlesque" consists of Jewish humor transferred to the burlesque wheel. This was a fairly late development. Not until the early 1900s did the flourishing American Yiddish theatre begin to provide comics for burlesque; though Frank Bush and Moore and Lessinger had performed Jewish acts in the 90s, even Weber and Fields appeared in blackface at the beginning of their careers. Then between West's birth and his twenty-first birthday, Jewish comedy became the leading force in burlesque humor. West certainly saw or heard about Fanny Brice, Barney Bernard and Alexander Carr (stars of *Potash* and *Perlmutter*), Bickle and Watson, the Welch brothers, Andy Rice, Lou Holtz, Julian Rose and numerous other Jewish comics. A great many explanations for the sudden efflorescence of Jewish comedy have been proposed. "There obviously must be something in the situation of the Jew . . . that results in the emergence of humor," Sig Altman writes.[14] In the context of a discussion of burlesque comedy and of West's fiction two reasons for the rise of Jewish humor are evident. In America between 1870 and 1885 various ethnic groups were placed in conflict, partly because no group would intentionally expose itself to another. As the only major non-Christian immigrant group, the Jews were especially mysterious and thus anxiety-producing to others. Humor "unmasked" the ethnic by revealing him fully to the "other." Second, the laughter produced by the release of anxiety in the process of unmasking helped to ease the tension of ethnic conflict. The audience experienced both an easing of suspicions and a release from their own insularity—and thus a birth of distancing self-irony. Humor, then, was a mode of cultural adjustment, a vehicle for survival. West adopted this repeated pattern of tension and release as a structural principle in each of his four novels. What is more, he used specifically Jewish materials in support of this pattern. He followed the tendency of Jewish burlesque comedians to concentrate their satire against the materialistic way of life. Like them he does not satirize Jewishness but the departure of some Jews from what it means to be Jewish, the replacement of Jewishness with empty materialism.[15] West's self-irony is *not* self-hatred. His Jewish characters are the Jews conventionalized by the burlesque stage. The famous wedding monologue written by Aaron Hoffman for Andy Rice is typical of the way that burlesque— and West—represents the undesirable Jew: "We had three detectives watch the presents—and my three brothers watched them! We had fine presents. Rosenbloom sent his card, the tailor his bill, Mrs. Bloom a fruit bowl, cut glass—cut from a dollar to ninety-eight cents! Stein the crockery man sent six little Steins—and *could they eat!*"[16] Sometimes the materialism has become so overpowering it has eaten into the brains: "Two Jews on a sinking ship. — Oi, the ship is sinking! —What are you crying for? Is it yours?"[17] But this is only one side of Jewish humor. Other jokes or characterizations demonstrate how hardship and the instinct for survival had produced cunning—and sometimes wisdom.

STRAIGHT MAN:	Mr. Cohen, what are you running for?
COHEN:	I'm trying to keep two fellow from fighting.
STRAIGHT MAN:	Who are the fellows?
COHEN:	An Irishman and me. Say, why don't you pay me for that suit? . . .
STRAIGHT MAN:	How much do you want?
COHEN:	I'd like enough to hire a lawyer to sue you for the balance.[18]

"Plunder is raging in the streets during the 1918 revolution. A middle-aged Jew is among the looters. 'For God's sake, Rubin, you too, looting?' 'Shhh, it's my own store.'[19]

"Mesritzer visits Pollack, who is sitting in his room naked, except for a top hat. Mesritzer: 'Why are you naked?' Pollack: 'Well, nobody comes here anyway.' 'But why the top hat?' 'Maybe somebody does come.' "[20] Such jokes as these cut both ways. According to Rabbi Nachman, "all joking is prohibited except jokes about idol worship." But Rabbi Baruch of Miedziborg says: "It is sinful to be sad." Jewish comedy repudiates the sin of melancholy, and so it must joke, but its humor is invariably directed against the idols of the tribe.

Comedy proceeds from the fearful to the funny by a natural process: and the process is one of healing. The power of comedy to effect cures is specifically evident in the Jewish burlesque—on the stage or in West's novels.

And today, it has begun to enter even psychotherapy. A glance at the practice of three psychotherapists who have been influenced by Jewish humor helps to illumine the deep structure and primary effect upon the auditor or reader of burlesque and West's burlesque fiction. These three psychiatrists have all dealt specifically with the connections between Jewishness, comedy, and mental health.

Freud acknowledged that *Jokes and their Relation to the Unconscious* (1905) was based on a collection of Jewish anecdotes he began collecting in the late 1890s. Arguing that jokes produced psychical and social pleasure as a result of their reliance upon associations as well as from the loosening of inhibitions— processes clearly observable in burlesque—Freud made a crucial distinction between jokes about Jews and Jewish jokes: the first, he says, are "brutal comic stories in which a joke is made unnecessary by the fact that Jews are regarded by foreigners as comic figures. The Jewish jokes which originate from Jews admit this too; but they know their real faults as well as the connection between them and their good qualities . . . ." Freud calls jokes "developed play,"[21] intelligible, coherent improvisation. This idea of comedy as play is especially important for an understanding of West's satire. The major butt of West's comic attack is vagrant wishing—wishing to be more beautiful, more excited, more loved—and play is just the opposite of wishing: play has a definite structure and a definable object, where wishing is loose, amorphous.

Thus, West's use of comic play is an integral part of his satiric mission in that it illustrates psychical coherence.

"Jokes grow best on the graves of old anxieties," Martin Grotjahn has written.[22] Grotjahn and Viktor Frankl have extended Freud's analysis of *Witz* by making comedy the center of therapeutic theory. Both attempt to laugh their patients out of neuroses by using comedy to aid in the growth of self-irony, to develop the powers of preconscious association, and to release aggressions. Comedy, they assume, is the most normal thing in the world, the best ground on which to stand, when the world seems crazy. Frankl calls his technique "paradoxical intention."[23] He encourages the patient to act out his symptom—to try for the moment to do what is most terrifying or embarrassing to him—to take the wind out of a phobia's sails. Here is one example: a thirty year old woman enters a psychotherapist's office and immediately states that she is going to die of a heart attack. The psychiatrist calls in her husband and requests that he hurry downtown to pick out a "nice coffin." Would the woman prefer a pink or green silk lining? Then he urges her: "Go ahead and try as hard as you can to die instantly of a heart attack." She tries, while doctor and husband roar with laughter, until she too joins in the mirth. The joke is the cure. In this kind of psychotherapy, the analyst himself becomes a comedian in order to heal. If need be he may even become the comic butt. When a worried patient strikes out against Grotjahn's argument that no business is worth the extraordinary devotion he gives to his and hisses: "Grotjahn, what would you do if I told you your mother is a whore?"—the doctor grins with relief and laughs: "I have suspected it all along!"

Laughter gives freedom and freedom increases laughter. No wonder that Nathanael West saw in burlesque comedy rich opportunities for the modern writer. No wonder that later Jewish writers, such as Delmore Schwartz in *Vaudeville for a Princess* and Sandra Hochman in *The Vaudeville Marriage*, have followed West's hints and applied burlesque to serious issues. No wonder, too, that the analysts have followed the novelist, and that for their model all have turned specifically to Jewish burlesque comedy, where paradoxical intention is most fully realized.

All this time Joe Weber's *derriere* has been descending toward that rubber tack and presumably you have been screaming with merriment because, as the comedians explain, the image of danger is present simultaneously with the knowledge that no pain will result, even to this sensitive area. The novel is like that rubber tack: all through his work West offers images of human pain and misery. But at last the pain is only an image: what endures is the way to take the pain, the comedy that flows from misery and defeat—burlesque comedy that hurts the heart but heals it in the end.

Notes

1. "Adventures in Human Nature," *The Associated Sunday Magazines*, June 23, 1912; quoted in Brett Page, *Writing for Vaudeville* (Springfield, Mass.: The Home Correspondence School, 1915), p. 103.
2. Quoted in Max Eastman, "There's the Humor of It"; clipping in Motion Picture Academy Library: "Comedy" file for 1930–1949.
3. Bernard Sobel, *Burleycue: An Underground History of Burlesque Days* (New York: Farrar and Rinehart, 1931), p. 134.
4. Seldes, Nathan and Wilson quoted in Sobel, *Burleycue*, pp. 219–20.
5. In Burns Mantle, ed., *The Best Plays of 1927–28* (New York: Dodd, Mead and Co., 1964), pp. 122–145.
6. Morton Eustis, in *Theatre Arts Monthly*, Sept. 1938, p. 675; clipping in Motion Picture Academy Library: "Comedy" file for 1930–49.
7. Letter to Geroge Milburn of April 6, 1939; quoted in my *Nathanael West: The Art of His Life* (New York: Farrar, Straus and Giroux, 1970), p. 335.
8. "Weber and Fields" file in Motion Picture Academy Library.
9. In particular see Douglas Gilbert, *American Vaudeville: Its Life and Times* (New York and London: Whittlesey House, 1940), especially pp. 263–65.
10. Gilbert, *American Vaudeville*, pp. 257–58.
11. Clifton Fadiman, "A New High in Low Comedy," *Stage*, Jan., 1936, p. 36.
12. Brett Page, *Writing for Vaudeville*, pp. 317–18.
13. Irving Kristol, "Is Jewish Humor Dead?", *Commentary*, Nov. 1951; quoted in Sig Altman, *The Comic Image of the Jew: Explorations of a Pop Culture Phenomenon* (Rutherford: Fairleigh Dickinson University Press, 1971), p. 18. See also Edith Menard, "Jewish Humorists of the 20s," *American Hebrew*, 156 (April 4, 1948), 32–78.
14. Altman, *Comic Image*, p. 18.
15. cf. Simon Halkin, *Modern Hebrew Literature* (New York: Schocken, 1950), p. 28 and *passim*.
16. Joe Laurie, Jr., *Vaudeville: From the Honky-Tonks to the Palace* (New York: Henry Holt and Co., 1953), p. 178.
17. Altman, *Comic Image*, p. 178.
18. Laurie, *Vaudeville*, pp. 454–55.
19. Altman, *Comic Image*, p. 166.
20. Altman, *Comic Image*, p. 167.
21. Sigmund Freud, *Jokes and their Relation to the Unconscious*, trans. by James Strachey (New York: W. W. Norton & Co., 1960), pp. 4, 118, 111, 179.
22. Grotjahn, "Jewish Jokes and their Relation to Masochism," in Werner M. Mendel, ed., *A Celebration of Laughter* (Los Angeles: Mara Books, 1970), pp. 135–44. See also Grotjahn, *Beyond Laughter* (New York: McGraw Hill, 1957).
23. Viktor E. Frankl, see *The Doctor and the Soul: From Psychotherapy to Logotherapy*, trans. Richard and Clara Winston (New York: Bantam Books, 1969), especially pp. 178–203. See also Arthur Burton, ed., *Modern Psychotherapeutic Practice: Innovations in Technique* (Palo Alto: Science and Behavior Books, 1965), pp. 361–79.

Nathanael West and *Seize the Day*

Gordon Bordewyk*

In *Love and Death in the American Novel* Leslie Fiedler inventories the legacy which Nathanael West has bestowed on subsequent practitioners of the art of fiction, and he singles out Saul Bellow as a legitimate heir of West's literary techniques: "The alientated *schlemiel*-heroes of Saul Bellow surely owe something to West's protagonists, whose anguish never quite overbalances their absurdity; and everywhere in the Jewish American novelists of the last two decades, West's influence is felt, if only as a temptation toward sheer terror rejected in favor of sentimentality or some abstract espousal of love."[1] Saul Bellow has never been accused of rejecting his literary patrimony, and his fiction is invariably loaded with direct references and veiled allusions to preceding generations of writers. For example, critics have pointed out that Bellow's fourth novel, *Seize the Day*, owes something to Shakespeare's seventy-third sonnet, Milton's "Lycidas," Keats's "Endymion," Miller's *Death of a Salesman*, and Perls, Hefferline and Goodman's *Gestalt Therapy*.[2] But the novel is also profoundly indebted to Nathanael West's *Miss Lonelyhearts* and *The Day of the Locust*, a fact which critics—Fiedler is an exception—have generally overlooked.

As readers, we can certainly enjoy *Seize the Day*—or any other Bellow novel, for that matter—without recognizing its kinship to earlier literature, because it does not depend on allusions for its success. But our understanding of the work is increased when we observe not only the breadth of Bellow's vision which is obvious on the surface, but also the depth of his literary resources. In *A Rhetoric of Irony* Wayne Booth notes that "as in reading metaphor, reconstruction of allusions adds to rather than subtracts from the surface meaning."[3] The verbal echoes of Nathanael West in *Seize the Day* are too significant to be ignored, and they offer another perspective and add another layer to this remarkable novel.

Nathanael West creates an imperfect universe in which the greater part of the population is deformed—intellectually, physically or morally. In *Miss Lonelyhearts* the grotesque characters cry out for help because of their physical and spiritual agony. Sick-of-it-all, Desperate, Harold S., Broken-Hearted,

*Reprinted with permission of Swets & Zeitlinger B.V. English Studies; A Journal of English Language and Literature Volume Sixty-four, pages 153–159.

Broad Shoulders—these are the characters about whom Shrike says, " 'Pain, pain, pain, the dull, sordid, gnawing, chronic pain of heart and brain. The pain that only a great spiritual liniment can relieve. . . .' "[4] Despite the editor's attempts to trivialize the torture faced by these letter writers, Miss Lonelyhearts steadfastly refuses to mock their condition or minimize their pain. If there is any comedy in the plight of Miss Lonelyhearts' correspondents, it is the nihilistic joke of cosmic indifference. When Betty protests that he is foolish to empathize so closely with his readers, Miss Lonelyhearts explains how his conception of the advice column has come full circle:

> The job is a circulation stunt and the whole staff considers it a joke . . . He too considers the job a joke, but after several months at it, the joke begins to escape him. He sees that the majority of the letters are profoundly humble pleas for moral and spiritual advice, that they are inarticulate expressions of genuine suffering. He also discovers that his correspondents take him seriously. For the first time in his life, he is forced to examine the values by which he lives. This examination shows him that he is the victim of the joke and not its perpetrator.
> (p. 32)

Hypersensitive to the pain of his readers, Miss Lonelyhearts internalizes their agony, attempting to carry their psychic burdens.

Grotesque characters also populate the world of *Seize the Day*. Dr. Tamkin, the psychologist-turned-investor, recites the case-histories of some of his abnormal patients to Tommy Wilhelm who thinks: "If you were to believe Tamkin, most of the world was like this. Everybody in the hotel had a mental disorder, a secret history, a concealed disease . . . Everyone was like the faces on a playing card, upside down either way."[5] But Tamkin's patients—like the neurotic dentist who is a confirmed nudist with Samson-like scruples against having his hair cut—are too bizarre, idiosyncratic and implausible to provoke the kind of compassionate response engendered by the grotesques in *Miss Lonelyhearts*.

Tommy Wilhelm's condition, however, is more complex. Sarah Blacher Cohen points out that an "obvious comic trait of the Bellow hero is his excessive involvement with self . . . If he cannot find any recent injuries to wince at, he picks at healed psychic scars to open up old wounds."[6] Although Tommy Wilhelm is a narcissistic schlemiel who almost savors the slings and arrows of outrageous fortune, there is also a serious element in his pain. Wilhelm is a post–World War II everyman: an economic failure, a victim of the American dream, a man alienated from his father, his wife, his sons and his mistress. Despite his forty-four years, he has not found a satisfactory answer to the question of self-identity. Indeed, it is not difficult to imagine Wilhelm as a character who would seek help from an advice columnist. During a conversation with his father, Wilhelm "felt as though he were unable to recover something. Like a ball in the surf, washed beyond reach, his self-control was

going out. 'I expect *help!*' The words escaped him in a loud, wild, frantic cry
. . ." (p. 53). This self-conscious burden of pain resembles that which is endured
by Miss Lonelyhearts' correspondents, like Sick-of-it-all who writes: "*I cry all
the time it hurts so much and I dont know what to do*" (p. 2).

Tommy Wilhelm and Miss Lonelyhearts both experience psychic trauma;
both are victims. And both are narcissistic although the factors which prompt
their introspective suffering are different. The universe has not been benevolent
to Tommy and he carries his burden of misfortune "like an accretion, a load,
a hump" on his back, an accumulation which threatens to crush him (p. 39).
Even Maurice Venice, that archetype of the unsuccessful talent scout, sees
Wilhelm as a natural for the role of a loser in the movies. Miss Lonelyhearts,
on the other hand, suffers the pain of inadequacy; he is acutely, desperately
aware of the world's suffering and is unable to atone for it. This causes him
to retreat into the self-flagellating pain of his own sensitive consciousness. It
would be a misleading oversimplification to claim that Wilhelm is just a self-
centered victim or that Miss Lonelyhearts is merely an altruistic, impotent
messiah. In fact, both are caught in an ambiguous tension between narcissism
and altruism.

In both novels the city is depicted as a chaotic, entropic environment
from which the main character, after witnessing the debilitating forces of
urban life, attempts to flee. Obsessed with order, Miss Lonelyhearts looks to
the city streets, "but there the chaos was multiple. Broken groups of people
hurried past, forming neither stars nor squares. The lamp-posts were badly
spaced and the flagging was of different sizes. Nor could he do anything with
the harsh clanging sound of street cars and the raw shouts of hucksters. No
repeated group of words would fit their rhythm and no scale could give them
meaning" (p. 11). Having seen the city as a repository for all the broken souls
who cannot endure what fate has dealt them, Miss Lonelyhearts follows Betty's
advice that he seek solace in the country. West's description of the holiday in
Connecticut is the most lyrical passage in the novel, and it seems that the
pastoral idyll may contribute to Miss Lonelyhearts' recuperation: "Betty
stopped with her arms high to listen to the bird. When it was quiet, she turned
towards him with a guilty laugh. He blew her a kiss. She caught it with a
gesture that was childishly sexual. He vaulted the porch rail and ran to kiss
her. As they went down, he smelled a mixture of sweat, soap and crushed
grass" (p. 38). The auditory suggestion of "crushed *glass*" in the final sentence
is a menacing hint that although nature may temporarily alleviate the symptoms, it cannot cure the disease. Indeed, Miss Lonelyhearts' crisis is exacerbated
when he, inevitably, returns to the city.

Tommy Wilhelm is also unable to withstand urban pressures; the chaotic
city often bewilders and upsets him. Because the city impinges on communica-
tion and interferes with restfulness, he longs for release from the city. He
misses his sales territory in the New England countryside, and he reminisces
about his ditch-digging days in the WPA. He tells his father: " 'I can't take

city life any more, and I miss the country. There's too much push here for me. It works me up too much. I take things too hard' " (p. 44). But Wilhelm cannot get very far: " 'Yesterday, late in the afternoon, my head was about to bust and I just had to have a little air, so I walked around the reservoir, and I sat down for a while in a playground. It rests me to watch the kids play potsy and skiprope' " (p. 44). Tommy Wilhelm is trapped in New York, his entire future resting on a last-ditch investment in rye and lard.

Pastoralism does not provide a solution, and both characters must confront the chaos of the city. As they come face to face with the city's horror, both have epiphanies in which they experience an ineffable, mystical love for their fellow men. Miss Lonelyhearts returns from Connecticut:

> When they reached the Bronx slums, Miss Lonelyhearts knew that Betty had failed to cure him and that he had been right when he had said that he could never forget the letters. He felt better, knowing this because he had begun to think himself a faker and a fool.
> Crowds of people moved through the street with a dream-like violence. As he looked at their broken hands and torn mouths he was overwhelmed by the desire to help them, and because this desire was sincere, he was happy despite the feeling of guilt which accompanied it. (pp. 38–39)

In a parallel scene, Tommy Wilhelm sits in the stock exchange, a microcosm which is emblematic of the city. Reflecting on the severity of urban alienation, he considers the possibility of order behind the chaos:

> The idea of this larger body had been planted in him a few days ago beneath Times Square, when he had gone downtown to pick up tickets for the baseball game on Saturday (a doubleheader at the Polo Grounds). He was going through an underground corridor, a place he had always hated and hated more than ever now. On the walls between the advertisements were words in chalk: "Sin No More," and "Do Not Eat the Pig," he had particularly noticed. And in the dark tunnel, in the haste, heat, and darkness which disfigure and make freaks and fragments of nose and eyes and teeth, all of a sudden, unsought, a general love for all these imperfect and lurid-looking people burst out in Wilhelm's breast. He loved them. One and all, he passionately loved them. They were his brothers and his sisters. He was imperfect and disfigured himself, but what difference did that make if he was united with them by this blaze of love? And as he walked he began to say, "Oh my brothers—my brothers and my sisters," blessing them all as well as himself. (pp. 84–5)

These epiphanies are nearly identical, and it is possible that Bellow was working directly from the text of *Miss Lonelyhearts*, when he was composing this scene. The parallels suggest that Tommy Wilhelm is not just a self-centered schlemiel; on the contrary, he is presented as a counterpart to Miss Lonelyhearts in his capacity to empathize with the crowd of disfigured people. Wilhelm's epiphany shows him as a potentially redemptive figure who has moved away from his earlier narcissism. But Wilhelm's character is not static and he does not linger on the rush of emotion he felt in the tunnel. In fact, as Sarah Blacher Cohen points out, he undercuts the experience with his crude explanation: "It was only another one of those subway things. Like having a hard-on at random" (p. 85).[7] After he depreciates the experience, his personal crisis is compounded, and it is not until the end of the novel that he recaptures this vision of himself as a redemptive lover of humanity.

In addition to creating these parallels to *Miss Lonelyhearts*, Saul Bellow also alludes to another work by Nathanael West. *The Day of the Locust*, West's last novel, is well-known for its depiction of Hollywood as a dream dump, of Southern California as a mecca for the displaced people of America: "All their lives they had slaved at some kind of dull, heavy labor, behind desks and counters, in the fields and at tedious machines of all sorts, saving their pennies and dreaming of the leisure that would be theirs when they had enough. Finally that day came. They could draw a weekly income of ten or fifteen dollars. Where else should they go but California, the land of sunshine and oranges?" (p. 177). Having arrived in the promised land, many of the pilgrims find that their dreams cannot be satisfied by sunshine and oranges, and they are hungry for novelty, eager for excitement, however artificial it may be: "When their stare was returned, their eyes filled with hatred. At this time Tod knew very little about them except that they had come to California to die" (p. 60). Bellow alludes to this vision of California when he describes Tommy Wilhelm's ill-fated pilgrimage to Hollywood: "Someone had said, and Wilhelm agreed with the saying, that in Los Angeles all the loose objects in the country were collected, as if America had been tilted and everything that wasn't tightly screwed down had slid into Southern California. He himself had been one of those loose objects" (pp. 14–15). Wilhelm's excursion to Los Angeles does not bring him stardom or success, and this initial failure becomes part of the pattern that characterizes his life after he returns to the East.

The parallel conclusions of *The Day of the Locust* and *Seize the Day* suggest that once again Bellow is borrowing from Nathanael West. At the end of West's novel, Tod Hackett has suffered from a number of psychic shocks. The whole nightmare quality of Los Angeles has overwhelmed him, and throughout the novel he has been forced to witness the spectacle of people engaging in aberrant behavior as an antidote to boredom. The fantasy and violence of the movie capital become West's metaphors for the hyperbolic surrealism of the "real world." As a mob waits for a premiere outside Kahn's Persian Palace Theatre, Homer Simpson goes berserk, stamping on the back of a young boy who has taunted him. This action jolts the crowd, transforming it into a huge, surging tide which sweeps Tod along. Grasping at the anchor of an iron railing, he mentally puts the finishing touches on "The Burning of Los Angeles," the apocalyptic painting he has been planning throughout the novel. Finally a policeman rescues Tod, offering him a ride home: "He was carried through the exit to the back street and lifted into a police car. The siren began to scream and at first he thought he was making the noise himself. He felt his lips with his hands. Thy were clamped tight. He knew then it was the siren. For some reason this made him laugh and he began to imitate the siren as loud as he could" (p. 185). The cathartic, primal scream is Tod's means of purging himself of the horrific situations he has witnessed. It is an ambiguous conclusion for the novel, raising the question of whether he has cracked up or gone totally, starkly sane. In either case, the elemental, emotional release of his scream is not only caused by his personal pain; rather, he stands apart from the mob, observing the fundamental sickness of society. Tod does not capitulate to violence. Instead, he has, for the moment, lost himself as he sees humanity's critical need for redemption. As a redemptive figure, Tod Hackett is inadequate; as a prophet, he sees that society needs to be saved from itself.

The conclusion of *Seize the Day* presents Tommy Wilhelm as the victim of severe emotional trauma. He has lost his final dollar in the commodities market; his father has refused to offer monetary assistance; his estranged wife has demanded that he send a support check. These financial crises are exacerbated by the alienation and betrayal they represent. Dr. Tamkin, the prophet of the here-and-now who was Wilhelm's mentor and "partner," has disappeared, leaving Wilhelm to bear the entire loss of their investment. Dr. Adler has withdrawn any semblance of paternal support, refusing to "carry" his son. Margaret is only concerned about her monthly checks and is unwilling to sympathize with Tommy's problems. Believing he has caught a glimpse of Dr. Tamkin on the sidewalk, Tommy tries to reach him but is trapped by the crowd and propelled into a funeral parlor. Similarly, a pivotal scene in *The Day of the Locust* occurs in a funeral chapel after Harry Greener's death. A small group of bored people who have never met Harry occupy the back rows, "hoping for a dramatic incident of some sort, hoping at least for one of the mourners to be led weeping hysterically from the chapel" (p. 127). Tod escapes from the mortuary when one of Harry's neighbors insists that the guests view the corpse. In *Seize the Day* Tommy is an uninvited guest but, afflicted with sorrow rather than boredom, he is not like the Los Angeles thrill-seekers.

At the end of *The Day of the Locust* a violent mob forces Tod to confront apocalypse; in *Seize the Day* a more peaceable crowd causes Tommy to come face to face with death. Wilhelm experiences a rush of emotion at the sight of the dead man, his initial fear giving way to sorrow which is mixed with admiration and envy: "A man—another human creature, was what first went through his thoughts, but other and different things were torn from him. What'll I do? I'm stripped and kicked out . . . Oh, Father, what do I ask of you? What'll I do about the kids—Tommy, Paul? My children. And Olive? My dear! Why, why, why—you must protect me against that devil who wants my life. If you want it, then kill me. Take, take it, take it from me" (p. 117). Like Tod's scream, Tommy Wilhelm's uncontrollable sobbing is cathartic. Attempting to purge himself of personal grief, Tommy cannot avoid mourning the condition of humanity. Although he is no Christ-figure, his thoughts— "you must protect me against that devil who wants my life. If you want it, then kill me. Take, take it, take it from me"—are a whisper of an allusion to Jesus' prayer in the garden of Gethsemane.

One of the funeral guests says that the dead man and Wilhelm cannot be brothers because they are as different as night and day. Tommy does not share the corpse's repose, but he is alive, and he must live in a social environment which extends beyond the narrow horizons of his own self-conscious misery. He has regained the sense of empathy for others which he experienced in his underground epiphany. Although he is not an adequate redeemer, he is more than a narcissistic schlemiel, and he has moved from the stage of "I want! I need!" to the stage of "They want. They need." This transformation marks the possibility of rebirth for Tommy Wilhelm who sinks "deeper than sorrow, through torn sobs and cries toward the consummation of his heart's ultimate need" (p. 118).

Philippe Soupalt claims that "Almost all American novelists, even if they do not admit it, adhere to the principle that we are born to be happy. Nathanael West has flatly rejected this principle."[8] So has Saul Bellow. The fundamental theme of Seize the Day is not that Tommy Wilhelm has failed to achieve happiness, although this certainly is true. Tommy has not, in that miserable life of his, found the measure of happiness which twentieth century America would regard as a norm. He has, however, by the conclusion of the novel, discovered something more significant. Through his sorrow, he senses that in order to be a human being he must transcend narcissistic self-pity and empathize with others, feeling their pain as well as his own. Bellow's allusions to Nathanael West in Seize the Day underscore this central theme.

Notes

1. *Love and Death in the American Novel*, rev. ed. (New York: Stein and Day, 1966), p. 490.

2. For example, see Keith Opdahl, *The Novels of Saul Bellow: An Introduction* (University Park: Pennsylvania State University Press, 1967); James C. Mathis, "The Theme of *Seize the Day*," *Critique*, 7, no. 3 (1965), 43–5; Donald Markos, "The Humanism of Saul Bellow," Ph.D. dissertation, University of Illinois, 1966; Leslie A. Fiedler, "Saul Bellow," *Prairie Schooner*, 31 (Summer 1957), 103–10.

3. *A Rhetoric of Irony* (Chicago: University of Chicago Press, 1974), p. 264, note 5.

4. *Miss Lonelyhearts & The Day of the Locust* (1962; rpt. New York: New Directions, 1969), p. 53. Subsequent references to the novels will be noted parenthetically.

5. *Seize the Day* (New York: Viking, 1956), p. 63. Subsequent references will be noted parenthetically.

6. Sarah Blacher Cohen, *Saul Bellow's Enigmatic Laughter* (Urbana: University of Illinois Press, 1974). pp. 7–8.

7. Cohen, p. 110.

8. "Introduction" to *Mademoiselle Coeur-Brise* (*Miss Lonelyhearts*), rpt. *Nathanael West: A Collection of Critical Essays*, ed. Jay Martin (Englewood Cliffs: Prentice-Hall, 1971), p. 113.

The Day of the Locust: An Apocalyptic Vision

GLORIA YOUNG*

In *The Day of the Locust* Nathanael West (born Nathan Weinstein) reveals an apocalyptic vision of impending twentieth-century Holocaust through his persona Tod Hackett, a painter who himself deteriorates throughout the novel. Allusions to Christian and Jewish apocalyptic works (Revelation to John, Daniel, Ezekial, Baruch, Enoch, Jeremiah, Esdras, and others); comparisons of Tod's on-going painting, "The Burning of Los Angeles," with the works of painters of madness, decay, and apocalypse (Goya, Rosa, Desiderio, Guardi, El Greco, Durer); and a setting in the grotesque and shadowy world of back-row Hollywood combine to provide a microcosmic background for the characters who have come to California to die, a background reminiscent of Sodom, Babylon, and Hell. The result is a novel whose vision is too black for satire, too bleak for hope.

Although Tod claims he is "an artist not a prophet," nevertheless, he refuses to "give up the role of Jeremiah." In "The Burning of Los Angeles" he paints himself into the picture, running wildly in the vanguard of the baseball-bat, torch-carrying horde, stopping to pick up a stone which he hurls at the approaching hysterical, crusading mob (West, pp. 65–66). Perhaps this novel is his prophetic stone thrown at the world in which he lived, a brilliantly accomplished revolutionary act.

In order to discuss *The Day of the Locust* as an apocalyptic vision, a background of apocalyptic literature is helpful. First, there is a distinction between apocalyptic and eschatological literature. Eschatology concerns the formal doctrine of last things: the end of time in terms of the destruction of the present world, the judgment of that world, and the salvation by God. Apocalypse (from the Greek word mean "unveiling" or "uncovering") is a revelation of the present as evil and of the end as both imminent and violent. The literature of Apocalypse, beginning with Daniel and Enoch and ending with the Revelation to John (written by John on the Isle of Patmos), has many elements, including "pagan imagery and even entire myths" which have entered into the literature of both Judaism and Christianity (Albright, 287–88).

The Old Testament prophets (Daniel, Joel, Zachariah, Isaiah, Ezekiel,

*Reprinted, with permission, from *Studies in American Jewish Literature* 5 (1986): 103–10.

and Jeremiah) and some books of the apocrypha are concerned "primarily if not exclusively with this life and this age of human history, rather than with the next life and the age to come" (Interpreter's Bible, XII, 347). Many of the visions of apocalypse do not include the coming of the messiah, the messianic reign, or the concept of the Anti-Christ. In all of the literature, however, by the time a given apocalypse "is revealed to the world it has reached the very depth of evil and corruption, and can become no worse" (XII, 348). The Book of Enoch (200–150 B. C.) describes the world as being completely and hopelessly evil: "For such a world there was no remedy, only destruction" ("Introduction," viii), and Abba Hillel Silver discusses the spiritual condition of the times during which the apocalyptic prophet Baruch was writing (a time contemporaneous with the writing of parts of the New Testament) as a time when "the crushed and beaten morale of the people [and] the danger of complete prostration" (103–4) made anarchy and chaos inevitable.

In the Old Testament, the apocalyptic visions never became dogma or theology but were simply "free expression of individuals allowing for a wide diversity of opinion" (Silver, 274); in the New Testament, the apocalypse became a firm creed, defined as the "eschatological belief that the power of evil (Satan), who is now in control of this temporal and hopelessly evil age of human history . . . is soon to be overcome and his evil rule ended by the direct intervention of God, who is the power of Good" (Interp. Bible, XII, 347).

In *The Day of the Locust* West utilizes the symbolic imagery of the New Testament within the context of Old Testament theology to reveal a corrupt world coming to a violent end, with no hope of salvation: a world with anti-christs but no Christ. Tod, playing Jeremiah, sees and paints this world. The title itself suggests Revelation 9:3,7: "Then from the smoke come locusts on the earth . . . like horses . . . their faces like human faces," and echoes the "dense swarm of locusts" Moses called forth to destroy the wickedness of Egypt (Exodus 10:14). The zeitgeist of the novel is that of a world rushing to destruction: a world of drugs, alcohol, cruelty, meaningless or perverted or vending-machine sex, violence, obscenity, insanity; a world peopled by characters who are deformed, corrupted, crippled, grotesque, autistic. Yet it is a world worthy of Tod's respect, since the "awful, anarchic power" of these deceived could "destroy civilization" (92).

In Revelation the opening of the first four Seals (closely paralleled in II Esdras) presents the Four Horsemen of the Apocalypse,[1] representing the woes to be visited upon mankind in judgment of his evil: the first, a white horse, whose rider "went out conquering and to conquer"; then, the red horse, whose rider with a great sword takes "peace from the earth, so that men should slay one another"; next, the black horse, whose rider "had a balance" to measure food in time of scarcity; and, finally, the pale horse, whose "rider's name was Death," followed by Hades who will "kill with sword and with famine and with pestilence." Traditionally, the white horse has represented invasion by warring enemies and / or anarchy; the red horse, war and / or civil war; the black horse, famine and / or pestilence; and the pale horse, death.

West's use of the symbols of Apocalypse is neither allegorical nor symbolic; rather, he uses images to parody, surrealistically, the Biblical prophecy of the doom to which the world is heading.

As the novel opens, setting as microcosm is immediately established along with the first allusion to horsemen: Tod hears the din of "a thousand hooves" and looks out his window to see a riot of fleeing English, Scotch, French, and German calvary, "jumbled together in bobbing disorder." Moving "like a mob," these Hollywood-set soldiers foreshadow the mob scenes to follow (p. 1). Setting as microcosm is reinforced as Tod goes home through streets bordered with a hodgepodge of Mexican, Samoan, Mediterranean, Egyptian, Japanese, Swiss, and Tudor cottages. These houses, built with plaster, lath and paper, "know no law" and, though comic, their horrible tastelessness is too sad for Tod to laugh at: the "truly monstrous" (p. 3) is beyond the limits of satire.

When Tod arrives at his apartment, he meets "Honest Abe Kusich," a sick, dishonest, dwarfed parody of Lincoln. Kusich gives Tod a tip on a horse race: "Tragopan" will be the winner, says Abe, perhaps foreshadowing the pandemic tragedy to come. Images of horses continue as a guest at the Estee's party tells Tod of the "millions starving" just prior to his finding the dead and bloated fake horse in the swimming pool, with its "enormous, distended belly" (p. 13), suggesting famine. The only character who might be expected to exert any control of horses is Earl, a drugstore cowboy who works, occasionally, in horse operas. When Tod goes to the set of *The Battle of Waterloo*, he is passed by a platoon of "big men mounted on gigantic horses" (p. 79) and then is almost run over by an Arab charging by on a white stallion (p. 80). Tod tries to call to him, but if there were an answer, it is lost in the tumult. During the battle at Mont St. Jean (St. John of Revelation), the hill itself collapses and everything becomes a rout.

Tod tries to follow Faye, who is playing a "Napoleonic vivandière" in "Waterloo," but he finds himself lost in a surreal, microcosmic world with an artificial desert, a canvas ocean liner with real life boats, a paper mache sphinx, a Western street with the "Last Chance Saloon," and a jungle compound. He goes through a fake door and comes out on a Paris street, bounded by a Roman courtyard where people are eating cardboard food before a cellophane waterfall (79–80).

In Revelation the opening of the fifth seal unveils the mob slain under the altar, perhaps parodied by Mr. Kahn's Pleasure Dome (129) where Homer is ultimately slain by the mob. The sixth seal reveals earthquakes and darkness, for "the great day of wrath has come, and who can stand before it?" (Rev. 6:17). (In II Baruch [6:4–8] this seal is accompanied by the firing of the city of Jerusalem.) The seventh seal[2] provides a prelude to a second series of woes, introduced by seven trumpets: woes of fire, blood, volcanic eruptions, waters of wormwood and gall, darkness, and demonic locusts with faces of people.

In the novel West continues to pervert—to turn upside down—words and symbols of religious apocalyptic imagery. He shows us a world without salvation, led by Mr. Know-All Pierce-All," the raw-food faddist (89); the "Church of Christ, Physical," where holiness is attained by weight-lifting; the "Church Invisible," where fortune-telling helps people find lost objects; the "Tabernacle of the Third Coming," where a woman impersonating a man preaches against salt; and the "Temple Moderne," where communicants learn the secret of Aztec brain-breathing. The message by an illiterate drifter whose "messianic rage" when he tells of having seen the "Tiger of Wrath and the Jackal of Lust" leads the gatherers to sing lustily "Onward Christian Soldiers" (92–3).

Harry Greener performs his own macabre dance of death, accompanied by his disintegrating laugh, which begins with an inorganic sound like the burning of sticks, progresses to the organic bark of an animal, and culminates in a mechanical, machine-like screech (42). Harry is buried to the solemn strains of Bach's "Now come, O our Saviour." The congregation's asking Christ to come changes from polite diffidence to impatience and "even a hint of a threat," since "the world had already been waiting for its lover more than seventeen hundred years" (78). In the meantime, the god Eros lies face downward in a pile of junk (80), and Mary becomes "Marie," the heroine of a porno film, perversely "fondling the child" (18) or "Mary Dove," a prostitute who works in Mrs. Jenning's callhouse.

West shows us a world in which Faye, the nubile, artificial product of her artificial environment, is loved by Tod who knows that his desire for her is closer to a desire to murder than a desire for sex; in which Mrs. Johnson (allusion to St. John of Revelation) loves funerals; in which pestilence is venereal disease; and in which the bored and restless crowd wait for a plane to crash so they can watch the passengers being "consumed in a 'holocaust of flame'" (131). The vicarious hunger of the Los Angeleans (the angels) is satisfied by a daily diet of "lynchings, murder, sex crimes, explosions, wrecks, love nests, fires, miracles, revolutions, wars" (132). It is the world of the Lord of the Flies. Homer watches for the dove-plumed quail but sees only lizards, spiders, and flies; the quail he does see is trapped, beheaded, and eaten. Hemingway's totemic rituals of the bullfight and Faulkner's of the bear hunt have degenerated to the horror of the cockfight in which the red, with its cracked beak, broken wing, and severed leg, dies and is eaten by the winning cock, while the dwarf screams, "Take off that stinking cannibal!" and Tod passes the whiskey (107).

The child Adore, with "his buttocks writhing" and his voice carrying "a top-heavy load of sexual pain," sings "Mama doan wan' no gin, / Because gin do make her sin" (90), and the transvestite sings "Little man, you've had a busy day." Faye can only sing of a "reefer five feet long" (p. 113), and Mig, the fighting cock keeper and the trapper of quail, sings a plaintive ballad,

> Las palmeras lloran por tu ausencia,
> Las laguna se seco—ay!
> La cerca de alambre que estaba en
> El patio tambien se cayo!
> Pues mi madre las cuidaba, ay!
> Toditito se acabo—Ay!

which translated means:

> the palm trees weep for your absence,
> The lake has dried up—Alas!
> The wire fence that used to be
> in the patio also has fallen down!
> Then my mother used to take care of them—Alas!
> Every little thing is finished—Alas!

which presents a picture of a lost Eden where the caretaker has gone.

In the lurid light of riots which open, occur and reoccur, and close the novel, Tod paints his apocalyptic vision of "The Burning of Los Angeles." "He was going to show the city burning at high noon . . . and the people . . . would be a holiday crowd" (65), writhing in a dance macabre, celebrating a black mardi gras as they wait to see the celebrities arrive at the Pleasure Dome. In Ingmar Bergman's *The Seventh Seal*, the artist paints a sea of faces in their Dance of Death, portraying Death dancing "off with all of them" (Bergman, 473). When Jons indicates that the horror of the picture is only the painter's view, the painter answers, "I'm only painting things as they are" (473).

Tod wants to paint as Alessandro Magnasco might have done, contrasting his figures in term of "their drained-out feeble bodies" with their "wild, disordered minds." He would not satirize them "as Hogarth or Daumier might" have done; he would paint his savage torch-bearers, stone-hurlers, and bat-carriers "with respect" (92). Tod mentions Goya as a model, and one imagines a painting like Goya's *The Colossus* (The Panic) in which people, like frightened ants, flee a world gone mad, a world where irrationality reigns. Or, Tod thinks, he might follow Francesco Guardi's style, and the reader sees the twisted trees, broken men, and forsaken landscapes of Guardi. Tod also alludes to Monsu Desiderios, and one envisions a painting like *The Destruction of Sodom*, with everything falling apart. "Looking down the hill now, he [Tod] would see compositions that might have actually been arranged from the Calabrian work of Rosa: "There were partially demolished buildings and broken monuments, half hidden by great, tortured trees, whose exposed roots writhed dramatically in the arid ground, and by shrubs that carried, not flowers, but armories of spikes, hooks, and swords" (81).

As Tod imagines other painters' conceptions, relating them to his own work, the reader's imagination recalls other apocalyptic works: El Greco's painting, *St. John's Vision of the Apocalypse*, with its lopsided, ecoplastic figures; and Dürer's series of woodcuts on the apocalypse, of which *The Four Horsemen*, with its great, brutal horses trampling the scurrying, terrified people, is the most powerful.

In the surreal world of *The Day of the Locust*, there is not even a Miss Lonelyhearts to serve as surrogate Saviour to Homer. Like one of Picasso's "great sterile athletes" (27) brooding hopelessly, Homer—compulsive, baby-talking, disassociated Homer, lusting with "only parts" of himself (47), crying "Momo" just before curling into his "Uterine flight" (124)—is doomed. His flight into autism cannot save him.

The crowd gathering before Mr. Kahn's Pleasure Dome, waiting for celebrities to arrive, becomes more and more lawless and violent.Tod knows that "at the sight of their heroes and heroines," it would "turn demoniac. Some little gesture . . . would start it moving and then nothing but machine guns would stop it" (130). It is Adore (love; adoration) who makes the gesture that sets it loose. Adore viciously teases and taunts Homer until Homer, maddened, stomps him to death; the mob then hysterically lynches Homer. Tod, witnessing Homer's death, is himself caught in the violent crowd, unable to reach Homer. Hurt and desperate, Tod can only ride the pace until he is finally slammed against an iron fence (138). Trying desperately to hang on, to avoid being swept back into the orgy of sex and violence, Tod closes his eyes and thinks of the "rough charcoal strokes" of his blocked out canvas: "Across the top, parallel with the frame, he had drawn the burning city, a great bonfire of architectural styles, ranging from Egyptian to Cape Cod colonial. Through the center . . . spilling into the middle foreground, came the mob. . . . In the lower foreground, men and women fled wildly before the vanguard of the crusading mob. . . . Faye ran proudly, and Tod himself picked up a small stone to throw before continuing his flight" (138).

The police arrive with sirens screaming. Tod begins to laugh and to "imitate the siren as loudly as he could" (140). The seventh seal, with its seven trumpets of woe, signaling chaos, is echoed as Tod is swept into madness. The book ends with his screaming, insane imitation of the siren.

West, casting Tod in the role of Jeremiah, wrote of the end. Jeremiah's own description of the end hauntingly reflects "The Day After" Nuclear Holocaust:

> I looked on the earth, and lo, it was waste and void;
>   and to the heavens, and they had no light.
> I looked on the mountains, and lo, they were quaking,
>   and all the hills moved to and fro.

> I looked, and lo, there was no man,
>   and all the birds of the air had fled.
> I looked, and lo, the fruitful land was a desert,
>   and all its cities were laid in ruins.

Paul Tillich in the title sermon of his book, *The Shaking of the Foundation*, uses this passage from Jeremiah to describe the existential condition of modern man. Tillich insists that the days are gone when we could listen to such words and not take them seriously. Although it is not easy to look into the chaos of possible destruction and although many men and nations "are compelled to escape, to turn away, to succeed in forgetting the end," nevertheless, he says, "we happen to live in a time when very few of us . . . will succeed in forgetting the end. For in these days the foundations of the earth *do* shake" (2–3).

St. John, after having envisioned the fall of the doomed city of Babylon that "in one hour . . . has been laid waste" (Rev. 18:19), also foresaw "a new heaven and a new earth" (21:1). West, in line with many Old Testament prophets, could only write of the destruction of the old. One thinks of Tod's comment about those waiting for the Saviour: "Perhaps Christ heard. If He did, He gave no sign" (78).

Notes

1. A classic film, *The Four Horsemen of the Apocalypse*, was made from Vincent Blasco Ibañez's novel of the same name.

2. Ingmar Bergman wrote an apocalyptic film called *The Seventh Seal*.

Works Cited

Albright, W. F. *From the Stone Age to Christianity*, quoted in *Where Judaism Differed*, by Abba Hillel Silver. New York: Macmillan, 1956.

Bergman, Ingmar. *The Seventh Seal*. In *Mirrors*. Ed. John Knott and Christopher Reaske. New York: Harper & Row, 1972.

The Book of Enoch. Translated R. H. Charles. London: S. P. C. I., 1976 (first published 1917). "Introduction" by W. O. E. Oesterley.

The Holy Bible. Revised Standard Version. New York: Thomas Nelson, 1953.

The Interpreter's Bible in XII vols. New York: Abingdon Press, 1957.

Silver, Abba Hillel. *Where Judaism Differed*. New York: Macmillan, 1956.

Tillich, Paul. *The Shaking of the Foundations*. New York: Scribner's, 1948.

West, Nathanael. *The Day of the Locust*. New York: Bantam, 1963.

The Art of Significant Disorder:
The Fiction of Nathanael West

JAN GORAK*

And of what consequence are the evils and the lunatic hours
And the vats of vice in which the city ferments
If some day, from the fog and the veils,
Arises a new Christ, in a sculptured light,
Who lifts humanity toward himself
And baptizes it by the fire of new stars?
                    —Emile Verhaeren, "L'âme de la ville"

The world is an oyster that but waits for hands to open it. Bare
hands are best, but have you any money?
                    —Shagpoke Whipple in *A Cool Million*

I

Nathanael West's ambitions reveal the fervor and the doubt of the godly
maker in a commercial world. Like Emile Verhaeren, he hopes to redeem the
secular city with the vision of a "new Christ" who "arises from the fog . . .
lifts humanity toward himself and baptizes it by the fire of new stars." Like
Shagpoke Whipple, he knows that any redeeming vision is likely to be the
means toward fresh expropriation conducted by grasping hands. Accordingly,
one of West's greatest fears—voiced repeatedly just before his death—was
that his work had been at best only half successful. Very late in his career, he
characterized his fiction as a "peculiar half world which I attempted to create,"
a description that reveals his diffidence about his procedure and final achievement. West thought that his fiction was unclassifiable, so that he completed
a book "only to find nowhere any just understanding of what the book is
about—I mean in the sense of tradition, place in scheme, method, etc., etc."[1]

*Copyright © 1987 by the Board of Trustees of the University of Illinois. Used with permission of the
University of Illinois Press. From Jan Gorak, *God the Artist: American Novelists in a Post-Realist Age* (Urbana:
University of Illinois Press, 1987): 37–45.

West need not have worried. Since his death the name West has come to mean whatever a commentator wants it to mean. This, at least, is the opinion of Maria Ujhazy, who alleges that "critics, with great effort, have managed to purge West's novels of their vital content, their critical realism, and have allegorized and interpreted them into kinship with the critics' own outlook."[2] Like his own Lemuel Pitkin, West has been dismantled and reconstituted according to the ideological persuasions of his commentators. Hence we have the Jungian West, the Freudian West, the Kierkegaardian West, and even Ujhazy's own critical-realist West.

Such critical strabysmus does West a double disservice, as this and the next chapter will argue. First, the picture that emerges of West is a grossly distorted one; instead of the living, breathing author we have the child of no natural parents described very wittily by Warwick Wadlington. "One influential critical portrait that has grown over the years is an intriguing Daumier creation: West as an exotic plant on our shores whose genus is really the Continental-Decadent-Existentialist family of literature."[3] The objection to this portrait lies not so much in the fact that it resembles no author yet sighted on sea or land—though that is certainly an important objection—but that it totally overlooks West's own uniqueness and ignores the conditions of the "peculiar half world" West attempted to create.

The nature of this half world is particularly interesting. West's drastically curtailed apprenticeship in Dada was followed by his prolonged eyewitness experience of the Great Depression at two of his father's New York hotels. His period as a Hollywood scriptwriter brought him into contact with a California that, as Edmund Wilson acknowledged, has always been a center for American class conflicts.[4] West's fiction consequently straddles categories that were increasingly investigated separately by his contemporaries. One of his signal achievements was to take the modernist cliché of the artist as hero, where the artist becomes "the higher example of and the only escape from the common predicament," and return him to the center of experience.[5] Max Schulz has pointed to the dual status of West's artists, as modernists in aspiration, but illusion makers by profession; out of that dualism West explored the limits and the potential of the artist as a godly maker in a commercial world.[6]

This achievement has not yet been given its due critical acknowledgment. Ever since James Light published his pioneering critical biography (*Nathanael West: An Interpretative Study*), West's critics have generally locked themselves inside their author's head.[7] Although Light was an incisive critic, the Jungian thrust of his interpretation had a disastrous effect on the course of West criticism. To watch Light's insights harden into Freudian orthodoxies, and then expire into Gnostic obscurity, one need only look at some of Light's successors. Stanley Hyman and Victor Comerchero, who prowl around the edges of West's fiction in search of a stray neurosis, still report on a recognizable author; but Harold Bloom, who finds in *Miss Lonelyhearts* "another displaced version of the Miltonic Romantic crisis-poem" with progenitors in Words-worth's *The Borderers* and Blake's *Milton*, clearly does not.[8]

But the most shameless—and the most brilliant—psychocritical reading of all belongs to W. H. Auden. Auden's famous essay "West's Disease" begins by pronouncing that West "is not, strictly speaking, a novelist; that is to say, he does not attempt an accurate description either of the social scene or of the subjective life of the mind." Confronted by the seemingly incontrovertible evidence that *Balso Snell* engages precisely with "the subjective life of the mind," Auden displays remarkable resourcefulness. The book, he argues, "adopted the dream convention, but neither the incidents nor the language are credible as a transcription of a real dream."[9] West's real gifts, Auden decides, belong not to fiction but to pathology; his fame rests on his authority in diagnosing the disease to which he gave his name. Just as he had rebuilt Dickens's Dingley Dell as the Garden of Eden, Auden refashions West's environment to suit the needs of his own parable.

Such criticism shrinks more than West's head; it shrinks the size of the fiction too. However, Leslie Fiedler's West promises much more. Fiedler sees West as a fictional innovator who becomes

> the inventor . . . of a peculiarly modern kind of book, whose claims on our credence are perfectly ambiguous. Reading his fiction, we do not know whether we are being presented with a nightmare endowed with the lineaments of reality, or with reality blurred to the uncertainty of a nightmare. In either case, he must be read as a comic novelist, and his anti-heroes understood as comic characters, still as much shlemiels as any imagined by Fuchs, though they are presented as sacrificial victims, the only Christs possible in our skeptical world. In West, however, humor is expressed almost entirely in terms of the grotesque, which is to say, on the borderline between jest and horror; for violence is to him technique as well as subject matter.[10]

Although anyone writing on West owes much to Fiedler, some murmurs of dissent are nonetheless in order. First of all, we might question the basis for Fiedler's rigid generic constraints. If we do not know what kind of world West is writing about, if we are uncertain whether it is nightmare or reality, how can we be so sure that "he must be read as a comic novelist"? Fiedler's generic certainties conceal a kind of scholastic disdain for the world in which his author operates. There is something Brahminical about Fiedler's approach to West; this critic enrolls his author in the ranks of genius without making clear the field in which that genius operates. It is all very well to call West "the inventor of a peculiarly modern kind of book," but under what peculiarly modern conditions does West make his innovations?

We are no nearer to an answer to this question after reading Jonathan Raban's essay "A Surfeit of Commodities: The Novels of Nathanael West."[11] Raban's West becomes a commodity to be exploited by all the flotsam of postindustrial society: graduate students, assistant professors, the *PMLA* index, and a host of others not too numerous for Raban to mention. From a sense that West merely looked into his troubled psyche and wrote, we move to the sense that he observed the monuments of trash around him, collated them in verbal form, and then buried himself and his words in them. Such responses are two sides of a common coin that devalue West's role as an artist whose disorder was significant in a way that more perfectly realized works perhaps were not.

At the heart of West's work lies his recognition of the changed relationship between the artist and his society. West's four books show the American economy moving from mass production to the production of illusion. His artists, however, cling to their goal of creating a world, even though the world they wish to create remains only an ideal memory in the America of the Great Depression. By the time West began to publish, the economic prosperity of the 1920s had vanished, leaving only the massive cultural and spiritual disillusionment that Miss Lonelyhearts diagnoses in Delehanty's speakeasy. As he drinks, West's hero reflects that he is one who, like his colleagues, "had believed in literature, had believed in Beauty and in personal expression as an absolute end." And, like them, he believes no longer, and now shares their disgust: "When they lost this belief, they lost everything. Money and fame meant nothing to them. They were not worldly men" (83). The role that they all play now requires them to become "machines for making jokes" (84).

The transformation of the artist from visionary deity to machine for making jokes rounds one crucial arc of West's imagination; the increasing disenchantment of an audience starved by an abundance of illusion completes the circle. West's peculiar half world is one where he becomes progressively more aware of the diminution of his powers and the growing aggression of his audience. Because of this his work reveals acutely—and very early—the kinds of strain that the idea of the artist as a godly maker will encounter in the kind of society where illusion is ubiquitous but unsatisfying. West's own peculiar kind of joking derives from his knowledge that what is happening all around him is hardly funny at all.

II

West's first novel, *The Dream Life of Balso Snell,* has generally been regarded as a nasty little squib, a juvenile *jeu d'esprit* that West somehow dragged out into his late twenties. Alan Ross, in his introduction to *The Complete Works of Nathanael West,* saw the book as "a sneer in the bathroom mirror at art," an assault that Randall Reid extended to an "attack on all art."[12] It has been usual to acknowledge that West's ambitions exceeded his capacities; Jay

Martin, who tactfully suggested that the book grasped "only tentatively" the themes of West's later fiction, shows—for a man dealing with a minor author—exemplary caution here.[13] On the other hand, all the existing evidence shows that West took much trouble with his books—and *Balso Snell* appears to have been no exception. Jack Sanford told James Light that most of the book was known to him as early as 1924, when West entertained him with an early version in a college dormitory.[14] Moreover, from 1927 to 1930, West revised the manuscript repeatedly, even making a very late change of title from *The Journal of Balso Snell* to *The Dream Life of Balso Snell.* The extended genesis of the book, its multiple revisions over a seven-year period, its tonal incongruities, and its strange oscillations between intensity and farce all point less to a jeu d'esprit than to a book (and an author) genuinely confused about its own identity.

Some hint of this confusion becomes apparent in the book's opening pages. We are introduced to West's first godly maker, Balso Snell, a lyric poet who has created a whole race of imaginary men. But Balso does not glory in his creation; he shudders at the thought of his *Phoenix Excrementi* because they "eat themselves, digest themselves, and give birth to themselves by evacuating their bowels" (5). Balso's dream life has a disturbingly visceral quality; the inspired man merges, as in *A Tale of a Tub,* with the flatulent man. Balso's imaginary men are as much the limits of his invention as the outcome of it; his shudder acknowledges the unwelcome duality that afflicts his imagination, his dual commitment to vision and profit.

Balso's authority as a godly maker is limited by the aspirations of his creation. As Balso tours his own interiors, he confronts truths he would rather not acknowledge: the contradictory impulses behind his own goals; the belatedness of his own imaginative life (so much a rescrambling of his own reading, so little the result of any genuine invention); the small margin that separates artistic self-assertion from simple violence. In the face of all this, the lyric poet and godly maker takes on the form of George F. Babbitt. "Stop sniffing mortality. . . . Eat more meat" (13), he tells Maloney the Areopagite, as the philistine stares down the martyr. West uses the dream journey and burlesque forms to explore the contradictory impulses in his own aesthetic and moral makeup. His own sense of the moral purpose of art (something West was never to overlook) can only emerge in Balso's leaden clichés; his own highly literary form of religious conviction has its bizarre reflection in the creation of Maloney and Gilson, a pair of dime-store martyrs. The journey begins as a structural device but gradually discovers an ethical purpose: through the journey West can make one side of his imagination talk to another, so that the angst-ridden young man can confront the dishonest commodity broker.

Balso's first guide hails him as "an ambassador from that ingenious people, the inventors and perfectors of the automatic water closet," a salutation that rams together Henry James's superior consciousness and Thomas Crapper's superior technology. Perhaps warming to these interdisciplinary fusions, Balso's guide now blends Hellenic classicism and Poe's romanticism in a somewhat aborted tribute to Balso's dual heritage as a child of Europe and the Americas, "My people are the heirs of Greece and Rome. As your own poet has so well put it, 'The Grandeur that was Greece and the Glory that was Rome'" (6).

Balso's mixed origins beget a mixed art. The book continually darts between high aspirations and low consequences, so that it blends farce and high symbolism in a fashion that troubles even its protagonists. Balso cannot be sure whether he is voyageur or tourist; wherever he goes he finds commerce ousting culture, as the commercialization of art steadily deteriorates into the corruption of art. In the *anus mirabilis* everyman is an artist. "The wooden horse," Balso realizes, "was inhabited solely by writers in search of an audience." Balso's reaction to this shows the competitive chain response this situation sets off. "He hit Miss McGeeney a terrific blow in the gut." If another story had to be told, "he would tell it" (36–37). Stripped of his special privileges, the American godly maker becomes a competitor amid a system of self-enhancing fictions; his task is to assert his authority, something he must do through violence rather than vision.

All art in *Balso Snell* tends to soliloquy in design, victimization in method, and mass circulation in distribution. Because artists must attract attention to survive, their means must become correspondingly elaborate. Maloney's flea, Gilson's precocity, Miss McGeeney's collapsible box of biographies—these are tertiary industries rather than contributions to the world of letters. But they are, as George Mowry's *The Urban Nation* shows us, an accurate reflection of American writing in the 1920s, which fed a public increasingly ravenous for life in the raw an endless diet of biography, or rehashed romanticism.[15] Gradually, West's book takes on the appearance of a novelization of "Tradition and the Individual Talent," with Balso hurled from specimen to specimen, each one a testimony to a half-digested art.

The artists in *Balso Snell* behave like spoiled suburban pets, biting the hands that uncomprehendingly feed them. Art is tranformed into anxiety as Gilson is attacked by "a fear so large that I felt I could not contain it without rupturing my mind" (21); Beagle Darwin wants to wrap his predicament round him, until he can snuggle into it, "letting it cover me completely"; Balso himself retreats into his less complicated youth, which in turn dissolves into his career-conscious present. Such art is always closer to hysteria than inspiration, the product of artists who can only becalm themselves by removal to the margins of experience. The case of John Gilson, an Olympian whose top-floor Schlegelian eyrie shelters a man just as remote from human sympathies, is typical here. Gilson's art insulates him from his own mother, whose grief he can then work up as material: "My mother visited me today. She cried. It is she who is crazy. Order is the test of sanity. Her emotions and thoughts are disordered. Mine are arranged, valued, placed" (14).

From a sardonic recycling of the works of other hands, the book turns to a recycling of its own structural devices, as if to confess that so massive a consumption of culture as that conducted in this novel inevitably accelerates the exhaustion of all resources but its own. Balso's journey through the *anus mirabilis* is reworked as Beagle's to Paris; Gilson's tyranny over his mother becomes Beagle's over Janey Davenport; Gilson's introversion becomes Darwin's lyrical drama; Balso's earlier recognition of the basically hostile relationship between artists and audiences (21–22) is reshaped into Gilson's Wildean parable, which in turn has been filched from Chekhov: "It would be more profitable [writes Chekhov] for the farmer to raise rats for the granary than for the bourgeois to nourish the artist, who must always be occupied with undermining institutions. In case the audience should misunderstand and align itself on the side of the artist, the ceiling of the theatre will be made to open and cover the occupants with tons of loose excrement. After the deluge, if they so desire, the patrons of my art can gather in the customary charming groups and discuss the play" (30). No wonder Balso Snell shudders; his *Phoenix Excrementi* are always on the point of returning to their original material. The parable that Beagle composes emphasizes once more the impotence of the artist; however heinous his devices, his patrons will "gather in the customary charming groups and discuss the play."

If art for a commercial audience becomes degraded art, what of the artist? The soliloquies of Gilson and Beagle Darwin reveal the nature of the artist's inner world. Both these artists have become deliverers of voids that are always threatening to consume them first, as Gilson's narrative discloses:

> My imagination is a wild beast that cries always for freedom. I am continually tormented by the desire to indulge some strange thing, perceptible but indistinct, hidden in the swamps of my mind. The hidden thing is always crying out to me from its hiding-place. "Do as I tell you and you will find out my shape. There, quick! what is that thing in your brain? Indulge my commands and some day the great doors of your mind will swing open and allow you to enter and handle to your complete satisfaction the vague shapes and figures hidden there." (16)

When the imagination takes on the shape of an emporium, its doors swinging open to allow easy access, what is left for West's artists but to take to trade themselves? Accordingly, the artists Balso encounters occupy themselves alternately with lofty aspirations and financial transactions. Maloney the Areopagite blends his unearthly interests with a desire to strike a hard bargain. He is, he tells Balso, occupied with "the biography of Saint Puce. If you are interested, I will give you a short précis of his life" (10). The summary, we have no doubt, will be shrewdly marketed. Similarly, Miss McGeeney, "a middle aged woman dressed in a mannish suit" (32), is conducting a number of projects, including a literary biography and "a novel in the manner of

Richardson." John Gilson, disturbingly precocious as well as murderous, be-comes almost predatory when he hears of Balso's magazine: "Maybe you run a magazine," he ponders. Would Balso perhaps buy his journal? "I need money" (23). The reason for his avarice is very revealing. "I'm fed up with poetry and art. Yet what can I do? I need women and because I can't buy or force them, I have to make poems for them. God knows how tired I am of using the insanity of Van Gogh and the adventures of Gauguin as can-openers for the ambitious Count Six-Times. And how sick I am of literary bitches. But they're the only kind that'll have me. . . . Listen Balso, for a dollar I'll send you a brief outline of my position" (23–24).

Gilson's head is a crematorium for postromantic styles. He houses jaded aestheticism, the embers of the decadence, the ashes of Nietzschean hyperbole, and a few stray live coals of Russian fiction. All of this to seduce women he hates. Similarly, Beagle Darwin's script for Janey Davenport reveals a revulsion for the very audience his career so sedulously courts. In this way, the book reflects its extended period of composition. It is the work of a precocious ingenu who has also studied the market, a man already tired of artistic milieus even before he has gained a foothold in them. And it is also the work of a man who knows that a godly maker in a commercial society cannot expect to have too much control of his own creation. . . .

Lotus Land or Locust Land?

David M. Fine*

Fifty years ago two slim novels appeared that put Los Angeles on the national literary map. Nathanael West's savage portrait of Hollywood, "The Day of the Locust," and the first of Raymond Chandler's seven hard-boiled L. A. detective stories, "The Big Sleep," appeared within months of each other in 1939. Chandler's achievement was to adapt the crime novel to the peculiar geographic and psychic terrain of Los Angeles. West's achievement, the larger one, was to transform and deepen the long-established but still crude Hollywood novel.

In the 1930s, when the talkies were invented, studio heads were scouring the East Coast (and Europe) for writers who could construct dialogue—as they were for actors who could speak it. Nathanael West, one of the eager recruits, made the first of his two sojourns to Hollywood in July of 1933.

A shy, lonely New Yorker ironically nicknamed "Pep," West had at the time two books behind him, both commercial failures. He had been working as a night manager in a Manhattan hotel owned by his father when "Miss Lonelyhearts," his second novel, was purchased by Darryl F. Zanuck. Hired to do the screenplay, West boarded a train for the coast, hoping to earn enough money in Hollywood to enable him to continue as a novelist.

His brother-in-law, the humorist S. J. Perelman, was already in Hollywood, having scripted the brilliant dialogue for the Marx brothers' films "Monkey Business" and "Horse Feathers." West's first Hollywood encounter ended before the year was up. His screenplay never materialized, and the novel was assigned to a team of hacks who managed, alchemically, to transmute a brilliant gem into a piece of innocuous fluff. When the picture, renamed "Advice to the Lovelorn," opened, the disheartened "Pep" West was on a train heading back to New York.

In 1935, he was back in Hollywood working as a salaried writer for Republic ("Repulsive," as it was called by the writers) Studios, scripting B movies, living in the tawdry Pa-Va-Sed apartment house on North Ivar Street and storing up the material for the Hollywood novel he had been thinking about. His Ivar Street neighbors were an assortment of Hollywood discards: has-been comics, bit players, stunt men and prostitutes.

*From *The Los Angeles Times Book Review* (31 December 1989): 4. Reprinted with the permission of the author.

One night he came home and saw a prostitute kick what appeared to be a bundle of laundry in the corridor. The bundle moved and a midget emerged from it. The incident found its way into the beginning of the novel. The surreal ambience of "The Day of the Locust," the grotesque "half world" of Hollywood outcasts and hangers-on West painted, was grounded in observed reality.

West never harbored the illusion that what he did at the studio had anything to do with art. Nor, he discovered, was the hack work to which he was assigned easy. He wrote in a letter that "this stuff about easy work is all wrong. . . . There's no fooling here. All the writers sit in cells in a row, and the minute the typewriter stops someone pokes his head in to see if you are still thinking."

West separated the two realms, working days in the "dream factory" and nights on his novel. It was completed in 1938 and published in 1939. Despite the praise of friends like F. Scott Fitzgerald and Dashiell Hammett, the book sold exactly 1,464 copies. A year after its publication, West was killed along with his wife (Eileen McKenney, of Ruth McKenney's "My Sister Eileen") when his car ran a stop sign in the Imperial Valley and struck another car. He was 37.

The Hollywood that West constructed out of the materials of observation, experience, and imagination was the symbolic center of an entire culture cheated and robbed by the puerile fantasies of the dream factory. He said in an earlier work on Hollywood that "everything that is wrong with the United States is to be found there in rare purity." Hollywood was source and symptom of a malady that was more than local. The novel is the severest literary indictment of the Hollywood dream we have and the most far-reaching in its implications for American culture. More relentlessly than other writers who were mining the materials of Hollywood for fiction, West traced the tangled connections between the fantasies produced by the studios and the fantasies so desperately pursued by the masses of dream seekers.

The landscape of West's novel is littered with illusion. Whole neighborhoods resemble movie sets, look like leftover props from completed or abandoned movies. The studio back lot is the "dream dump," the "Sargasso of the imagination." Beyond the studio walls the city appears as a vast annex to the lots. It's as though the sets had spilled over onto the surrounding landscape. Tod Hackett, West's spokesman, climbs to his apartment in the Hollywood Hills past a melange of "Mexican ranch houses, Samoan huts, Mediterranean villas, Egyptian and Japanese temples, Swiss chalets, Tudor cottages, and every possible combination of these styles that line the slopes of the canyon."

In this movie-like landscape, West's characters act out their roles. Teenage would-be starlet Fay Greener, dreaming of fame and glamour, shuffles her deck of dream cards and draws a different role daily, playing everything from Daddy's girl in a white sailor suit to tough whore. Meanwhile, her father, Harry Greener, ex-vaudeville performer, tap-dances his way to exhaustion, collapses, fakes his own heart attack and then dies from it.

The line here between living and acting has disappeared. Life has been reduced to a series of roles. One becomes what one pretends to be. All the world is a sound stage. Even the natural landscape is rendered in terms of a movie set. The setting sun against the edge of trees appears like the "violet piping" of a neon tube. The moon puts in a cameo appearance as a "bone button" poking through a "blue serge sky." The organic world has been preempted, upstaged, by the inorganic. Nature is the work of well-placed props, technical skill, and effective lighting.

But illusion breeds disillusion, and disillusion breeds violence. While the performers play out their roles, all those tired, jaded Midwesterners who "had come to California to die" stare with resentment and burn with rage. They are the cheated, the ones who have been fed on the dream and find that oranges and sunshine are not enough to satisfy their palates. They are the ones who hang out at airports hoping to see a plane crash and attend the funerals of strangers hoping to witness some extraordinary display of grief.

When Hollywood dreams fail to materialize, a feeling of betrayal sets in, and with it the kind of fury that erupts in the orgiastic mob violence that brings the novel to a screaming halt. The thousands of bit players, those without speaking parts, the locusts of the title, become, in the final reel, the leading performers, tearing the Hollywood props down. It is one of the most devastating last scenes in American fiction.

Like Chandler but more profoundly than Chandler, West gave us a way of "reading" the West Coast Metropolis—a mythic, symbolic reading that stands in direct opposition to the California-as-Eden myth fabricated in those same years by the railroad companies, real-estate developers, city boosters, Chamber of Commerce and the movies themselves.

California was not simply the land of the fresh start and the happy ending. There was a dark, shadow side to the American Dream and to the intensified, California version of it—to the dream that one can escape the past, reinvent one's life at will, be what one wishes to be.

The writers who would write about Los Angeles in the decades ahead—Evelyn Waugh, Budd Schulberg, Norman Mailer, Joan Didion, Alison Lurie, John Gregory Dunne, Stuart Kaminsky and others—all took their starting point from the same sense of the dream gone haywire. The promise of new beginnings can be an elusive one, can in fact sour into an invitation to sure disaster. One can lose as well as find oneself in the fluidity of Southern California.

Nathanael West's *Miss Lonelyhearts*

BEVERLY JONES*

In a discussion of Nathanael West's *Miss Lonelyhearts* in *American Apocalypses,* Douglas Robinson challenges the conventional alignment of Miss Lonelyhearts with Christ and Shrike with Satan, pointing out that such a thematic reduction overlooks the evidence that West more often aligns his antagonists the other way by presenting Lonelyhearts as a restless Satan wandering through chaos and Shrike as the Christ figure whose rhetoric becomes "his image of order, his rock, which guarantees his invulnerability throughout the novel" (126). Although Robinson does not elaborate on this concept, a close textual study of the novella will show that his reversal of traditional roles is viable, especially in the character of Shrike, who exposes the hypocrisy and irrationality of Lonelyhearts' religious mania with an unrelenting nihilism that identifies him as the modernist antihero.

A general note on the nature of heroism in modern fiction seems appropriate here. In *Radical Innocence* Ihab Hassan asserts that, because part of the make-up of the hero in American fiction of the past was his ability to mediate between the Self and the World, the restlessness and rebellion in the heroic soul remained quiescent, and the hero's struggles affirmed the harmony of the inner life of man and the external world of God, nature, and society. Today, however, that harmony is rapidly disappearing: "The World, in our time, seems to have either vanished or become a rigid and intractable mass. The anarchy of nihilism and the terror of statism delimit the extremes between which there seems to be no viable mean. Mediation between Self and World appears no longer possible—there is only surrender or recoil. In his modern recoil, the hero has become an anti-hero" (327).

In West's novella, one of Lonelyhearts' newspaper associates alludes to this breakdown of mediation between Self and World: "The trouble with him, the trouble with all of us, is that we have no outer life, only an inner one, and that by necessity" (15). Man's inner life, or Self, has become so alienated from society that his outer life, or World, no longer exists in any meaningful way. In Hassan's view, however, the estranged antihero reacts to the modernist dilemma by recoiling from nihilism, whereas in *Lonelyhearts,* Shrike embraces it as his system of order.

*From *Modern Fiction Studies* 36 (Summer 1990): 218–24. Reprinted with the permission of Purdue Research Foundation.

Lonelyhearts' response to the modernist predicament is the fever of religious hysteria, and because it leads not to redemption through Christian love but to violence and death, he fails in his messianic role and ironically becomes the agent of chaos. On the other hand, Shrike's impious modernist response, because it enables him to function and thrive in a world where the good, the true, and the beautiful do not exist, becomes the source of a virtually unassailable stability. An unabashed voluptuary, a debauchee, and a dead-pan but otherwise very lively satyr, Shrike resolutely refuses to allow his pagan pleasures to be displaced by Lonelyhearts' ideas of Christian asceticism. To that end, he undertakes his own mock apologia in Delehanty's bar, prefacing his drunken declamation by disclosing that he can walk on his own water and inquiring whether his audience has heard of "Shrike's Passion in the Luncheonette or the Agony in the Soda Fountain" (7). What follows could be referred to as his Sermon in the Speakeasy: "Under the skin of men is a wondrous jungle where veins like lush tropical growths hang along over-ripe organs and weed-like entrails writhe in squirming tangles of red and yellow. In this jungle . . . lives a bird called the soul. The Catholic hunts this bird with bread and wine, the Hebrew with a golden ruler, the Protestant on leaden feet with leaden words, the Buddhist with gestures, the Negro with blood. I spit on them all. Phooh! And I call upon you to spit. Phooh!" (7–8).

Shrike does not intend his discourse to be spiritually uplifting but sexually titillating, because it is engendered by his lechery for his latest conquest, Miss Farkis. His grandiloquent utterance is punctuated by periodic nuzzling and rump-patting designed to result not in faith but fornication: "His caresses kept pace with the sermon. When he had reached the end, he buried his triangular face like the blade of a hatchet in her neck" (8).

Lawrence DiStasi writes that Shrike applies the deflated concept of Christianity to sexual seduction in a parody of the tradition of courtly love: "Where the latter moved toward non-violence and gentilesse, however, this parody illustrates the counter movement in the modern world. This simultaneous demystification of religion and love results in the unbinding of the aggressive component in each of them, leaving only violence in their place" (87).

In a modernist society where carnality and the appetites of the flesh have consigned courtly love to the scrap heap, Shrike rules with supreme authority. He encourages his frigid wife Mary to see other men, as she points out, "To save money. He knows that I let them neck me and when I get home all hot and bothered, he climbs into my bed and begs for it. The cheap bastard!" (22). Yet the marriage remains intact. Shrike freely admits that his love is "of the flesh flashy" (21) and that if he suffers, it is only because he must endure the indignity of having to wait while Lonelyhearts arouses his wife for him. After a date featuring many long, wet kisses, Mary disappears into the apartment, and Shrike emerges momentarily to inspect the corridor, wearing only the top of his pajamas. Following the transubstantiation, by proxy, of body and blood into lust, Shrike the modernist priest, clad in his pajama-top chasuble, prepares for the sacrament of predatory sex. In an alarming reduction of Christian anthropomorphism to pagan atavism, Shrike's apotheosis of the libido is figured forth in the iconography of the Mexican War obelisk, an enormous phallus of stone, perpetually rigid, "lengthening in rapid jerks . . . red and swollen in the dying sun, as though it were about to spout a load of granite seed" (19).

As the modernist antihero, Shrike has his own system of order to shore against ruin, an uncompromising cynicism made all the more impenetrable by the fact that there is nothing arcane about its major tenet. There is no meaning in anything, especially suffering, and there is no escape from it in this or any other life. With the gleam of polished parody, Shrike blocks every conceivable retreat from pain, including the pastoral: "You buy a farm and walk behind your horse's moist behind. . . . To this rhythm you sow and weep and chivy your kine between the pregnant rows of corn and taters"; the South Seas à la Gauguin: "The tourists envy you your breech clout and carefree laugh and little brown bride and fingers instead of forks"; the pleasure dome: "You fornicate under pictures by Matisse and Picasso, you drink from Renaissance glassware and often you spend an evening beside the fireplace with Proust and an apple"; and the sanctuary of timeless Art: "You know that your shoes are broken and there are pimples on your face, yes, and that you have buck teeth and a club foot, but you don't care, for tomorrow they are playing Beethoven's last quartets in Carnegie Hall and at home you have Shakespeare's plays in one volume" (34–35). Shrike's flamboyant oratory delineates a modernist epistemology proclaiming the wisdom of a chilling contempt which mocks Camus's pronouncement that "There is no fate that cannot be surmounted by scorn" (90). I sneer, therefore I am.

The main thrust of Shrike's messianic mission as the modernist antihero is to expose the hypocrisy of Lonelyhearts' Christianity, with its neurotic fixation of the dark mysteries of blood and martyrdom. Removing the ivory figure from its cross, Lonelyhearts essays the recrucifixion of Christ by nailing him to the wall with spikes, but "Instead of writhing, the Christ remained calmy decorative" (8). Lonelyhearts' vision of the disastrous attempt to kill a lamb, emblematic of Christ, complete with ritual butcher knife and incantation over an altar strewn with buttercups and daisies, reveals his preoccupation with blood sacrifice and his horror at being unable to consummate it properly. The knife snaps, and the mutilated lamb crawls away into the bushes, where Lonelyhearts later returns to crush its head with a stone, "leaving the carcass to the flies that swarmed around the bloody altar flowers" (10). Lonelyhearts' bungled sacrifice, it turns out, is made ironically not to God but to Beelzebub, Lord of the Flies. It is characteristic of Shrike's acuity that he perceives this attraction to sadism and violence beneath Lonelyhearts' mask of piety, and he calls upon Lonelyhearts to stop wearing the hair shirt and pondering the Passion: "You're morbid, my friend, morbid. Forget the crucifixion, remember the Renaissance. There were no brooders then. I give you the Borgias. What a period! What pageantry! Drunken popes . . . Beautiful courtesans . . . Illegitimate children . . ." (5–6, ellipses West's).

Shrike also sees through the pretense of Lonelyhearts' crusade to alleviate human suffering, and so does Lonelyhearts, who knows very well that his humble Father Zossima posturing is all in the name of greed: "His column would be syndicated and the whole world would learn to love. The Kingdom of Heaven would arrive. He would sit on the right hand of the Lamb" (8), in the glorious fulfillment of the Puritan American Dream updated to the twentieth-century. To Shrike, the concept of fame and fortune as a syndicated columnist is rational enough, because self-aggrandizement is after all the sole motive of man's endeavor, but he objects to Lonelyhearts' sanctimonious, breast-beating altruism as the avowed driving force of his ambition. With a pragmatism that is totally incorruptible, Shrike refuses to compromise the purity of his self-interest by disguising it as anything else. He advises Lonelyhearts to avoid recommending suicide in the column, not because life is worth living or because his readers should give a damn about anything but because, as Shrike puts it, "your job is to increase the circulation of the paper. Suicide, it is only reasonable to think, would defeat this purpose" (18). In the same spirit, Goldsmith, one of Shrike's disciples, suggests that Lonelyhearts should satisfy the sexual needs of one of his frustrated correspondents in order to "get the lady with child and increase the potential circulation of the paper" (26).

Shrike also decries Lonelyhearts' self-righteous obsession with providing spiritual sustenance to the wretched soul in pain, and to that end he manages to debunk the profundities of the Lord's Prayer, the French aristocracy, and the Eucharist all in one fell spoof: "I advise you to give your readers stones. When they ask for bread don't give them crackers as does the Church and don't, like the State, tell them to eat cake. Explain that man cannot live by bread alone and give them stones. Teach them to pray each morning: 'Give us this day our daily stone' " (5). Gerald Nelson explains that Shrike's shrill insistence is based on his messianic mission to reveal the truth, foul as it is: "He is not a black priest; there is no perversion in him. He does not try to cover up or delude his parishioners. He preaches with a beautifully pristine, deliberate ruthlessness. It is not his fault if he drives his flock mad" (82).

In order to ensure the triumph of his own gospel of negativism, Shrike also demolishes the reality of suffering, not only of Lonelyhearts but also of the letter writers, and he burlesques their imbecilic utterances to reduce them to the level of absurdity: "This one is a jim-dandy. A young boy wants a violin. It looks simple; all you have to do is get the kid one. But then you discover that he dictated the letter to his little sister. He is paralyzed and can't even feed himself. He has a toy violin and hugs it to his chest, imitating the sound of playing with his mouth. How pathetic. However, one can learn much from this parable. Label the boy Labor, the violin Capital and so on. . ." (53).

Shrike is able to handle the letters and the banality of Lonelyhearts' response to them with equally derisive facility because, as Jeffrey Duncan notes, both bear the same message: "the human race is a poet that writes the eccentric propositions of its fate, and propositions, fate, the race itself amount only to so much noisy breath, hot air, flatulence" (118).

In the modernist world, which Jonathan Raban describes as "the urban industrial environment of pulp media and cheapjack commodities" (222), Shrike reigns supreme as the Primum Mobile, the first mover, for neither Lonelyhearts nor his correspondents has any existence outside the artificial framework of clichés created by Shrike and the newspaper to define them. Once set in motion, his mechanical media universe can only operate according to the linguistic laws he has set down.

Shrike's crowning achievement is his unmasking of Lonelyhearts as a vengeful, Calvinistic Jonathan Edwards for the mass media, eager to preach his hellfire and brimstone sermon, perhaps edited to "Sinners in the Hands of an Angry Columnist," and featuring such highlights as "Suffer, you wretched bunch of freaks. Neither God nor I can stand to have you in our sight because you are uglier than you can imagine in your wildest nightmares" (116–127). Gerald Nelson points out that Lonelyhearts, whose Christianity is actually closet voyeurism, enjoys the suffering of his letter writers and offers to supply a spiritual dimension that will heighten rather than alleviate their physical and mental pain: "Instead of merely moaning, he wants them to really face the agony of emptiness, and die. So that he can watch" (87). As the chief agent and overseer of this abyss of misery, Lonelyhearts emerges as the modernist Satan.

Shrike, on the other hand, has no desire to feed the repulsive little spiders into the flames of perdition; instead, he would offer his readers the insipid tripe they want to hear, the kind of bromide he dictates with relish to Lonelyhearts and which Lonelyhearts can only mimic later: "Do not let life overwhelm you. When the old paths are choked with the debris of failure, look for newer and fresher paths. Art is just such a path. Art is distilled from suffering. Art is One of Life's Richest Offerings. For those who have not the talent to create, there is appreciation. For those. . . . Go on from there" (4). Shrike's glib rhetoric becomes the Logos; his irony is transmitted as the modernist Word. The Antichrist is the monomaniacal Lonelyhearts, described by Shrike as the "still more swollen Mussolini of the soul" (52), bloated by a surfeit of pseudo-divinity, corruption incarnate.

The clash between the modernist responses of Shrike and Lonelyhearts is a fight to the finish, and the introduction of Fay and Peter Doyle into the fray signals the onset of the apocalyptic showdown. Shrike immediately acknowledges the truth that the Doyles are living the reality of an American nightmare from which it is impossible to awaken them. When he asks Doyle, whom West describes as a "partially destroyed insect" (44), to speak for humanity from the vantage point of a gas meter reader, Doyle replies with a leer that his profession has replaced the defunct iceman in the stories about sexual dalliance in the suburbs. Vastly amused, Shrike roars, "What? I can see you are not the man for us. You know nothing about humanity; you are humanity. I leave you to Lonelyhearts" (45). Shrike knows that the diabolical, death-ridden heretic, whose bony chin is "cleft like a hoof" (4), is waiting in a vengeful delirium to claim both Doyle and his wife.

Merging the motif of the loathsome insect suspended over the fire with his blood sacrifice fixation, Lonelyhearts postulates a dialectic of transfiguration through pain: "Christ died for you. He died nailed to a tree for you. His gift to you is suffering and it is only through suffering that you can know him" (39). Lonelyhearts renounces the Christian doctrine of deliverance through the redemptive love of the Son of God, whom he describes as the "black fruit that hangs on the crosstree" (49) and touts a cheapened mimicry of the savior's transcendent agony and death as a nostrum for the torments of his correspondents' souls. In a "stage scream," Lonelyhearts then hysterically invokes the serpent of temptation in the Garden: "Man was lost by eating of the forbidden fruit. He shall be saved by eating of the forbidden fruit. The black Christ-fruit, the love fruit" (49). The apostasy of Lonelyhearts' exhortation to corrupt divine grace with dimestore carnality does not inspire the hoped-for regeneration but a lewd ritual of seduction, as the lickerish Mrs. Doyle "waved her behind at him like a flag" and "after doing a few obscene steps in front of him . . . opened the neck of her dress and tried to force his head between her breasts" (50). With the Christian compassion twisted into a fury of sadistic violence, Lonelyhearts can only respond by inflicting pain: "He struck out blindly and hit her in the face. She screamed and he hit her again and again. He kept hitting her until she stopped trying to hold him, then he ran out of the house" (50).

Shrike is much more Christ-like in his understanding that, in twentieth-century America, the downtrodden want ways to hang onto life and enjoy their puerile amusements, not ways to suffer and die. The sixteen-year-old girl who writes Lonelyhearts about her misfortune of being born without a nose only wants the nose she never had, or failing that, the illusion of a nose and a few nights out on the town, not plastic surgery of the soul that leaves her with the same hole in her face where a nose should be. And Lonelyhearts, blinded by his delusion, fails to see that he is involved not in a miraculous revelation of his power to heal but in the oldest, tackiest story in the dirty joke book, the adulterous triangle with Doyle as the gun-toting cuckold threatening murder and mayhem. He has no real desire to kill Lonelyhearts; he just wants to be talked out of it and go on home where he can bark like a dog at his wife, tear open the fly of whatever man happens to be in the apartment at the time, roll over on his back, and howl to be scratched. Then dragging his club foot up and down cellar stairs to read meters won't seem so bad after all. In a world where faith is dead, West seems to suggest, what Doyle wants to do is what most of the rest of us really want to do in order to survive. Mark Conroy writes: "The stories we tell ourselves, like the stories we tell others, are as necessary as they are fraudulent; and the more irrelevant they become, the more necessary they may well seem. The narrative of *Miss Lonelyhearts* is the story of this cruel calculus. It is a tale where Shrike has the last laugh, because he has already written the first line" (124).

The confidence and strength of Shrike's laughter are the measure of his successful demystification of man's spiritual longing to merge with the absolute. Miles D. Orvell explains Shrike's victory over Lonelyhearts' attempts to restore the suffering world around him:

> Walt Whitman had tried—in his own time, and with a precedent conception of the relatedness of the physical and the spiritual lives—to move from the inner vision to the world, and with a hard, underlying view of the speedy progress America was making toward a muscle-bound, impoverishing materialism; but for Whitman the move had been chiefly imaginative, a matter of poetry and prophecy, and so buoyed by a resurgent optimism. West was heir to Whitman's insight that in our modern industrial society, spiritual, sexual and institutional energies are bound together; but it was West's twentieth-century view that regeneration is an agony, and, it would seem, a deception. (167)

Perhaps, then, it is time to leave Whitman behind and to listen to the word of a later prophet, Yeats, who heralded the second coming of a savior more suited to our times. And so, its hour come round at last, the rough beast slouches not toward Bethlehem but toward twentieth-century America, where he is born in *Miss Lonelyhearts* and is named Shrike, after the bird that mercilessly impales its prey on thorns.

If we doubt that Shrike is the true modernist Christ, who the prophet tells us has a "gaze blank and pitiless as the sun," we have only to look into his face: "Although his gestures were elaborate, his face was blank. No matter how fantastic or excited his speech, he never changed his expression. Under the shining white globe of his brow, his features huddled together in a dead, gray triangle" (6).

Works Cited

Camus, Albert. *The Myth of Sisyphus*. New York: Vintage, 1955.

Conroy, Mark. "Letters and Spirit in *Miss Lonelyhearts*." *Nathanael West's "Miss Lonelyhearts": Modern Critical Interpretations*. Ed. Harold Bloom. New York: Chelsea, 1987. 111–124.

DiStasi, Lawrence. "Agression in *Miss Lonelyhearts*: Nowhere to Throw the Stone." *Nathanael West: The Cheaters and the Cheated*. Ed. David Madden. Deland: Everett / Edwards, 1973. 83–101.

Duncan, Jeffrey L. "The Problem of Language in *Miss Lonelyhearts*." *Iowa Review* 8 (1977): 116–127.

Hassan, Ihab. *Radical Innocence*: *Studies in the Contemporary Novel*. Princeton: Princeton UP, 1973.

Nelson, Gerald B. *"Lonelyhearts."* *Ten Versions of America*. New York: Knopf, 1972. 79–90.

Orvell, Miles D. "The Messianic Sexuality of *Miss Lonelyhearts*." *Studies in Short Fiction* 10.2 (1973): 159–167.

Raban, Jonathan. "A Surfeit of Commodities: The Novels of Nathanael West." *The American Novel and the Nineteen Twenties*. Ed. Malcolm Bradbury and David Palmer. New York: Arnold, 1971. 215–231.

Robinson, Douglas. "The Ritual Icon." *American Apocalypses*: *The Image of the End of the World in American Literature*. Baltimore: Johns Hopkins UP, 1985. 198–232.

West, Nathanael, *Miss Lonelyhearts*. New York: New Directions, 1969.

The Shrike Voice Dominates *Miss Lonelyhearts*

DAVID MADDEN*

The attentive reader of Nathanael West's *Miss Lonelyhearts* will find the cynical tough-guy voice of the narrator essentially discordant: Miss Lonelyhearts' own actions, thoughts, and dialogue are incongruent with the style in which West as narrator describes them. West uses what Henry James called the third-person, central-intelligence point of view. It enables the reader to experience everything the author presents as filtered through the perceptions of the protagonist, here, Miss Lonelyhearts. But West's hard-boiled style reflects Shrike's mental processes more closely than it does the mind of Miss Lonelyhearts. In fact, West's Shrike-like narration differs sharply from Miss Lonelyhearts' voice in dialogue, which in turn differs sharply from Shrike's blunt idiom. West's style is then most effective, not when he simulates Miss Lonelyhearts' mental processes, but when he lets Shrike speak.

Nathanael West the artist was too self-conscious to have intended this vocal incongruity. It would appear to be an unconscious result of a division in his personal life and in his vision of life in general. Miss Lonelyhearts and Shrike express the poles of that division, with Shrike's vision being the more powerful. Evaluating the consequences of this incongruity, the reader will find the novel to be aesthetically flawed. But he or she also will discern some interesting "imagined" secondary readings.

West's four short novels appeared between 1931 and 1939. He was only 33 years old when *Miss Lonelyhearts*, his second novel, appeared. Most critics have stressed the similarities among the four narratives, encouraging readers to imagine them as constituting a single work. Irving Malin believed that all of West's characters are cracked mirror images of each other.[1] His four protagonists (Balso Snell, Miss Lonelyhearts, Lemuel Pitkin, and Tod Hackett) are essentially the same young man. Together, they reveal one side of the author himself. Like him, they are caught—as Jay Martin, West's major biographer, stated—"in their own or others' illusions."[2] Yet Victor Comerchero pointed out that the novelist's much darker, pessimistic side is expressed in another "Westian persona": Shrike.[3] Martin agreed, declaring that West "could be his own Shrike."[4]

Personally and professionally, West seemed to be trying to pass Fitzger-

*This essay was written specifically for this volume.

ald's "test of a first-rate intelligence." To Fitzgerald this meant "the ability to hold two opposed ideas in the mind at the same time and still retain the ability to function."[5] Consciously and unconsciously, in life and work, West made a near-compulsive use of disguises: Nathan Weinstein's transformation into Nathanael West was only the start. In early drafts, Miss Lonelyhearts had a name—Thomas Matlock. In the published novel, he has none. Many of West's personal acquaintances have noted his role-playing. In his introduction to the Avon Books edition of *Miss Lonelyhearts*, for example, Malcolm Cowley observed that "Pep was never more himself than when he became a fictitious character. His friends watched him play the successive roles. . . . With his talent for projecting himself into a variety of roles, West in person is Miss Lonelyhearts, and he is also Shrike, the cynical managing editor who keeps tormenting him."[6]

Jay Martin described S. J. Perelman's assessment of his brother-in-law. "There are really two Wests, Perelman intimates. . . . [H]e hinted that West's personality was divided between self-deluding fantasy and scorn for illusions. . . . But the West who wrote the novel, Perelman continued, only apparently joking, 'is only eighteen inches high. He is very sensitive [and] somewhat savage.' He is a kind of eternal figure of revolt—having been seen at Austerlitz and Jena—savage, close to madness, a man out of the world of dreams, the creative dwarf, the inner man." Martin added: "In *Balso Snell*, West wrote a similar speech in which he tried to explain his own duality. 'When you think of me,' a character says, 'think of two men.'"[7]

The source of West's complex personality, said Martin, "lay in the contrast between his intellectual and emotional life." Most acquaintances regarded West's "supposed cynicism" as

"a cover-up for a real desire to make contact." Such people were, of course, shocked by the difference they felt between the person and the author, and concluded that his books are basically unlike him. On the other hand, West had, according to others an "intellectual brutalism" which emerged surprisingly at times—in his humor, which was often cruel; in his absolute intolerance of pretense and his refusal even to talk to people he regarded as dull or superficial; in his mockery of the emotions of others and his anxiety to suppress all expressions of sentiment. . . . This predisposition toward a tough intellectualism at the expense of tender emtion constituted the source of West's satiric point of view.[8]

One may well offer the above as a description of Shrike. Indeed, as early as 1957, the critic C. C. Hollis saw what West's friends had seen: "Miss Lonelyhearts was what West dared not be: Shrike was what he dreaded to become."[9] For even though the schizophrenia of both West and Miss Lonelyhearts has often been noted, it is not always clear whether Shrike is a facet of Miss Lonelyhearts or if Miss Lonelyhearts is a facet of Shrike. Did West consciously come to abhor his own Shrike-like voice, which created the other character? That question raises another: Did Shrike abhor his own voice and thus create Miss Lonelyhearts?

In his *The Dream Life of Balso Snell*, West employs dream and surrealism, burlesque and other techniques to attack, in the Shrike manner, his literary heroes and enemies alike. In *Miss Lonelyhearts*, he tries to balance meditations on events with coldly objective observations, but he allows Shrike's speech-as-action to overwhelm the meditative elements. In *A Cool Million*, he uses the Alger myth satirically, to attack, again as Shrike would, the American dream of success. As did Fitzgerald in *The Great Gatsby*, West at least once passed the test of a first-rate intelligence—in his art, if not in his life. Only in *The Day of the Locust* did this youthful writer make his third-person style congruent with the emotions, imagination, and intellect of the protagonist. But though less of an artistic achievement than this final novel, *Miss Lonelyhearts* may finally prove the more interesting work.

As noted, the reader may find it illuminating to imagine West's four novels as constituting a single work and his four protagonists as one young man resembling the author himself. The reader may then imagine that composite novel as written by Shrike, the butcher-bird, the bird of prey. Victor Comerchero suggested this West-Shrike reading when he inadvertently equated author and character as phrase-mongers: "In passages full of the brilliant puns, cliches, and rhetoric in which West excelled, he [Shrike] cruelly and systematically destroys one of Miss Lonelyhearts' potential escapes after another." Comerchero also pointed out that while certain motifs appear in all four novels, the first two works are personal, psychological, and philosophical; the latter two, more social-psychological and political."[10] In *Miss Lonelyhearts*, however, Shrike's comments include all those perspectives.

Comerchero saw in *Miss Lonelyhearts* a balance of elements that characterize all four novels. Tragic-comic and pathetic-satiric elements are "inseparably fused." The novel presents a balance of "compassion, contempt, and suffering," said Comerchero, "complex harmonies of meaning" that result "from the counterplay of the literal and symbolical." Hence the narrative is for him "delicately poised between agonizing pessimism and ironic amusement."[11] However, it is possible to see a radical *imbalance* among all those elements because they derive from the discord between West's point of view strategy and his style.

Martin often described West and his purposes in Shrike-like terms. While writing the chapters of the novel for *Contact*, West was looking to *Americana* magazine "for Shrike-like attitudes."[12] It was with such an attitude that Susan Chester first showed him some of the letters she received for her advice column. Miss Lonelyhearts himself begins his job thinking of it as a joke. West's early choice of a comic-strip technique for the novel was also a Shrike-like gesture. (West was himself a talented cartoonist.) West had a compulsion to read his latest work on *Miss Lonelyhearts* aloud. "He had to speak it," a friend said. The novel's Shrike-like style lends itself to such readings. This compulsion to speak directly to the reader, as Shrike speaks directly to Miss Lonelyhearts ("He did not want to listen to Shrike"), moved West to experiment with Miss Lonelyhearts' first-person narrative, which sounded even more obviously like Shrike.

Perelman's reaction to the first four chapters (three years' work) was that they were "Too psychological, not concrete enough."[13] Shrike's speeches and West's Shrike-like, hard-boiled metaphors were intended as concrete elements in the published version. Only two pages into the novel, West's metaphor for the letters that all sound alike is Shrike-like and out of key with Miss Lonelyhearts' point-of-view. He describes them as "stamped from the dough of suffering with a heart-shaped cookie knife." Other examples abound. One evocative one is "flowers that smelled like feet." Another is "As he followed her up the stairs to his apartment, he watched the action of her massive hams; they were like two enormous grindstones."[14]

West writing is like Shrike speaking. "I am a great saint. . . . I can walk on my own water. Haven't you ever heard of Shrike's Passion in the Luncheonette, or the Agony in the Soda Fountain? Then I compared the wounds in Christ's body to the mouths of a miraculous purse in which we deposit the small change of our sins. It is indeed an excellent conceit" (74). Indeed, it may be too excellent for Shrike the character; it seems more typical of West the literary satirist. After Shrike's long speech, West ends the chapter with a Shrikean simile: "he buried his triangular face like the blade of a hatchet in her neck" (74). The incongruities continue. For example, a perception of Mrs. Shrike attributed to Miss Lonelyhearts sounds more like West and Shrike, and it is descriptive of both at their best: "She always talked in headlines" (90). On the other hand, Miss Lonelyhearts is best described in this passage: "his tongue had become a fat thumb. To avoid talking" (79). Miss Lonelyhearts seldom speaks to Shrike. "Miss Lonelyhearts always found it impossible to reply to him." When he does make "a desperate attempt to kid back," he speaks with no Shrikean edge or pointedness: " 'And you,' he said, 'you're an old meanie who beats his wife' "(91).

Miss Lonelyhearts sounds like Shrike only when he imitates Shrike and tries to reverse roles. For instance, he echoes Shrike when he torments "the clean old man" by declaring: "But you are a pervert, aren't you?" (86). A few pages later, he speaks of seeing himself as the butt of Shrike's jokes. At that point the reader understands why the willfully compassionate Miss Lonelyhearts made a joke of the old man. Another example occurs when he tries to violate the vulnerable Betty's insufferable innocence. He sounds much like Shrike when the latter is violating Miss Lonelyhearts' own compulsion to escape from evil into innocence: " 'What a kind bitch you are. As soon as any one acts viciously, you say he's sick. Wife-torturers, rapers of small children, according to you they're all sick. No morality, only medicine. Well, I'm not sick. I don't need any of your damned aspirin. I've got a Christ complex.

Humanity . . . I'm a humanity lover. All the broken bastards.' " He then gave "a short laugh that was like a bark" (81). Then later, for contrast, West has Miss Lonelyhearts explain his job to Betty without Shrikean phrases. But that scene is immediately justaposed to the scene in which Shrike bursts into the room to deliver his longest set speech. Here he uses another West-like suggestion as a spring board: " 'Art! Be an artist or a writer' " (109). Predictably, Miss Lonelyhearts offers no response and evokes Shrike's ridicule.

In the pastoral, edenic episode, "in the country," West omits any conversation between Miss Lonelyhearts and Betty, juxtaposing that chapter to the "return." His style is at its best here, as when he observes: "Crowds of people moved through the street with a dream-like violence" (115). Striking a Shrikean tone, West comments elsewhere on violence in general: "In America, violence is idiomatic . . . in America violence is daily."[15] Even the chapter titles (where the author speaks directly to his reader) reveal a more Shrike-like than Miss Lonelyhearts-like phrasing: "Miss Lonelyhearts and the dead pan," "Miss Lonelyhearts and the fat thumb," "Miss Lonelyhearts on a field trip," and "Miss Lonelyhearts has a religious experience."

West relies on a Shrikean metaphor to describe his hero: "Miss Lonelyhearts . . . was smiling an innocent, amused smile, the smile of an anarchist sitting in the movies with a bomb in his pocket. In a little while he would leave to kill the president" (83). It is hardly the kind of perception this character would have of himself. But this minor lapse in the prevalent point of view strategy is another example of a style that churns out metaphors—that is, metaphors sounding like headlines or jokes. A more Miss Lonelyhearts-like passage is found on the next page. A long passage about a childhood memory, it ends: "Every child, everywhere; in the whole world there was not one child who was not gravely, sweetly dancing" (84). Is this sentimental lapse the inevitable gaff to be heard in the tough-guy voice of a Hemingway, Traven, Cain, McCoy, Hammett, or Chandler? Or, is West finally lapsing into a mode appropriate to Miss Lonelyhearts and that—given West's choice of point of view—should characterize the novel overall?

Usually, Miss Lonelyhearts' tongue becomes a "fat thumb." For instance, he talks with Mrs. Doyle at some length, but only to make negative replies and weak small talk: "She waited for him to comment, but he remained silent until she nudged him into speech with her elbow. 'Your husband probably loves you and the kid,' he said" (99). When Mrs. Doyle tells Miss Lonelyhearts that she was once pretty but now must "spend her life with a shrimp of a cripple," he reluctantly responds. " 'You're still pretty,' he said without knowing why, except that he was frightened" (104). When the pathetic Mr. Doyle comes to Miss Lonelyhearts for help, it is Shrike who talks to him, at great length and in his usual "dead pan" manner. Even when Miss Lonelyhearts and Doyle go to Doyle's apartment, West does not allow Miss Lonelyhearts to speak. In the apartment, Mrs. Doyle speaks, primarily shrieking at both of them. When Miss Lonelyhearts pleads, "Please don't fight" (128), it is one of the few lines he speaks in 25 pages. A few pages from the end, Miss Lonelyhearts makes a telling reference to Shrike. " 'Why are you mad at me, Betty? I didn't do anything. It was Shrike's idea and he did all the talking' " (136). From beginning to end, the Shrike voice dominates not only Miss Lonelyhearts but also West's style. On his first appearance in the novel Shrike states: " 'Here, I'll dictate. Art Is a Way Out' " (69). Thus he immediately sounds the Westian satirical note struck on every page of *The Dream Life of Balso Snell*, whose hero tries desperately to find a way out of the anal canal of art. But Art does not provide a way out, neither for Miss Lonelyhearts nor for Shrike. West himself may have been better served by art, but the mesmerizing Shrike voice appears to have distracted him from noticing this particular artistic incongruity.

In an early version of the "dismal swamp" episode, West tried "to give his hero complexity," said Jay Martin, "by making him a character divided against himself. Miss Lonelyhearts contains, as aspects of one personality, both Thomas Matlock and Shrike."[16] Martin offered the reader one of the best and most sustained commentaries on Shrike (178–79). He noted that it was not Shrike but Miss Lonelyhearts and Betty who gave West the "greatest difficulty" throughout the novel's many revisions. Martin reported also that at the time of his death West was planning a new novel about "a Shrike-like writer . . . whose subject is the absurdity of the actual."[17] Hence West the novelist spoke most easily and convincingly in the Shrike voice. It was in his movie scripts— where he articulated ideals such as the American dream—that, as Martin astutely showed, West found a place to express his Miss Lonelyhearts side, an idiom free of Shrike-like attitudes (206).

But Martin, like most West critics, seemed not to understand how point of view works in the published novel. He called it "third person, omniscient."[18] More precisely, it is, as noted above, third person, central intelligence, with a few minor lapses. The first lapse comes in the early, physical description of Miss Lonelyhearts. Here the style is not particularly Shrikean, although the paragraph does end with a comment by Shrike: "On seeing him for the first time, Shrike had smiled and said, 'The Susan Chesters, the Beatrice Fairfaxes and the Miss Lonelyhearts are the priests of twentieth-century America' " (69). There is a second brief lapse in West's use of the third-person, central-intelligence point of view. It occurs when Miss Lonelyhearts leaves the room and West continues the scene in his absence, with Shrike finishing his long speech, "the gospel according to Shrike" (135). Marcus Smith argued that the shift provides a necessary ironic distance.[19] Yet that does not justify shattering the psychological and aesthetic unity of effect that the third-person, central-intelligence point of view is designed to create.

Martin did deal with revisions that affect point of view. He stated that at one point in the revision process, West tried interior monologue. He published the result in *Contempo* as "The Dismal Swamp." He then changed his mind and revised that chapter for the novel, retaining the same title. There Shrike speaks in dialogue some of the same ideas Miss Lonelyhearts had expressed about himself in the interior monologue version.[20] In another revision, West tried to convert the third-person narration into Miss Lonelyhearts' first person. Why, one may wonder, did he not then revise the style to sound more like Miss Lonelyhearts? In any event, West found that the change to first-person narration did not work.

Carter A. Daniel reasoned that the "first person narration would be largely unsuitable in a novel which derives most of its impact from the author's implied ironical judgments of the main character." Apparently he saw no problem inherent in West's use of the third-person, central-intelligence point of view. The Shrike-like style is there in both the first-person and the third-person versions, though it is appropriate to neither. Daniel concluded that the novel's various versions reveal West to have been "an astute reader and reviser of his own work."[21] Be that as it may, West still failed to detect the major incongruity described here. Those passages dealing with Shrike that Daniel quoted for comparison show few significant changes. Admittedly, some of West's revisions produced many of the striking (mostly Shrikean) metaphors for which he is justly praised. Still, most changes are simply pronoun substitutions—that is, from first person back to third person. They merely suggest West's commitment to the Shrike voice.

There is one possibility that does appear plausible: West did see his narrative's aesthetic incongruity, but he deliberately wanted to have it both ways. He wanted to tell the acceptable story of Miss Lonelyhearts' conversion to compassion (despite its inherent irony), while retaining Shrike's more authentic satirical voice. With that possibility in mind, one might argue, in defense of the published novel, that the incongruity of a cynical voice narrating the mental torment of a compassionate young man is West's ingenious way of creating a simultaneous expression of two contrasting views of life. In other words, the Shrike-like cynical style is there to cancel out, line by line, Miss Lonelyhearts' progress toward a deluded compassion. That is one reading, and it is an appealing one. Of course, it does not preclude the reading described in the opening of this essay. However, it is more likely that even this self-conscious artist was not in total conscious control here. As a result, he was a better writer, and what he wrote is effective though artistically flawed.

West may have realized, as he tried Miss Lonelyhearts' first-person narration, that his protagonist was too articulate. For it was central to this character that he remain rather inarticulate as may be seen in his dialogue. It is illuminating to think of West changing back to third person because the first person voice he heard sounded far more like Shrike's (and his own) than like Miss Lonelyhearts'. The third person enabled him to often repeat the mocking of Miss Lonelyhearts in the Shrikean mode; this mocking idiom had a major effect on intent, producing a tone of sadistic satire. But through the various revisions, that voice remains inappropriate to focus on Miss Lonelyhearts' mental processes. It is inappropriate unless the reader imagines, as one secondary reading, that after Miss Lonelyhearts' death, Shrike is imagining his vision of life, his emotions and thoughts. Hence Shrike becomes the writer of the story of Miss Lonelyhearts (and thus of himself), as if from that character's point of view. In essence, Shrike then becomes Miss Lonelyhearts.

Shrike appears in only one-third of the 15 chapters, but his presence is felt throughout. Noting that Miss Lonelyhearts speaks to Shrike only a few times, the reader may wonder if West is making satirical use of the secret-sharer concept. James W. Hickey argued that "As an extension of Miss Lonelyhearts' consciousness, *Miss Lonelyhearts* records Miss Lonelyhearts' exaggerated and often perverse perception of reality. The Shrike we see through Miss Lonelyhearts' eyes is not the 'real' Shrike of some objective 'real' world; he is an extension of the relentless, merciless Shrike of Miss Lonelyhearts' psychotic imagination. What is revealed to us is not so much intensified by Shrike's actual personality but by those aspects of Shrike which most affect Miss Lonelyhearts." Shrike's attitude, said Hickey, is "a sort of alter ego to Miss Lonelyhearts." This is suggested by West's transference to Shrike of observations about Miss Lonelyhearts which that character made himself in the interior monologue version described by Martin above. "[I]t is an easy misconception to assume that Shrike's surface callousness negates his despair," Hickey added. "Indeed, it confirms Shrike's self-tortured involvement as, like the wounded animal of a later chapter, he tears at the wound to hurt the pain. . . . If Shrike is depicted as a jeering, sniveling sadist, it is because that is the way in which Miss Lonelyhearts' demented consciousness perceives him."[22]

Irving Malin saw yet another pun on Shrike's name that is apt here. Shrike sounds like "shriek," Malin noted, suggesting a cry for help. The editor's first words in the novel come in the form of a prayer (let us prey). The words are printed on white cardboard at which Miss Lonelyhearts is staring as the novel begins: "Soul of Miss L, glorify me. . . . Help me, Miss L, help me, help me" (65). In many inverted ways, Miss Lonelyhearts does glorify Shrike, but is Shrike to some extent seriously crying out for help? Is he speaking of himself when he speaks to Goldsmith, who is, like Shrike, "a machine for making jokes"? "Shrike . . . appeared to be offended. 'Goldsmith, you are the nasty product of this unbelieving age. You cannot believe, you can only laugh. You take everything with a bag of salt and forget that salt is the enemy of fire as well as of ice. Be warned, the salt you use is not Attic salt, it is coarse butcher's salt. It doesn't preserve; it kills" (122). Shrike, the butcher bird, begins one of his longest satirical speeches with yet another of several phrases that may suggest his own need: "Every man his own Miss Lonelyhearts" (132).

If Hickey's interpretation was appealing, most critics agreed with Marcus Smith that "Both Shrike and Betty establish 'norms' for which their apparent 'flatness' of caricature is an advantage. Shrike withdraws from the world's evil into cynical mockery and there is no suggestion that he can ever emerge as a humane person."[23] But Stanley Edgar Hyman offered a radically different view of Miss Lonelyhearts' relationship with Shrike, a relationship that for him is spun in a matrix of technical and thematic ambiguity. He argued that this is a novel about homosexuality.[24]

The speaking voice dominated the popular arts of the 1930s. The first-person narrators of the tough-guy novels were one of several types of storytellers who provided a voice for readers of mass-market fiction. *Miss Lonelyhearts* is one of the few novels in which the hard-boiled style of that decade is effective in the third person. Yet it has been argued here that that style is inappropriate. Because West uses the controlled third-person, central-intelligence point of view, his style should be true to Miss Lonelyhearts' manner of expressing himself. But the reader who examines Miss Lonelyhearts' speeches will discover few lines similar to West's narrative style or Shrike's dialogue. Given the evidence in the novel, the reader can only conclude that Shrike's vision and idiom are more convincing than Miss Lonelyhearts' (as Lucifer is often more convincing than Christ in Milton's *Paradise Lost*). In fact, Shrike's style is repeatedly like that of a black mass. "Let us pray" is a possible pun, in a novel full of puns, on the meaning of his name, bird of prey. West's style, said Jay Martin, "is made to illuminate character."[25] Yes, but exactly *which* character is thus illuminated? The foregoing has been offered not as a primary reading but as a qualified, secondary reading of *Miss Lonelyhearts*. Perhaps the interested reader will let this light fall on a second or third re-reading of the novel, as one among several challenging experiences of it.

Notes

1.   Irving Malin, *Nathanael West's Novels* (Carbondale: Southern Illinois University Press, 1972), 133. [Reprinted in part in this volume.]

2.   Jay Martin, *Nathanael West: The Art of His Life* (New York: Farrar, Staus, and Giroux, 1970), 113.

3.   Victor Comerchero, *Nathanael West, The Ironic Prophet* (Seattle: University of Washington Press, 1967), 12. [Reprinted in part in this volume.]

4.   Martin, *Nathanael West*, 117.

5.   F. Scott Fitzgerald, *The Crack-up* (New York: New Directions, 1945), 69.

6.   Malcolm Cowley, Introduction. *Miss Lonelyhearts* (New York: Avon, 1959), ii, iv.

7.   Martin, *Nathanael West*, 202.

8.   Martin, *Nathanael West*, 94–95.

9.   C. C. Hollis, "Nathanael West and Surrealist Violence," *Fresco* 7 (1957): 5–13.

10.   Comerchero, *Nathanael West*, 78, 73.

11.   Comerchero, *Nathanael West*, 72.

12.   Martin, *Nathanael West*, 215.

13.   Martin, *Nathanael West*, 118.

14.   *The Complete Works of Nathanael West*. Introduction by Alan Ross (New York: Farrar, Straus and Cudahy, 1957), 66, 70, 101; hereafter cited in the text.

15.   "Some Notes on Violence," *Contact* 1 (1932): 132–33.

16.   Martin, *Nathanael West*, 152.

17.   Martin, *Nathanael West*, 395.

18.   Martin, *Nathanael West*, 154.

19. Marcus Smith, "The Crucial Departure: Irony and Point-of-View," in *Nathanael West: The Cheaters and the Cheated*, ed. David Madden (DeLand, Florida: Everett / Edwards Press, 1973), 106–07.

20. Martin, *Nathanael West*, 153.

21. Carter A. Daniel, "West's Revision of Miss Lonelyhearts," *Studies in Bibliography* 16 (1963): 233, 243.

22. James W. Hickey, "Freudian Criticism and Miss Lonelyhearts," in *Nathanael West: The Cheaters and the Cheated*, ed. David Madden (DeLand, Florida: Everett / Edwards Press, 1973), 115, 118.

23. Smith, "The Crucial Departure," 10.

24. Stanley Edgar Hyman, *Nathanael West* (Minneapolis: University of Minnesota Press, 1962), 22–24.

25. Martin, *Nathanael West*, 131.

Nathanael West: A Jewish Satirist in Spite of Himself

Daniel Walden*

In 1940 Nathanael West died in an automobile accident. Few newspapers noticed. Those that did invariably got the basic facts wrong. They spelled his name as "Nathaniel," gave his age as 34 or 40, described him as a "Hollywood scenarist," and credited him with writing *The Day of Locusts* and *Miss Lovely Hearts*.[1] Since 1940, however, his reputation has grown, even as the dispute continues over the proper label or category for his work. Was he a black humorist? a parodist? a satirist? or (dare it be said?) an American-Jewish novelist?

In his Introduction to a recent collection of essays on West, Harold Bloom dismissed *The Day of the Locust* as "an overpraised work, a waste of West's genius." He referred to *The Dream Life of Balso Snell* as "squalid and dreadful, with occasional passages of rancid power." He had kinder words for *A Cool Million*. For though this novel is "an outrageous parody of American picaresque," it is also "a permanent work of American satire" that seems to him "underpraised." Bloom reserved his primary praise for *Miss Lonelyhearts*, which he termed a "remorseless masterpiece."[2] Bloom has often proved an astute reader, and he was right about *Miss Lonelyhearts* and *A Cool Million*. But on *The Dream Life of Balso Snell* and *The Day of the Locust* he was clearly wrong. Is *Balso Snell* a masterpiece? No. Yet it is an extraordinarily creative feat by a young novelist, and it deserves recognition for that fact alone. Is *The Day of the Locust* a masterpiece? Some critics say it is; at the least it is a major work, albeit a flawed one.

Bloom again strained to be offbeat when he noted that "West, born Nathan Weinstein, is a significant episode in the long and tormented history of Jewish Gnosticism." This observation emboldened him to suggest that Gershom Scholem's essay "Redemption Through Sin" (from Sholem's *The Messianic Idea in Judaism*) was the best commentary on *Miss Lonelyhearts*.[3] But Bloom need hardly have turned to a scholar of Jewish mysticism for a key to West's novel. As West's college friend I. J. Kapstein had observed, Nathanael West had no meaningful Jewish heritage. Still, the American society in which

*This essay was written specifically for this volume.

he lived treated him as a Jew and an outsider. He wished to be neither. Consequently, he chose to strike back at those societal forces that he deemed responsible for his rejection: American democracy, Judaism, and Christianity. In fact, said Kapstein, the driving force behind all his work was the belief that "his writing was not an end in itself, but a means to an end: the achievement of acceptance, the dream life of Nathanael West come true."[4]

The basic facts of Nathanael West's life are well known, but they merit retelling from a Jewish perspective. West did not have a traditional Jewish upbringing, and he did not want to be Jewish. He became an angry young man because of the "cruel" trick fate and his family had played on him. Yet he could not have written as he did had he not been Jewish. He tried to laugh through his tears at his "misfortune," but his outrage and despair overwhelmed his laughter so that, as Victor Comerchero has observed, he kept "breaking into a sob."[5] West's attitude is not surprising. His businessman father, a secularized German Jew, strived mightily, if unsuccessfully, to gain acceptance as an American rather than a Jew.

West's life was a quest. Indeed, his writings reveal his quest for a home as insistently as do those of James Joyce. "After all, my dear fellow, life is a journey," says Anaxogoras at the outset of *Balso Snell*. Born in 1903, the son of Max and Anna Wallenstein Weinstein, West grew up in an affluent New York City home in which being "American" was all-important. Refusing to speak Russian or Yiddish at home, his parents taught German to their children. Their house, on 110th Street across from Central Park, was part of what was called "The Gilded Ghetto." A successful contractor, Max Weinstein named his buildings the Arizona, the Colorado, and the Colonnade. He did not send his children to Hebrew school, and before Nathan was 10, he gave the boy a set of Horatio Alger's books. These actions reflected his patriotic zeal. The Weinsteins may have started out as impoverished immigrants from Kovno, Lithuania, but they made their way in the best "melting pot" tradition.

Young Nathan was an enthusiastic but inept athlete who loved the outdoors and wanted very much to be a good baseball player. During his high school summers he attended Camp Paradox, a middle-class Jewish camp. There he earned the ironic nicknames of "Pep" and "Home Run Weinstein" because he was awkward and spoke slowly. In the lower grades he was an ordinary student, but at DeWitt Clinton High School he revealed an interest in film, theatre, and literature. Even so, he failed Spanish, History, Latin, Plane Geometry, and Physics, and he left high school before graduating. Determined to go to college, he used a forged transcript and the name of "Nathaniel" Weinstein to gain entry to Tufts College in 1921. Several months later he was asked to withdraw. Again employing another student's transcript, this time one belonging to a Nathan Weinstein who had gone on to medical school, he applied to Brown University. In Spring 1922, he was admitted to Brown, with 57 credits earned by his namesake. At Brown University a new Nathan Weinstein emerged. He now accepted "the rules of the game," said one roommate, which meant "He got through college, as I did, on brains and hard work." He also interested himself in alcohol, women, food, football, and good times. He always dressed like the campus dandies of the day. None of this seeming good fellowship, however, gained him his heart's desire: fraternity membership. For when he asked to join DKE, he was turned down. Intellectually, he refused to accept the rejection. Years later he confided to his friend Lester Cole that he had already rejected "them." But the wound was deep. As a student of literature and culture, he had developed a sense of superior status; he felt himself part of the elite minority of the well-dressed and truly cultured. He thought of himself as a gentleman and author. In effect, he now thought of himself as "Nathanael West," although he would not change his name legally until 1926.[6]

He formed his own university group and called it the "Hanseatic League." He intended the name to recall the free German towns of the thirteenth century that had come together to protect and promote commerce. (The territories included Kovno, the town from which his father had come.) He meant the group to reflect his enlightenment and modernism and to counterbalance his Joe College image. He always appeared ready to laugh at himself, as dude or modernist. In the meantime, he read widely and deeply in Greek and Roman classics, religious literature, French symbolists, Russian realists, and American and British modernists. He was preparing to be a writer. He already exhibited his special brand of Westian humor. When he wrote a term paper on "Euripedes—A Playwright"—published in *Casements* (July 1924), the Brown literary magazine—he used his new knowledge to accuse Euripedes, with tongue in cheek, of plagiarism. In June 1924, he wrote another seriocomic piece, this time for his friend Quentin Reynolds. He here recounted the adventures of a flea named Saint Puce (French for flea) who was born under Christ's armpit, fed on his body, and died at the moment of Christ's death. This tale became the central metaphor for *The Dream Life of Balso Snell*, on which he worked sporadically from 1924 to 1930.

West spent three months (from October 1926 to January 1927) in Paris, dividing his time unequally between the "bohemian" clubs and writing. It was prior to this trip that he changed his name officially to Nathanael West. Years later, I. J. Kapstein offered his view of West's thinking in those years. He elaborated on two themes. On the one hand West "had no Jewish heritage," Kapstein observed, thus "it was likely less hostility than complete indifference to it that finally made it burdensome to him." On the other hand, Kapstein added,

> What I do find is his getting even with a world that made him an outsider because he was a Jew, something he did not want to be anyway. He got even with Christianity. It professed to love all men (except Jews) and it kept him from belonging to fraternities and clubs and enjoying everywhere at any time the simple pleasure of belonging with [the] right people: hence the mockery of

Christianity in *The Dream Life of Balso Snell* (St. Puce, etc.) and the expose in *Miss Lonelyhearts* of Christianity as a stupid illusion having nothing to do with the reality of human nature and the hard truths of life.[7]

Kapstein also felt that West, in *The Day of the Locust*, was getting even, not only with American democracy, but also with humanity itself. This is most specific in the imagery of "The Burning of Los Angeles" painting. But to his credit, West turned his emotional negativism into aesthetic positivism. As Kapstein stated,

> In fiction West could discharge all the resentment he could not discharge in fact. In fiction he could rise above the world of fact and manipulate it to his will. As an artist in fiction he could prove to the world that had rejected him that it was wrong and that he deserved to be accepted by it. Indeed, having gone this far, I would say that this last was the driving force in the production of his work. His writing was not an end it itself, but a means to an end: the achievement of acceptance, the dream life of Nathanael West come true.[8]

He started "getting even" in his first novel. For *The Dream Life of Balso Snell* is a satirical attack against literary games and the perversion of art in a mass culture. West intended his scatological images to shock both the pompous avant-garde and the "booboisie." He directed his barbs at the pseudo-sophisticates he met in Paris in the 1920's who opted for escape to "Anywhere Out of This World" (the title of his hero's first song). Balso Snell himself is a kind of Babbitt who finds absurdity in all the major historical events of the Western civilization. Hence he concludes that "Art is a sublime excrement." Yet even as he lampoons art as escapism, Balso criticizes the dream makers who divert art from society. Of course *Balso Snell* was an experimental first novel that was intended to do much, perhaps too much. Thematically, it strikes at "[e]very weakness in the World's religions," noted William Bittner, "and then swings into religious love."[9] Norman Podhoretz has called it "a brilliantly insane surrealist fantasy that tries very hard to mock Western culture out of existence."[10] Malcolm Cowley has observed, somewhat ironically, that "escape from the mass was becoming a mass movement."[11] These would-be escapees were part of West's target.

Hence when West had Balso Snell enter the Trojan horse's anus, he meant not only to shock the reader but also to symbolize man's deterioration to a subhuman level. When he satirized the classical past, Catholic religion, Joyce, Doestoevsky, and Freud, West aimed at those (Jews and Gentiles alike) who had perverted the heritage of these gifted individuals and cultural forces. To shock and shatter the reader's complacency were important to West. To evoke the reader's disgust was also part of West's plan. Could the reader fail to react as Balso does? The latter "had good cause to tremble, for the Phoenix Excrementi eat themselves, digest themselves, and give birth to themselves by evacuating their bowels." Balso Snell is the grotesque product of the commercialized world West had come to know in New York and Paris.

Despite the reactions of some critics, *Balso Snell* was a carefully written and structured novel. West rewrote it many times to say precisely what he intended. This becomes clear when Balso meets a "Guide" with the word "Tours" on the front of his cap. West wished this figure to be seen as a confidence man eager to publicize any culture for a profit. When Balso mentions anti-Semitism, the Guide screams: "I am a Jew! and whenever anything is mentioned, I find it necessary to say I am a Jew. I'm a Jew! A Jew!" (7–8). When Balso attempts to placate the Guide with the cliche that "some of my best friends are Jews," the latter responds with meaningless chitchat. In short, West offered the reader this "Jewish Guide" as a grotesque incongruity, an atomized person whose life is a sham. West ridiculed affectation wherever he met it by creating incidents and images at once grotesque and comical. For example, he did so again at the end of the third episode. Here Balso writes a play for the art theatres, those patronized by art lovers, book lovers, school teachers, sensitive young Jews who adore culture, librarians, homosexuals, newspaper men, and advertising copy people. His purpose is to insult their intelligence. But on the chance that they do not get his message, Balso would have the ceiling of the theatre open "and cover the occupants with tons of loose excrement. After the deluge, if they so desire, the patrons of my art can gather in the customary charming groups and discuss the play" (31).

The entire novel is a satiric attempt to use the past to explain the present and future in a world that is one vast dungheap. A brilliantly conceived comic novel, *The Dream Life of Balso Snell* is obsessively scatological, anti-Catholic, and anti-Jewish. In addition, the reader who takes seriously John Rasknolnikov Gilson's declaration that "I need women and because I can't buy or force them, I have to make poems for them" (23), can only conclude that the novel is also sexist and misogynistic. As Max Schulz has insightfully noted, unlike so many of the post–World War II "Jewish" writers, West was unable to rest content suspended between heavenly aspirations and earthly limitations, belief and skepticism, order and disorder. Confronted by conflicting imperatives offered as moral norms as well as by the realization that any societal balance would be supplanted by the supremacy of one individual over the other, West structured each novel as a search for absolutes, for values. "If I could only discover the Real," cries Gilson. "A Real that I could know with my senses" (14). West had the same need. Disillusioned and embittered, unhappily poised between two cultures, he searched for something real in which to believe, even as he ended each novel with a mocking denunciation of false dreams. As an outsider, a Jew who did not want to be a Jew, he became almost instinctively a moral teacher, that most Jewish of vocations.

According to his friend John Sanford, West had his own way of dealing with "truth" or reality. "So far as I know, he never denied that he was a Jew,"

Sanford recalled, "and so far as I know he never changed his faith (it's a joke to call it that, because he had as much faith as an ear of corn). But he changed his name, he changed his clothes, he changed his manners (we all did). In short he did everything possible to create the impression in his own mind— remember that, in his own mind—that he was just like Al Vanderbilt. It never quite came off."[13] A personal experience illustrates this point. When a boy, West dropped an easy fly at a critical point in a baseball game, and was chased off the field by a mob of angry spectators. Years later, Wells Root, another of West's friends, recalled that whenever he heard the story, after West went to Hollywood in the 1930s, he remembered that West had felt that if the mob "had caught him they would have killed him."[14]

For most people this would have been a forgettable, even amusing, incident. But given West's personal insecurities, it is not hard to imagine the experience leaving him with an internalized image of himself as a persecuted individual fleeing from his tormentors. It is tempting to link the chase to a long history of archetypal images of Jews. In the 1930s, Hitler's persecution of the Jews tormented West. Like it or not, Nathanael West could not forget that he was a Jew, a member of a frequently despised minority. It is worth recalling Will Herberg's description of the second-generation Jew as one to whom the question "Who am I?" was too often answered with ambition, anxiety, and self-hatred. Like the early Saul Bellow hero, West was a dangling man who doted on order, as did Miss Lonelyhearts. Everett Stonequist has put it quite specifically. This second generation wanted nothing more than to be Americans. Tied to the old country by their parents, they realized that they were fated to remain marginal Americans. West was such a marginal individual. Inhabiting or having "ties of kinship with two or more interacting societies," he could not " 'belong' or feel at home in either group."[15]

Clearly, West's life and fiction were part of his quest for a home. West may have rejected his Jewish heritage, but that heritage shaped his search. In *Balso Snell* his obsession with flux is clear: shapes constantly alter before Balso's eyes. At the same time West blurred the distinction between performer and spectator. Almost all his characters are changing or trying to be someone else. Uncertain of the ideals of American life, they find their dream of a better day shattered by bitter reality. West's own Jeremiah-like search for permanent values was blocked repeatedly by the pathos of the Depression victims he saw all around him. Thus the Westian man, wrote Max Schulz, "is an early species on the evolutionary scale of *genus victima*. . . . West's involvement with him is that of the prophet. . . . He hates what will not heed his jeremiads."[16]

Josephine Herbst, who knew him well, made the same point. "The horror of this age was in West's nerves, in his blood,"[17] she stated. He searched with passion for something in which to believe. At the same time, he struggled always to show he was neither a typical bohemian nor Jew, nor a typical anything else. What he did exhibit was the desperate commitment of the 1930s idealists who felt betrayed by existing societal ideas and disillusioned by New Deal liberalism. While literary realists like Mike Gold, Samuel Ornitz, and Henry Roth were portraying various aspects of Jewish life, West felt compelled to define the larger American experience with a negative symbolism. His shattered dreams and repeated disappointments fed his personal bitterness and irony, as well as his sense of cosmic injustice. Such convictions were not exclusively Jewish, but they could substantiate the collective Jewish experience. Feeling alienated from both Jewish and Christian humanitarianism, West chose to jeer at both.

In *Miss Lonelyhearts* West makes his anti-Semitism quite clear and leaves no doubt in the reader's mind that he does not want to be a Jew. Nor does anyone else in the novel. The attendant at the Aw-Kum-On Garage blames even the absence of deer at the local pond on "the Yids." Yet West employs his virulent skepticism to attack not only the professed value system of the American populace but also their pretentious, vulgar, and often sadistic wielders of power. His central characters are no better. Shrike, as his name suggests, is a predator. Even Miss Lonelyhearts is morally lacking. He may change from a cynical newspaper writer to a would-be dispassionate columnist and compassionate human being. But even as he grows painfully aware of God's love for man and achieves an emotional union with Christ, he reveals himself to be a homophobe, a seducer, and abuser. West seemingly wanted to believe that love and religion might be a solution to life's problems. But his underlying doubts are revealed in his hero's spurious conversion, as in his conviction that "true compassion" is an impossibility in the Waste Land that is human existence. For Miss Lonelyhearts to believe that God has sent him to embrace and so cure the crippled Doyle is less a miracle than a harbinger of God's death, in West's vision. Just as *The Dream Life of Balso Snell* is a mockery of the bardic dream, so *Miss Lonelyhearts* proves a denunciation of the Christ dream.

Not surprisingly then, *A Cool Million* is a secularized version of the religious and cultural dreams played out in these first two novels. In true Horatio Alger, Jr. fashion, Nathan "Shagpoke" Whipple, an ex-President with a phony cracker-barrel philosophy, assures Lemuel Pitkin that everyone can be a Rockefeller or a Ford. But in West's view of things, the average, honest American Boy is likely to achieve very little. Cunning, craft, power, fraud, and aggression (as seen in Wu Fong's fancy "American" brothel) are more likely keys to success. For West, the Horatio Alger myth is more likely to destroy the individual than reward him. West may or may not have drawn upon early images of his father as entrepreneur, but certainly he had before him the lessons of the Depression. He reacted to the capitalist dream with disdain, for, like it or not, he had assimilated the Judeo-Christian value system. Hence he criticized the prevailing economic system and the sanctimonious, greedy, and dehumanizing movers and shakers so prevalent even then. That "Shagpoke" criticizes the "sophisticated aliens," or that his minions resemble those of Mussolini or Hitler, is no coincidence. As disillusioned and frustrated as the most Jewish or Christian idealist, West wanted desperately to believe in love, the American Dream, and even God. But life kept getting in his way.

West was keenly aware of the conflicting elements in his own nature and interests. In *The Day of the Locust* he attributes these dichotomies to Tod Hackett, whom he describes as "a very complicated young man with a whole set of personalities, one inside the other like a nest of Chinese boxes" (260). Robert M. Coates called him a pessimist. Clifton Fadiman was among the first to term him a surrealist. Edmund Wilson wrote that West derived rather from those postwar French writers who had specialized in the delirious and diabolic fantasy that had in turn come out of Rimbaud and Lautréamont. West often relied upon incongruities to make his points. Unlike the Surrealists, however, he distilled his perceptions into images and situations stripped painfully barren of minutiae.[18] Perhaps, as Daniel Aaron has suggested, West belonged to that select company of socially committed Depression writers who drew revolutionary conclusions in highly idiosyncratic and undoctrinaire ways. He was an exorcist of a kind, as he recognized that comedy is cathartic. Clearly he tried on occasion to be a "satiric propagandist." At his most authentic, Aaron concluded, West was indeed a truly "universal satirist."[19]

In the 1930s Hollywood was enough of a boomtown to render unreal the news of breadlines and starvation plaguing most of the country. But corruption and destruction are persistent in West's movie town. Violence is largely sexual. His Southern California is where people come to die. They find that here one means of survival is role-playing, a discovery made by Jews centuries back. West suggested this knowledge through a series of minor characters and symbols. These include the absurd Chief Kiss-My-Towkus with his Yiddish accent, the bigots at Claude's party who discuss how to "get rid of the illiterate mockies that run the movie industry," the huge sign above the riot that parodies Coleridge—"Mr. Kahn a Pleasure Dome Decreed," and a face named Ikey Cohn as a symbol of New York's Rockaway Playland. Most significant and obvious is the cock named Juju (Jew Jew) that gaffs the cock Hermano (brotherhood) in the brain. These elements alone suggest that West was trying hard to be a parodist, a heretic, and a moralist. Randall Reid saw him as a man "afflicted with a moral impulse whose traditional forms have collapsed." For the pleasures some value and pursue, said Reid, became for West the graveyard of the American Dream.[20]

Originally, West planned to call his final novel *The Cheated* and to base it on the true story of a California soldier of fortune who had been implicated in a local murder. His book was to have described the adventures of a motley group of bored, sensation-starved Angelenos taken on a trip by the protagonist. Gradually he shifted the emphasis to Homer Simpson and Tod Hackett, who found themselves enmeshed in a demimonde of lying, cheating, and pretense. His people are masqueraders and dreamers who finally realize they have been tricked and that life is little more than a cheap Mardi Gras. Burning with anger and frustration, they find release only in mob violence. West admitted that he avoided depicting Hollywood's talented and industrious individuals, as they were not proper targets for satire. He focused instead on the movie town's "peculiar half-world" which fed his creative imagination. "I believe there is a place," he wrote to Jack Conroy, "for the fellow who yells fire and indicates where some of the smoke is coming from without actually dragging the hose to the spot."[21]

West could see fire and smoke everywhere. For in 1939, as he sat finishing *The Day of the Locust,* World War II was growing in intensity. Hitler's troops were advancing, the Nazi-Soviet Pact was signed, and Germany invaded Poland. Life seemed to consist increasingly of political betrayal, communism, fascism, opportunism, and, as Dorothy Parker noted, the only "ism" in which Hollywood really believed, plagiarism. West revised his manuscript several times, retitling it in the process. In addition to "The Cheaters," he considered calling it "The Grass Eaters," "Cry Wolf," "The Wrath to Come," and "Days to Come," before settling on "The Days of the Locust," which he then modified to *The Day of the Locust.* He had in mind the verses in Exodus in which Moses warns Pharaoh that unless he frees the Hebrews, "tomorrow I will bring locusts into your country" (10:3–6, 13–15) and in Revelations "and out of the smoke there came forth locusts upon the earth" (9:3–11). From Exodus, therefore, West derived the idea of the "release" of the Hebrews into the Promised Land. From Revelations he borrowed the idea of the dream apocalypse.[22]

Some who knew West tried to explain the inner forces that drove him. He had "some furious hunger," said Philip Wylie, "for a different humanity that was hidden by his deep, empathetic, outraged yet somehow, at bottom, loving regard for people."[23] He had a "queer grin" and was very "self-deprecating," recalled Matthew Josephson. He also had a "vicious interest in the cockeyed religions of California," but at the same time he was "a master of compassionate irony."[24] West offered his own insights. While awaiting reviews of his new novel, for example, he described himself in a letter to editor Saxe Commins as a "Jeremiah." Convinced that "Few things are sadder than the truly monstrous," he had focused his gaze on man's more monstrous characteristics. He was keenly aware, noted Jay Martin, that "there is nothing to root for in his books, and what is even worse, no rooters." His final novel was an almost complete bust. The was hardly news. His profits from his four novels and a decade of writing fiction came to $1,280.[25]

Taken together, these elements suggest that Nathanael West discharged his frustrations with life and his resentments against the world in his writing. In his fiction he could manipulate people and events as he wished and, as Jay Martin observed, prove "to the world that had rejected him that it was wrong and that he deserved to be accepted by it." His novels were his means of achieving acceptance; they added up to the dream life of Nathanael West come true. Laughing through his tears, often "breaking into a sob," this Jew who did not want to be a Jew became one in spite of himself. In his strenuous efforts to find himself, he exposed with the fury and piercing wit of an Old Testament prophet the falseness and vapidity of many of America's dreams and values. His novels not only reflect his era, noted Martin, but they also, and more importantly, are "perennial and true explorations into the Siberia of the human spirit."[26] They represent a significant, if ironic, accomplishment for this driven young man whose parents had been born in Kovno, Lithuania.

Notes

1. Jay Martin, *Nathanael West: The Art of His Life* (New York: Farrar, Straus & Giroux, 1970), 10–13.
2. Harold Bloom, ed., *Modern Critical Views: Nathanael West* (New York: Chelsea House, 1986), 1.
3. Bloom, *Modern Critical Views*, 1.
4. I. J. Kapstein, unpublished Letter to Daniel Walden, 9 March 1970.
5. Victor Comerchero, *Nathanael West, The Ironic Prophet* (Seattle: University of Washington Press, 1967), 71. [Reprinted in part in this volume.]
6. Martin, *Nathanael West*, 30–52, 56–57.
7. Kapstein, Letter to Walden.
8. Kapstein, Letter to Walden.
9. William Bittner, "A la recherche d'un ecrivain perdu," *Les Langues Modernes* 54 (July–August 1960): 280.
10. Norman Podhoretz, "Nathanael West: A Particular Kind of Joking," in *Doings and Undoings: The Fifties and After* (New York: Farrar, Straus & Giroux, 1957), 65–66. [Reprinted in this volume.]
11. Malcolm Cowley, Introduction to *Miss Lonelyhearts* (New York: Avon, 1950), ii–iv.
12. *The Complete Works* (New York: Farrar, Straus & Cudahy, 1957), 5; hereafter cited in the text.
13. John Sanford, "Nathanael West," *The Screen Writer* 2 (December 1946): 10–13.
14. Wells Root, Letter to Richard Gehman, c. 1947, in James Light, *Nathanael West: An Interpretation* (Evanston: Northwestern University Press, 1961), 145.
15. Everett Stonequist, "The Marginal Character of the Jews," in *Jews in a Gentile World*, ed. Isacque Graeber and Steuart H. Bart (New York: Macmillan, 1942), 307.
16. Max Schulz, *Radical Sophistication: Studies in Contemporary American Jewish Novelists* (Athens: Ohio University Press, 1969), 53. [Reprinted in part in this volume.]
17. Josephine Herbst, "Nathanael West," *Kenyon Review* 23 (Autumn 1961): 611. See also Herbst, *"Miss Lonelyhearts*: An Allegory," *Contempo* (25 July 1933): 5. [Reprinted in this volume.]
18. Edmund Wilson, "The Boys in the Back Room," in *Classics and Commercials: A Literary Chronicle of the Forties* (New York: Farrar, Straus and Giroux, 1950), 51–56. [Reprinted in this volume.]
19. Daniel Aaron, "Late Thoughts on Nathanael West," *Massachusetts Review* 6 (Winter–Spring, 1965): 316.
20. Randall Reid, *The Fiction of Nathanael West* (Chicago: University of Chicago Press, 1967), 6–7, 9.

21. Letter from Nathanael West to Jack Conroy, quoted in Martin, 336.

22. Nathan Scott, *Nathanael West: A Critical Essay* (Grand Rapids: W. B. Eerdmans, 1971), 31. See also Martin, 258–66.

23. Martin, 320.

24. Daniel Walden, interview with Matthew Josephson, 3 May 1971.

25. Martin, 341.

26. Martin, 10.

Index

♦